Envision It! | Visual Skills Handbook

Author's Purpose

Cause and Effect

Compare and Contrast

Draw Conclusions

Fact and Opinion

Generalize

Graphic Sources

Literary Elements

Main Idea and Details

Sequence

Author's Purpose

An author writes for many purposes, some of which are to inform, to entertain, to persuade, or to express feelings or a mood. An author may have more than one purpose for writing.

Cause and Effect

An effect is something that happens. A cause is why that thing happens. An effect sometimes has more than one cause. A cause sometimes has more than one effect. Clue words such as *because*, *as a result*, *therefore*, and *so that* can signal causes and effects.

Cause

Effect

Compare and Contrast

To compare and contrast is to look for similarities and differences in things. Clue words such as *like* or *as* show similarities. Clue words such as *but* or *unlike* show differences.

Draw Conclusions

When we draw conclusions, we make sensible decisions or form reasonable opinions after thinking about the facts and details in what we are reading.

Fact and Opinion

A statement of fact can be proved true or false. Facts are based on evidence. A statement of opinion expresses a judgment, belief, or way of thinking.

Generalize

To generalize is to make a broad statement or rule that applies to many examples.

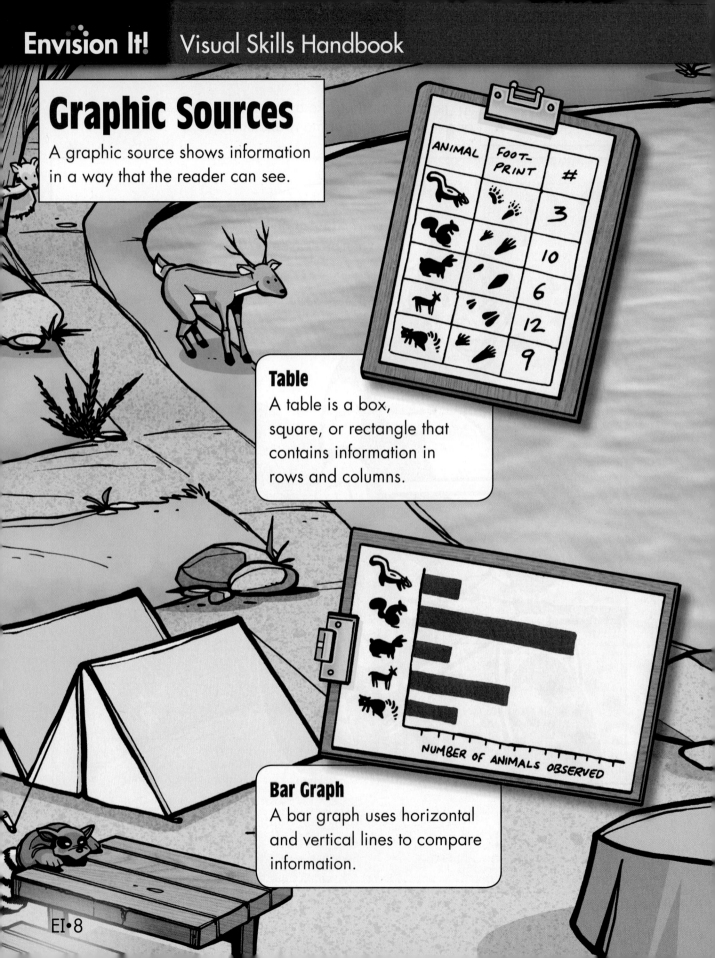

Graphic Sources

A graphic source shows information in a way that the reader can see.

Table

A table is a box, square, or rectangle that contains information in rows and columns.

Bar Graph

A bar graph uses horizontal and vertical lines to compare information.

Map

A map is a drawing of a place that shows where something is or where something happened.

Diagram

A diagram is a drawing, usually with parts that are labeled.

Literary Elements

A **Day** at the **Beach**

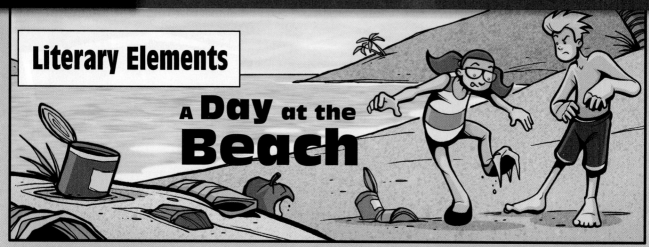

Understanding a story requires knowing the four main parts of a story: character, setting, plot, and theme.

Setting - the time and place in which a story happens

Character - a person or animal in a story

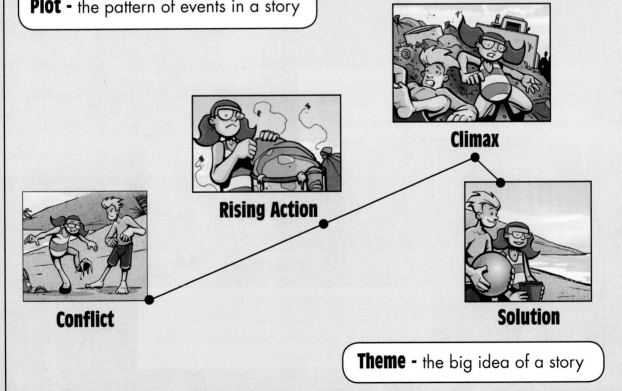

Plot - the pattern of events in a story

Rising Action

Climax

Conflict

Solution

Theme - the big idea of a story

Main Idea and Details

Main idea is the most important idea about a topic. For example, it takes a lot of people to put on a big rock concert.

Details are smaller pieces of information that support the main idea. Musicians, technicians, and fans are all part of the rock concert experience.

Sequence

Sequence refers to the order that events happen.
We use sequence when we list the steps in a process.

Envision It! | Visual Strategies Handbook

Background Knowledge

Important Ideas

Inferring

Monitor and Clarify

Predict and Set Purpose

Questioning

Story Structure

Summarize

Text Structure

Visualize

Background Knowledge

Background knowledge is what you already know about a topic based on your reading and personal experience. Make connections to people, places, and things from the real world. Use background knowledge before, during, and after reading.

To use background knowledge
- with fiction, preview the title, author's name, and illustrations
- with nonfiction, preview chapter titles, headings, graphics, and captions
- think about what you already know
- think about your own experiences

Let's Think About Reading!

When I use background knowledge, I ask myself
- Does this character remind me of someone?
- How is this story or text similar to others I have read?
- What else do I already know about this genre or topic?

Important Ideas

Important ideas are essential ideas and supporting details in a nonfiction selection. Important ideas include information and facts that provide clues to the author's purpose.

To identify important ideas

- read all titles, headings, and captions
- look for words in italics, boldface print, or bulleted lists
- look for signal words and phrases: *for example, most important,* and others
- use photographs, illustrations, or other graphic sources
- note how the text is organized—cause and effect, problem and solution, question and answer, or other ways

The deadline is important to know!

Let's Think About Reading!

When I identify important ideas, I ask myself

- What information is included in bold, italics, or some other special lettering?
- What details support important ideas?
- Are there signal words and phrases?
- What do illustrations, photos, diagrams, and charts show?
- How is the text organized?
- Why did the author write this?

Inferring

When we **infer** we use background knowledge with clues in the text to come up with our own ideas about what the author is trying to present.

To infer
- identify what you already know
- combine what you know with text clues to come up with your own ideas

You got the part in the talent show!

Let's **Think** About **Reading!**

When I infer, I ask myself
- What do I already know?
- Which text clues are important?
- What is the author trying to present?

Monitor and Clarify

We **monitor** comprehension to check our understanding of what we've read. We **clarify** to find out why we haven't understood what we've read and to fix up problems.

To monitor and clarify

- use background knowledge
- try different strategies: ask questions, reread, or use text features and illustrations

When I monitor and clarify, I ask myself
- Do I understand what I'm reading?
- What doesn't make sense?
- What strategies can I use?

Predict and Set Purpose

We **predict** to tell what might happen next in a story or article. The prediction is based on what has already happened. We **set a purpose** to guide our reading.

To predict and set a purpose
- preview the title and the author's name
- preview any illustrations or graphics
- identify why you're reading
- use what you already know to make predictions
- check and change your predictions based on new information

Let's **Think** About **Reading!**

When I predict and set a purpose, I ask myself
- What do I already know?
- What do I think will happen?
- What is my purpose for reading?

Questioning

Questioning is asking good questions about important text information. Questioning takes place before, during, and after reading.

To question
- read with a question in mind
- stop, think, and record your questions as you read
- make notes when you find information
- check your understanding and ask questions to clarify

Let's **Think** About **Reading!**

When I question, I ask myself
- Have I asked a good question with a question word?
- What questions help me make sense of my reading?
- What does the author mean?

Story Structure

Story structure is the arrangement of a story from beginning to end. Most stories involve a conflict and a resolution. You can use this information to summarize a story.

To identify story structure

- note the conflict, or problem, at the beginning of a story
- track the rising action as the conflict builds in the middle
- recognize the climax when the characters face the conflict
- identify how the conflict gets resolved and the story ends

Let's Think About Reading!

When I identify story structure, I ask myself

- What are the characters' goals?
- What is the story's conflict?
- How does the conflict build throughout the story?
- How is the conflict resolved in the end?

Summarize

We **summarize,** or retell, to check our understanding of what we've read. A summary is a brief statement—no more than a few sentences.

To summarize fiction
- tell what happens in the story
- think about the characters and their goals, the setting, and the plot

To summarize nonfiction
- tell the main idea, leaving out supporting details
- think about text structure and how the selection is organized

Let's **Think** About Reading!

When I summarize, I ask myself
- What is the story or selection about?
- In fiction, what are the characters' goals? Are they successful?
- In nonfiction, how is the information organized?

Text Structure

We use **text structure** to look for the way the author has organized the text; for example, cause and effect, problem and solution, sequence, or compare and contrast. Analyze text structure before, during, and after reading to locate information.

To identify text structure
- before reading: preview titles, headings, and illustrations
- make predictions
- during reading: ask questions, identify the structure, and notice the organization
- after reading: recall the organization and summarize the text

Let's Think About Reading!

When I identify text structure, I ask myself
- What clues do titles, headings, and illustrations provide?
- How is information organized?
- How does the organization help my understanding?

Visualize

We **visualize** to form pictures in our minds as we read. This helps us monitor our comprehension.

To visualize

- combine what you already know with details from the text to make pictures in your mind
- use all of your senses to put yourself in the story or text

Let's **Think** About **Reading!**

When I visualize, I ask myself

- What do I already know?
- Which details create pictures in my mind?
- How can my senses put me in the story or text?

READING STREET

GRADE 6

COMMON CORE

Program Authors

Peter Afflerbach
Camille Blachowicz
Candy Dawson Boyd
Elena Izquierdo
Connie Juel
Edward Kame'enui
Donald Leu
Jeanne R. Paratore

P. David Pearson
Sam Sebesta
Deborah Simmons
Susan Watts Taffe
Alfred Tatum
Sharon Vaughn
Karen Kring Wixson

Glenview, Illinois

Boston, Massachusetts

Chandler, Arizona

Upper Saddle River, New Jersey

ALWAYS LEARNING

PEARSON

We dedicate Reading Street to
Peter Jovanovich.

His wisdom, courage,
and passion for education
are an inspiration to us all.

Accelerated Reader®

Acknowledgments appear on pages 494–497, which constitute an extension of this copyright page.

PEARSON

ISBN-13: 978-0-328-72457-4
ISBN-10:   0-328-72457-2
8 9 10 V057 17 16 15 14

Dear Reader,

A new school year is beginning. Are you ready? You are about to take a trip along a famous street—*Scott Foresman Reading Street*. During this trip you will learn about loyalty and respect, space and time, and different challenges and obstacles. You will meet a girl who finds a stray dog, a boy who learns to survive alone in the wilderness, and the great American singer Marian Anderson. You will visit places from the past, such as ancient Egypt, and learn about a boy who lives on the moon.

As you read about rain forests, archaeologists who are studying early American sites, and a dog that has become a symbol for an entire nation, you will gain new information to help you in science and social studies.

While you're enjoying these exciting pieces of literature, you will find that something else is going on: you are becoming a better reader who is gaining new skills as you polish old ones.

Have a great trip— and send us a postcard!

Sincerely,
The Authors

Loyalty and Respect

What draws us to people and things around us and makes us care?

OLD YELLER
by **FRED GIPSON**
author of "Hound Dog Man"

Week 2

Week 3

Unit 1 Contents

Week 6

Unit 1

Envision It! A Comprehension Handbook

Envision It! Visual Skills Handbook EI•1–EI•13

Envision It! Visual Strategies Handbook EI•15–EI•25

Words! Vocabulary Handbook W•1–W•15

Unit 2 Contents

Space and Time

Why might things far away and long ago be important to us now?

Week 1

Let's **Think** About **Reading!**

Week 2

Week 3

Unit 2 Contents

Week 6

Unit 2

Envision It! A Comprehension Handbook

Envision It! Visual Skills Handbook EI•1–EI•13

Envision It! Visual Strategies Handbook EI•15–EI•25

Words! Vocabulary Handbook W•1–W•15

Unit 3 Contents

Challenges and Obstacles

How are the results of our efforts sometimes greater than we expect?

Week 1

Let's **Think** About **Reading!**

realistic fiction • social studies

13

Unit 3 Contents

14

Week 6

Unit 3

Envision It! A Comprehension Handbook

Envision It! Visual Skills Handbook EI•1–EI•13

Envision It! Visual Strategies Handbook EI•15–EI•25

Words! Vocabulary Handbook W•1–W•15

Don Leu
The Internet Guy

Right before our eyes, the nature of reading and learning is changing. The Internet and other technologies create new opportunities, new solutions, and new literacies. New reading comprehension skills are required online. They are increasingly important to our students and our society.

Those of us on the Reading Street team are here to help you on this new, and very exciting, journey.

See It!

- **Big Question Video**

- **Concept Talk Video**

- **Envision It! Animations**

- **eReaders**

Hear It!

- **eSelections**

- **Grammar Jammer**

- **Vocabulary Activities**

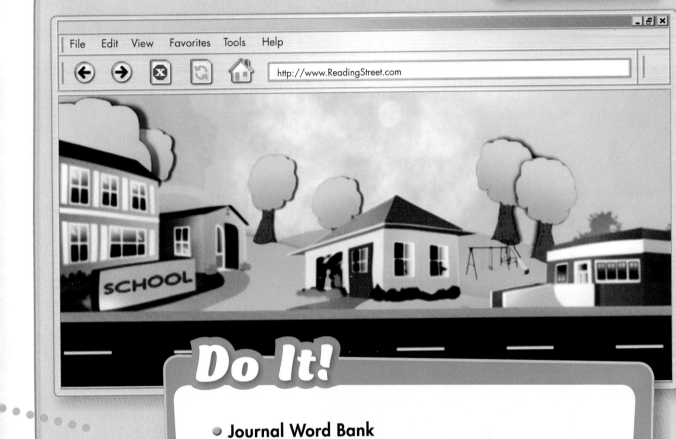

Do It!

- **Journal Word Bank**

- **Story Sort**

- **21st Century Skills Activities**

- **Vocabulary Activities**

- **Online Assessment**

http://www.ReadingStreet.com

SCHOOL

Loyalty and Respect

What draws us to people and things around us and makes us care?

Common Core State Standards
Language 6. Acquire and use accurately grade-appropriate general academic and domain-specific words and phrases; gather vocabulary knowledge when considering a word or phrase important to comprehension or expression.
Also Speaking/Listening 1.c.

Let's Talk About

Protecting

- Express opinions about what protecting a person or animal means.

- Ask questions about when a person or animal might need to be protected.

- Share how you have felt when you've protected a person or animal.

READING STREET ONLINE
CONCEPT TALK VIDEO
www.ReadingStreet.com

Common Core State Standards

Literature 3. Describe how a particular story's or drama's plot unfolds in a series of episodes as well as how the characters respond or change as the plot moves toward a resolution.

Envision It! | Skill Strategy

Skill

Strategy

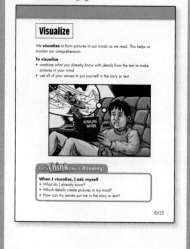

Comprehension Skill

Literary Elements: Setting and Plot

- Setting is the time and place in which a story occurs. Setting can shape events and behaviors.

- Plot is the pattern of events in a story. Usually events happen in a sequential order.

- A plot has a conflict or problem; rising action when the conflict builds; a climax, the most exciting part of a story; and a resolution.

- Use a graphic organizer like the one below to identify setting as you read "High Plains Childhood."

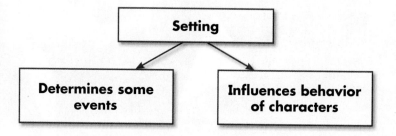

Comprehension Strategy

Visualize

Good readers visualize, or create mental pictures of, what they read. They picture themselves in the text, using any or all five of their senses. Words and phrases in the text help form pictures in their minds. Visualizing is a good way to understand the setting of a story and how the setting affects the plot and the characters.

High Plains Childhood

My parents moved us to the treacherous high plains of West Texas in 1853, when I was seven and my sister Jenny was twelve. We lived in the middle of a gigantic, rolling prairie and were stunned by how dry and hot it was and by how many wild animals were around. We encountered many challenging circumstances.

One time we were caught in a violent sandstorm. It was around noon, and Jenny and I were walking back to our cabin. Suddenly the wind picked up, the sky blackened, and blowing grains of sand struck our faces and arms. I screamed; Jenny pulled me to the ground. The storm pounded us for about ten minutes. All we could do was lie there. When it ended, sand covered our bodies and filled our clothing.

Then, just three days later, I was stopped in my tracks by a rattlesnake. I stood there like a statue, eyes unblinking, as the snake stared menacingly at me. After a few horrifying moments it slithered off, and I ran like the wind back home. I then sat down and wept the fear out of my body.

Skill The author states the place and time in this first sentence. What is the setting?

Strategy What images come to mind when you read the author's description of the high plains of Texas?

Skill Could this event have occurred in other settings? Why or why not?

Your Turn!

⏸ **Need a Review?** See the *Envision It! Handbook* for help with literary elements—setting and plot—and with visualizing.

Let's **Think** About..

▶ **Ready to Try It?** Use what you've learned about setting and plot as you read *Old Yeller*.

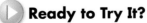

Common Core State Standards
Language 4.c. Consult reference materials (e.g., dictionaries, glossaries, thesauruses), both print and digital, to find the pronunciation of a word or determine or clarify its precise meaning or its part of speech. **Also Language 4., 5.**

Envision It! | Words to Know

lunging

slung

speckled

nub

romping

rowdy

READING STREET ONLINE
VOCABULARY ACTIVITIES
www.ReadingStreet.com

Vocabulary Strategy for
Synonyms

Thesaurus A synonym is a word that has the same or almost the same meaning as another word. You can find synonyms for a word by looking up the word in a thesaurus.

Choose one of the Words to Know and follow these steps.

1. Identify the word and think about its meaning.

2. Look up the word in a thesaurus.

3. Examine the synonyms listed and consider what each of them means.

4. Use a dictionary to be sure of each synonym's exact meaning.

5. Choose the synonym that makes the best sense in the sentence.

Read "A Best Friend." Look for Words to Know that might have synonyms listed in a thesaurus. Look them up to see what the synonyms are.

Words to Write Reread "A Best Friend." Does a dog live with you? Or would you like to get a dog? Think about fun things you can do with a dog. Write a description of how you and a dog might play. Use words from the Words to Know list in your description.

A Best Friend

The bond between people and dogs runs deep and strong. Owners just fall in love with their dogs. These four-legged friends return the feeling many times over. The size, shape, and breed of the dog do not seem to matter. It might be a speckled, sleek Dalmatian. It might be a stubby-legged, wiry-haired Scottie with a nub of a tail. All dogs adore their people.

Romping with the kids on the lawn, the family dog shows joy with its whole body. Lunging for a tossed ball in the park, it leaps higher and farther than muscles should allow. Happiness seems to give the dog extra lift. Even a quiet old dog sitting by its master's feet seems to want nothing more.

Worn out after a shared run or walk, owner and dog lie down together for a nap. A child sleeps with a trusting arm slung over the dog's back. This picture says a lot about the connection we feel with these family members with fur. Whether the time together has been rowdy or calm, the dog is content. It seems to say with every inch of its being, nothing makes me happier than spending time with you!

Your Turn!

Need a Review? For help using a thesaurus to find synonyms, see *Words!*

Let's Think About..

Ready to Try It? Read *Old Yeller* on pp. 26–39.

Old Yeller

by Fred Gipson
illustrated by Lori Lohstoeter

Historical fiction is fiction that takes place in the past. What clues tell you that *Old Yeller* takes place in the past?

Question of the Week
How can we help protect those we love?

Let's Think About Reading!

Let's **Think** About...

From this first illustration, what image comes to mind about Old Yeller's family?

🔁 **Visualize**

The year is 1867 on the frontier of Texas. Fourteen-year-old Travis takes charge of the family homestead while his father is away. Left behind with Travis, his mother, and five-year-old brother named Arliss, is a stray yellow dog. The family calls him Old Yeller.

That little Arliss! If he wasn't a mess! From the time he'd grown up big enough to get out of the cabin, he'd made a practice of trying to catch and keep every living thing that ran, flew, jumped, or crawled.

Every night before Mama let him go to bed, she'd made Arliss empty his pockets of whatever he'd captured during the day. Generally, it would be a tangled-up mess of grasshoppers and worms and praying bugs and little rusty tree lizards. One time he brought in a horned toad that got so mad he swelled out round and flat as a Mexican *tortilla* and bled at the eyes. Sometimes it was stuff like a young bird that had fallen out of its nest before it could fly, or a green-speckled spring frog, or a striped water snake. And once he turned out of his pocket a wadded-up baby copperhead that nearly threw Mama into spasms. We never did figure out why the snake hadn't bitten him, but Mama took no more chances on snakes. She switched Arliss hard for catching that snake. Then she made me spend better than a week taking him out and teaching him to throw rocks and kill snakes.

That was all right with Little Arliss. If Mama wanted him to kill his snakes first, he'd kill them. But that still didn't keep him from sticking them in his pockets along with everything else he'd captured that day. The snakes might be stinking by the time Mama called on him to empty his pocket, but they'd be dead.

Let's Think About…

What does this description of Little Arliss's behavior tell about the role he plays in the family?
Important Ideas

Let's Think About...

How does the author use descriptions to bring this scene to life?
Story Structure

Then, after the yeller dog came, Little Arliss started catching even bigger game. Like cottontail rabbits and chaparral birds and a baby possum that sulked and lay like dead for the first several hours until he finally decided that Arliss wasn't going to hurt him.

Of course, it was Old Yeller that was doing the catching. He'd run the game down and turn it over to Little Arliss. Then Little Arliss would come in and tell Mama a big fib about how he caught it himself.

I watched them one day when they caught a blue catfish out of Birdsong Creek. The fish had fed out into water so shallow that his top fin was sticking out. About the time I saw it, Old Yeller and Little Arliss did too. They made a run at it. The fish went scooting away toward deeper water, only Yeller was too fast for him. He pounced on the fish and shut his big mouth down over it and went romping to the bank, where he dropped it down on the grass and let it flop. And here came Little Arliss to fall on it like I guess he'd been doing everything else. The minute he got his hands on it, the fish finned him and he went to crying.

But he didn't turn the fish loose. He just grabbed it up and went running and squawling toward the house, where he gave the fish to Mama. His hands were all bloody by then, where the fish had finned him. They swelled up and got mighty sore; not even a mesquite thorn hurts as bad as a sharp fish fin when it's run deep into your hand.

But as soon as Mama had wrapped his hands in a poultice of mashed-up prickly-pear root to draw out the poison, Little Arliss forgot all about his hurt. And that night when we ate the fish for supper, he told the biggest windy I ever heard about how he'd dived 'way down into a deep hole under the rocks and dragged that fish out and nearly got drowned before he could swim to the bank with it.

But when I tried to tell Mama what really happened, she wouldn't let me. "Now, this is Arliss's story," she said. "You let him tell it the way he wants to."

I told Mama then, I said: "Mama, that old yeller dog is going to make the biggest liar in Texas out of Little Arliss."

But Mama just laughed at me, like she always laughed at Little Arliss's big windies after she'd gotten off where he couldn't hear her. She said for me to let Little Arliss alone. She said that if he ever told a bigger whopper than the ones I used to tell, she had yet to hear it.

Well, I hushed then. If Mama wanted Little Arliss to grow up to be the biggest liar in Texas, I guessed it wasn't any of my business.

Let's **Think** About...

What do you know about family relationships that helps explain why Travis feels so frustrated?
Background Knowledge

31

All of which, I figure, is what led up to Little Arliss's catching the bear. I think Mama had let him tell so many big yarns about his catching live game that he'd begun to believe them himself.

When it happened, I was down the creek a ways, splitting rails to fix up the yard fence where the bulls had torn it down. I'd been down there since dinner, working in a stand of tall slim post oaks. I'd chop down a tree, trim off the branches as far up as I wanted, then cut away the rest of the top. After that I'd start splitting the log.

I'd split the log by driving steel wedges into the wood. I'd start at the big end and hammer in a wedge with the back side of my axe. This would start a little split running lengthways of the log. Then I'd take a second wedge and drive it into this split. This would split the log further along and, at the same time, loosen the first wedge. I'd then knock the first wedge loose and move it up in front of the second one.

Driving one wedge ahead of the other like that, I could finally split a log in two halves. Then I'd go to work on the halves, splitting them apart. That way, from each log, I'd come out with four rails.

Swinging that chopping axe was sure hard work. The sweat poured off me. My back muscles ached. The axe got so heavy I could hardly swing it. My breath got harder and harder to breathe.

An hour before sundown, I was worn down to a nub. It seemed like I couldn't hit another lick. Papa could have lasted till past sundown, but I didn't see how I could. I shouldered my axe and started toward the cabin, trying to think up some excuse to tell Mama to keep her from knowing I was played clear out.

That's when I heard Little Arliss scream.

Well, Little Arliss was a screamer by nature. He'd scream when he was happy and scream when he was mad and a lot of times he'd scream just to hear himself make a noise. Generally, we paid no more mind to his screaming than we did to the boggle of a wild turkey.

Let's Think About...

What mental picture do you see when you read about Travis splitting logs?

▶ Visualize

But this time was different. The second I heard his screaming, I felt my heart flop clear over. This time I knew Little Arliss was in real trouble.

I tore out up the trail leading toward the cabin. A minute before, I'd been so tired out with my rail splitting that I couldn't have struck a trot. But now I raced through the tall trees in that creek bottom, covering ground like a scared wolf.

Little Arliss's second scream, when it came, was louder and shriller and more frantic-sounding than the first. Mixed with it was a whimpering crying sound that I knew didn't come from him. It was a sound I'd heard before and seemed like I ought to know what it was, but right then I couldn't place it.

Then, from way off to one side came a sound that I would have recognized anywhere. It was the coughing roar of a charging bear. I'd just heard it once in my life. That was the time Mama had shot and wounded a hog-killing bear and Papa had had to finish it off with a knife to keep it from getting her.

Let's **Think** About...

Based on what has happened so far, what do you think will happen next?
Predict and Set Purpose

My heart went to pushing up into my throat, nearly choking off my wind. I strained for every lick of speed I could get out of my running legs. I didn't know what sort of fix Little Arliss had got himself into, but I knew that it had to do with a mad bear, which was enough.

The way the late sun slanted through the trees had the trail all cross-banded with streaks of bright light and dark shade. I ran through these bright and dark patches so fast that the changing light nearly blinded me. Then suddenly, I raced out into the open where I could see ahead. And what I saw sent a chill clear through to the marrow of my bones.

There was Little Arliss, down in that spring hole again. He was lying half in and half out of the water, holding onto the hind leg of a little black bear cub no bigger than a small coon. The bear cub was out on the bank, whimpering and crying and clawing the rocks with all three of his other feet, trying to pull away. But Little Arliss was holding on for all he was worth, scared now and screaming his head off. Too scared to let go.

How the bear cub ever came to prowl close enough for Little Arliss to grab him, I don't know. And why he didn't turn on him and bite loose, I couldn't figure out, either. Unless he was like Little Arliss, too scared to think.

But all of that didn't matter now. What mattered was the bear cub's mama. She'd heard the cries of her baby and was coming to save him. She was coming so fast that she had the brush popping and breaking as she crashed through and over it. I could see her black heavy figure piling off down the slant on the far side of Birdsong Creek. She was roaring mad and ready to kill.

And worst of all, I could see that I'd never get there in time!

Mama couldn't either. She'd heard Arliss, too, and here she came from the cabin, running down the slant toward the spring, screaming at Arliss, telling him to turn the bear cub loose. But Little Arliss wouldn't do it. All he'd do was hang with that hind leg and let out one shrill shriek after another as fast as he could suck in a breath.

Let's Think About...

How does the author use language of the senses to tell how upset the two bears are at Little Arliss?
Story Structure

34

Let's **Think** About...

How does this illustration reinforce the words the author uses?

Visualize

35

Now the she bear was charging across the shallows in the creek. She was knocking sheets of water high in the bright sun, charging with her fur up and her long teeth bared, filling the canyon with that awful coughing roar. And no matter how fast Mama ran or how fast I ran, the she bear was going to get there first!

I think I nearly went blind then, picturing what was going to happen to Little Arliss. I know that I opened my mouth to scream and not any sound came out.

Then, just as the bear went lunging up the creek bank toward Little Arliss and her cub, a flash of yellow came streaking out of the brush.

It was that big yeller dog. He was roaring like a mad bull. He wasn't one-third as big and heavy as the she bear, but when he piled into her from one side, he rolled her clear off her feet. They went down in a wild, roaring tangle of twisting bodies and scrambling feet and slashing fangs.

As I raced past them, I saw the bear lunge up to stand on her hind feet like a man while she clawed at the body of the yeller dog hanging to her throat. I didn't wait to see more. Without ever checking my stride, I ran in and jerked Little Arliss loose from the cub. I grabbed him by the wrist and yanked him up out of that water and slung him toward Mama like he was a half-empty sack of corn. I screamed at Mama. "Grab him, Mama! Grab him and run!" Then I swung my chopping axe high and wheeled, aiming to cave in the she bear's head with the first lick.

But I never did strike. I didn't need to. Old Yeller hadn't let the bear get close enough. He couldn't handle her; she was too big and strong for that. She'd stand there on her hind feet, hunched over, and take a roaring swing at him with one of those big front claws. She'd slap him head over heels. She'd knock him so far that it didn't look like he could possibly get back there before she charged again, but he always did. He'd hit the ground rolling, yelling his head off with the pain of the blow; but somehow he'd always roll to his feet. And here he'd come again, ready to tie into her for another round.

Let's Think About...

How is the author building suspense during the battle between Old Yeller and the she bear?
Story Structure

Let's **Think** About...

What does this illustration suggest will happen? **Predict and Set Purpose**

I stood there with my axe raised, watching them for a long moment. Then from up toward the house, I heard Mama calling: "Come away from there, Travis. Hurry, son! Run!"

That spooked me. Up till then, I'd been ready to tie into that bear myself. Now, suddenly, I was scared out of my wits again. I ran toward the cabin.

But like it was, Old Yeller nearly beat me there. I didn't see it, of course, but Mama said that the minute Old Yeller saw we were all in the clear and out of danger, he threw the fight to that she bear and lit out for the house. The bear chased him for a little piece, but at the rate Old Yeller was leaving her behind, Mama said it looked like the bear was backing up.

But if the big yeller dog was scared or hurt in any way when he came dashing into the house, he didn't show it. He sure didn't show it like we all did. Little Arliss had hushed his screaming, but he was trembling all over and clinging to Mama like he'd never let her go. And Mama was sitting in the middle of the floor, holding him up close and crying like she'd never stop. And me, I was close to crying, myself.

Old Yeller, though, all he did was come bounding in to jump on us and lick us in the face and bark so loud that there, inside the cabin, the noise nearly made us deaf.

The way he acted, you might have thought that bear fight hadn't been anything more than a rowdy romp that we'd all taken part in for the fun of it.

Let's Think About...

Which words create the most vivid pictures in your mind about Old Yeller's return to his family?

Visualize

39

Common Core State Standards
Literature 1. Cite textual evidence to support analysis of what the text says explicitly as well as inferences drawn from the text. **Also Literature 2., Writing 9.**

Envision It! | Retell

Think Critically

1. On page 36, when the bear is charging at Little Arliss, Travis says, "I think I nearly went blind then. . . ." What can you infer about the relationship Travis has with Little Arliss? Compare their relationship to that of brothers in a different story you have read. **Text to Text**

2. Reread the incident with Little Arliss and the bear cub, paying special attention to the verbs the author uses to describe the action. Make a list of five of these verbs and explain their effect on the reader. **Think Like an Author**

3. Analyze how the setting of *Old Yeller* contributes to the story. Could this have taken place in a setting such as a desert? a city? Explain. **Literary Elements**

4. Look back to page 32 and reread the passage that describes Travis splitting rails. When you visualize this scene, how do you picture Travis? Describe what you see. **Visualize**

5. **Look Back and Write** Look back at page 30. Write a paragraph using your own words to describe the setting of this scene of *Old Yeller*. Provide evidence to support your answer.
Key Ideas and Details • Text Evidence

Meet the Author

Fred Gipson

Frederick Benjamin Gipson was born on a farm in Mason, Texas. He said that as a boy he liked to hunt, fish, and follow his hounds in search of fox, raccoon, and wildcat. Fred Gipson became a journalist and then a writer of short stories and novels. His most famous novel, and his favorite, is *Old Yeller,* a Newbery Honor Book that has sold more than three million copies. When it was made into a movie, Mr. Gipson was invited to Los Angeles to work on the screenplay. He is well known as a Southwest writer, and he was honored by many different groups for his writing. He died in 1973.

Other books by Fred Gipson:
Curly and the Wild Boar and *Little Arliss*

Use the Reading Log in the *Reader's and Writer's Notebook* to record your independent reading.

Common Core State Standards

Writing 3.a. Engage and orient the reader by establishing a context and introducing a narrator and/or characters; organize an event sequence that unfolds naturally and logically. **Also Writing 3.b., Language 1., 2., 3.**

Let's Write It!

Key Features of a Personal Narrative

- focuses on a real event from the writer's life

- written in the first person, "I"

- uses appropriate sensory details

READING STREET ONLINE
GRAMMAR JAMMER
www.ReadingStreet.com

Personal Narrative

A **personal narrative** recounts a memorable event or series of related events from the writer's life. The student model on the next page is an example of a personal narrative.

Writing Prompt In *Old Yeller*, Travis tells a story about his younger brother, Arliss. Think about something important, funny, or exciting that happened to you when you were younger. Now write a personal narrative about that experience.

Writer's Checklist

Remember, you should ...

☑ tell about something from your life.

☑ express your own style and tone.

☑ use descriptive details to capture readers' attention.

☑ use complete sentences.

My Birthday Surprise

When I was eight, Mom asked Dad and me to meet her at our favorite restaurant for dinner. We always drove there together, so I felt like something strange was going on.

When we got there, my mom met us at the door. She seemed nervous. She was giggling and peering out the window, and her hands kept fidgeting with the menu. She was also super speedy with everything—ordering and eating. At one point, she even excused herself from the table. Dad didn't seem to notice.

Why was my mom so excited? I thought maybe she was going to tell us that I was going to get a new baby brother or sister. Boy, was I wrong!

After dinner, we went outside. My mom gestured to her car.

"Ride with me."

I piled into the back seat. Suddenly, I was covered by a soft, furry, wiggling creature. Mom didn't want to leave my new puppy in the car for too long! What a surprise!

Genre
A **personal narrative** tells about an event in the writer's life.

Writing Trait
Author's **voice** may be revealed through description.

The four kinds of sentences are used correctly.

Conventions

Four Kinds of Sentences

Remember A **declarative sentence** makes a statement and ends with a period, an **interrogative sentence** asks a question, an **imperative sentence** gives a command, and an **exclamatory sentence** shows strong feeling with an exclamation mark.

Common Core State Standards
Informational Text 2. Determine a central idea of a text and how it is conveyed through particular details; provide a summary of the text distinct from personal opinions or judgments. **Also Writing 9.**

Social Studies in Reading

Genre
Expository Text

- Expository text tells about real people and events.

- Expository texts communicate information about the natural or social world.

- Read "A Dog's Life" and look for factual information that shows how dogs can be very important to people, from the fourteenth-century story to the present day.

A DOG'S LIFE

By Iain Zaczek

In the fourteenth century, a French historian named Froissart told the story of a prince who had to find a husband for his younger sister. The girl in question had three suitors, each of whom was brave, noble, and chivalrous. Indeed, these knights had so many fine qualities that the prince found it impossible to choose among them. So in the end, he decided to leave the final choice up to fate. Remembering his sister's fondness for her pet greyhound, he had the dog brought before the suitors and declared that the princess would marry whichever man the animal preferred.

It was a short contest. As soon as the greyhound was let off its leash, it ran over to the tallest of the three, started to

Greyhound

44

sniff his leg, and then began licking his hand with great affection. With this, the matter was decided. The princess accepted her brother's decision and the wedding took place within a week.

Bulldog

Let's **Think** About...

What point is the author making about the relationship of dogs to people, and what facts support his point?
Expository Text

What the prince didn't realize, of course, was that his sister had been meeting the lucky suitor in secret for some time, and that the young man had already befriended the dog. All of which goes to show that you should never underestimate the usefulness of keeping a dog. Ever since the beginning of time, dogs and humans have lived together and helped each other. Dogs can do many things better than people: they can run faster, their hearing is more acute, and their sense of smell is much stronger. Because of this, they have often been used for hunting, to provide food for their owners, or else as alert guard dogs. Some have helped detectives track down criminals, while others are sent out to rescue mountaineers trapped in snowdrifts. Shepherds always have dogs to keep their sheep under control, and guide dogs are equally invaluable to the blind.

Search-and-rescue worker talks on walkie-talkie, with German shepherd on duty.

45

Let's **Think** About...

Different dog breeds with different traits have been deliberately developed. How does the author explain this fact?
Expository Text

Poodle

There are many different breeds of dog because some are better than others at carrying out certain types of tasks. Today, most dogs are kept as household pets, so their original purpose has often been forgotten. Poodles, for example, were originally bred as water dogs, helping huntsmen to fetch their prey from lakes and rivers. Their hair was clipped short so that they could move more easily through the water, but it was left longer at the joints to prevent rheumatism. The name comes from *puddeln*, a German word for "splashing about." Similarly, dachshunds were deliberately bred with short legs and long bodies so that they could wriggle down holes and chase badgers (*dachs-hund* means "badger dog"). Dalmatians were used as carriage dogs, running alongside their owners' horse-drawn coach to protect them against highwaymen. Fortunately, all these practices have long since been abandoned, and the animals can lead a much more pleasant life as pets.

Dachshund

Dalmatian

Why are dogs so keen to help us? Apart from the fact that we give them food, they are used to living in packs and are adaptable enough to think of humans as part of this extended family. So when your pet tries to convince you that he would rather sleep in your bedroom than in the kitchen or the yard, he is following a perfectly natural instinct. He is trying to remain as close as possible to you, the honorary leader of his pack.

Let's Think About...

Reading Across Texts From what you read about Old Yeller, which of the dogs mentioned in "A Dog's Life" seems most like him?

Writing Across Texts Write a comparison of Old Yeller with the dog you chose.

Vocabulary

Synonyms

Thesaurus Remember that a thesaurus is similar to a dictionary. Words are organized in alphabetical order. A thesaurus is useful because it lists synonyms, or words with nearly identical meanings. Some thesauruses also list antonyms, or words with opposite meanings.

Practice It! Look back at *Old Yeller* and select two words from the Words to Know list. Use a thesaurus to find a synonym for each word. Use a dictionary to be absolutely sure of the meanings of the synonyms you find. Then find the Words to Know that you selected in *Old Yeller* and replace them with their synonyms.

Fluency

Expression

Remember that when you read aloud, you can use different tones and expressions in your voice to show emotion. Reading with expression lets you show the suspense, concern, or excitement in a story.

Practice It! With a partner, read aloud paragraphs 2–4 on page 31 of *Old Yeller*. Pay attention to the words of Mama and Travis and read them with expression. Take turns reading and offering each other feedback.

48

Listening and Speaking

Whether you are telling or listening to a story, pay attention to tone and mood.

Storytelling

Storytelling is a way of sharing information orally. Stories have a beginning, a middle, and an end. They also use vivid language to keep listeners' attention.

Practice It! In a small group, make up a story about an animal that helps people, such as a service dog. Tell what this animal's life might be like. Plan your story so that everyone in the group makes a contribution to what will happen. Tell your story to the class.

Tips

Listening . . .

- Listen attentively to each speaker.
- Listen to identify tone and mood.
- Take notes so that you can ask relevant questions.

Speaking . . .

- Speak to entertain the audience.
- Use clear, vivid language.
- Use appropriate tone and mood.

Teamwork . . .

- Pay close attention to the storytellers before you.
- Don't take up too much time.

Common Core State Standards

Language 6. Acquire and use accurately grade-appropriate general academic and domain-specific words and phrases; gather vocabulary knowledge when considering a word or phrase important to comprehension or expression. **Also Speaking/Listening 1.c.**

Oral Vocabulary

Let's Talk About

Community

- Describe the community where you live.

- Ask questions about what makes a community.

- Express opinions about why communities are important to people.

READING STREET ONLINE
CONCEPT TALK VIDEO
www.ReadingStreet.com

Common Core State Standards

Literature 2. Determine a theme or central idea of a text and how it is conveyed through particular details; provide a summary of the text distinct from personal opinions or judgments. **Also Literature 1.**

Envision It! | Skill Strategy

Skill

Strategy

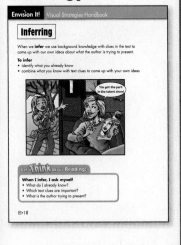

Comprehension Skill

Literary Elements: Character and Theme

- Characters are the people who take part in the events of the story.

- Theme is the main idea or central meaning of a piece of writing. The theme is often not stated. You can find it using evidence from the story as clues.

- Use a graphic organizer like the one below to identify characters and theme as you read "Linda and Val" on page 53.

Characters	Val and Linda
Theme	
First clue	Linda does not want to work with Val because of her physical challenge.
Second clue	When Val's fingers will not open, the girls cooperate as Linda pries Val's hand open.
Third clue	Linda decides to be friends with Val and that she likes working with her.

Comprehension Strategy

Inferring

Authors do not always directly tell readers everything about the characters, events, and theme in a story. Sometimes you need to infer, or figure out, what is not stated directly.

LINDA AND VAL

"Today we'll weigh objects. For homework, you'll make a graph of the weights," Mr. Daniels said. "Linda, you work with Val."

Linda's eyes widened in disbelief. "Val?" Linda said. Val had joined the class just last week. She had cerebral palsy.

Linda looked at Val, who was attempting to stand up. Her arms and legs shook. Linda rolled her eyes. Val slowly wobbled over and said, "Hi, Linda." Linda did not reply.

Once Val sat down, Linda asked, "Have you ever weighed an object?"

"Sure, even shaky old me," Val joked. The humorous reply surprised Linda, and she relaxed a little.

Val tried to place a weight on the scale, but her hand stayed closed. Then her clenched fist began to shake. "Could you pry that open for me?" Val asked. Linda slowly peeled Val's fingers back until the weight dropped. "Nice job," Val said, smiling. "You didn't even need a crowbar." Linda smiled. "Do you want me to put the next weight on?" she asked.

"Sure, this time I might never let go!" Val quipped. Both girls laughed and continued working. At the end of the class, Val asked, "Do you want to come over to my home after school? We could work on the graph together."

Linda didn't even hesitate. "Sure."

Skill Remember that you can learn about a character by the way he or she acts. What does Linda's facial expression tell you about her?

Skill Linda has begun to change her actions and words toward Val. What does this tell you about Val's character?

Strategy Linda and Val may become friends after this experience. What do you think caused this to happen?

Your Turn!

⏸ **Need a Review?** See the *Envision It! Handbook* for help with literary elements—theme and character—and inferring.

▶ **Ready to Try It?** Use what you've learned about character and theme as you read *Mother Fletcher's Gift*.

Mother Fletcher's Gift

53

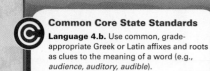

Common Core State Standards
Language 4.b. Use common, grade-appropriate Greek or Latin affixes and roots as clues to the meaning of a word (e.g., *audience, auditory, audible*).

Envision It! | Words to Know

fixtures

flimsy

incident

apparently

subscribe

survive

Vocabulary Strategy for

🎯 Greek and Latin Roots

Word Structure When you come across a word you don't know, look for word parts you have seen in words that you do know. Many words are built from Greek or Latin roots. For example, *scribe* is the root of the Latin word *scribere*, meaning "to write." A scribe is a person who writes. You can often figure out a word's meaning by examining its Greek or Latin root.

1. Check a word for any recognizable Greek or Latin word parts.

2. Use a dictionary to look up Greek or Latin roots you do not know.

3. Use the meaning of the root, as well as other word parts, to help you figure out the meaning of the word.

4. Reread the sentence. Does this meaning for the word make sense?

Read "Saving the Past." Look for Greek and Latin roots to help you figure out the meanings of words. You may also use the glossary to help you figure out the meanings of this week's Words to Know.

Words to Write Reread "Saving the Past." What building or location in your community is a part of history? Write about this place and tell why it should never be destroyed. Use as many words from the Words to Know list as you can.

Saving the Past

Have you ever known people who are trying to save an old building from being torn down? You may have said, "So what? What's the big deal?" As far as you can see, it apparently is worthless. The roof is caving in, and the paint has faded and peeled. It looks tired and ugly and flimsy. Why not tear it down, you ask? Something cool like a mini-mall or a bicycle store could go there.

The building may be a historic landmark. You probably have several in your area. These are buildings that are rich in history. They have importance to the people of the community. Perhaps some historic incident took place there, like the birth of a President or the creation of an important invention. Maybe the building shows the details and style of a time we want to remember. Its roof, trim, and antique fixtures capture the charm of an era that is past.

Most people subscribe to the idea that we should save these buildings. They need to be preserved and treasured. While they survive, we can take pride in remembering part of who we were and are.

Your Turn!

 **Need a Review?** For help using Greek and Latin roots to define unfamiliar words, see *Words!*

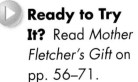 **Ready to Try It?** Read *Mother Fletcher's Gift* on pp. 56–71.

Realistic fiction includes stories about imaginary people and events that could happen in real life. Look for realistic actions and events as you read.

Mother Fletcher's Gift

by *Walter Dean Myers*
illustrated by *William Low*

Question of the Week
Why should we care about people we don't know?

It was rumored that Mother Fletcher was well over ninety years old. She had become a legend on 145th Street. If anybody wanted to know what the neighborhood looked like in the twenties, where Jack Johnson had lived, perhaps, or where James Baldwin's father had preached, Mother Fletcher could tell you. Patrolman William Michael O'Brien had heard about her shortly after his assignment to the precinct, but it wasn't until nearly three months later that he actually met the old woman.

He was on foot patrol and had stopped to pass a few words with one of the local shopkeepers when a young black girl came running up to him and told him that Mother Fletcher was sick and needed an ambulance. O'Brien knew that in this neighborhood it was nearly impossible to get a doctor who would make house calls. But he had also been told that sometimes the people used ambulances just to go downtown.

He followed the girl into one of the buildings and into a first-floor apartment. The place was small but spotless. The floor was covered with a linoleum rug that was worn through in several spots. The porcelain in the kitchen sink was discolored but the brass fixtures were shining brightly.

"She's in here," the girl said, and went into the adjoining room.

Mother Fletcher sat upright in the white-sheeted bed, her pale green housecoat pinned at the neck. O'Brien had never seen as black a person in his entire life. Her skin was a dull ebony that seemed almost purple in the light of the lamp by her bed.

Her gray hair, still streaked with wisps of black and thinner on the sides than on the top, framed her face and, catching the light, made her look like a black version of a painted medieval saint. She was a small person, in the delicate way that a child is small, but with the quiet grace of her years. But what stood out most on the old woman were her eyes.

They were, if it was possible, even darker than her skin. Black shiny eyes that darted brightly about, checking the room for anything that might have been out of place.

"Didn't my great-great-grandchild there tell you I was sick?" Mother Fletcher shot a glance in the direction of the girl. "I gave her a dime to tell you."

"I mean," O'Brien said, "what *exactly* is the matter?"

"How do I know? I'm not a doctor." Mother Fletcher pulled the housecoat tighter around her thin shoulders.

"What's your name, please?"

"Mother Fletcher."

"What's your first name?"

"I'm Mother Fletcher, that's all. Now, are you going to get me an ambulance or do I have to send that child out for another officer?"

"We can't just call an ambulance any time someone says to call one," O'Brien said.

"Boy, I am not someone," the old woman said. "I am Mother Fletcher and you can call for an ambulance. You know how to use that radio you got."

"What is your age?" O'Brien flipped out his radio and called the emergency network.

"Full-grown," came the flat reply.

O'Brien stepped into the next room and told the operator what he had. The ambulance arrived some fifteen minutes later. Two slim attendants carried the old woman out. O'Brien wrote up the incident in his book and promptly put it out of his mind.

A week later he was called into one of the precinct offices, where a lieutenant and two patrolmen were waiting for him.

"O'Brien." Lt. Stanton rolled a cigar from one side of his mouth to the other. "What's this I hear about you taking graft?"

"I don't know what you're talking about," O'Brien answered.

"Well, this package just came in from someone on your beat and it's addressed to your shield number." The lieutenant was enjoying this. "Looks like graft to me, O'Brien. Open it up."

O'Brien looked at the childish scrawl on the top of the box. *To Officer 4566.* There was no return address. He flipped open the flimsy box and took out the contents. It was a knitted green cardigan. Instead of a brand name on the label it simply repeated his badge number, 4566. O'Brien tried it on and was surprised to discover that it fit even his long arms.

"I wonder who it's from?"

"Mother Fletcher," the lieutenant said. "You do anything for her?"

"Mother Fletcher? Oh, yes, the old black lady. I called an ambulance for her. No big thing."

"She probably started making that sweater for you on the way to the hospital," Lt. Stanton said. "We had another guy here about two years ago that straightened out a hassle she had with her landlord. She made him a sweater too. Then she decided that the landlord was right after all and she made *him* a sweater. I guess it makes her feel good. You can put a couple of bucks in the precinct fund to make up for the sweater. And don't forget to go around and thank Mother Fletcher. It's good for community P.R."

O'Brien got around to thanking the old woman a few days later, telling her how his wife had been jealous of such a fine sweater. Three weeks later another package arrived at the station house. It was a sweater for his wife. When he went over to thank Mother Fletcher for the second sweater he was careful not to mention that he had a six-year-old daughter.

Over the next months O'Brien learned more about Mother Fletcher from people on his beat. Some stories were a bit far-fetched, but they were all told in a way that said that people loved the old woman. She did her own shopping, always carrying the same blue cloth shopping bag, and always walking on the sunny side of the street "to keep the bones warm." Once O'Brien met her on the corner of 147th Street and asked how she was feeling.

"I'm feeling just fine. I'm not cutting the rug," she said, "but I'm not lying on it, either."

O'Brien talked to her now and again when he saw her on the street, and started writing down everything she said, trying to piece together enough information to determine her true age. In truth, Mother Fletcher was the only one in his precinct that he thought of during his off-duty hours. The struggle and hassles of Harlem were not what he wanted to bring home with him. It didn't take O'Brien long to subscribe to the precinct motto—Eight and Straight. Eight hours on the job and straight out of the neighborhood.

To O'Brien, "out of the neighborhood" meant home to a ranch-style house in suburban Staten Island. He looked forward to the day when his wife, Kathy, could quit her job with the utility company and stay home with their daughter, Meaghan. He had told Kathy about Mother Fletcher and they had gone over his notes in the evenings trying to figure her age. Beyond this O'Brien was careful to keep his job apart from his family. At least he was until just before Christmas.

"Hi, honey," Bill called out as he ducked in from the light snow.

"Dinner's almost ready," Kathy answered as she came from the kitchen. "Did you ask Mother Fletcher if she remembered when Woodrow Wilson was elected President?"

"Yep."

"Well, what did she say?" Kathy wiped her hands on her apron.

"She said she remembered it."

"Did she remember how old she was then?"

"Nope, unless you can figure how old ''bout half grown' is," Bill said. He tousled his daughter's hair and sat on the couch.

"What else did she say?" Kathy folded one leg under herself and sat on it.

"Not much. I think she knows that I'm trying to figure out her age, and she's playing with me." Bill glanced toward the kitchen and sniffed the air. "Is that roast beef?"

"Chicken," Kathy answered. "So that's all she said today?"

"No, she complained about how loud the teenagers play their radios and, oh, yes, she invited us to Christmas dinner."

"Who invited us to dinner?" Meaghan looked up from her book.

"A lady Daddy knows in Harlem, sweetheart."

"Can we take presents over?"

"We won't be going over," Bill said.

"Why, Daddy?"

"We have other plans. We're going to . . . what are we doing for Christmas, Kathy?"

"Nothing."

"Then we can go!" Meaghan said.

"Kathy, will you deal with your daughter?" Bill smiled as he reached for the paper. "She's too much for me."

"No, I won't." Kathy got up. "I'm going to start serving dinner. And Meaghan has a right to ask a question."

"Hey, let's not make an issue of this," Bill said.

64

"She just asked for a simple explanation, Bill." Kathy was annoyed.

"The lady is a little different, that's all." Bill spoke to his daughter. "The place she lives in isn't very nice, and Daddy would rather not spend his Christmas in that kind of a neighborhood."

"Is she a poor lady?"

"Yes, she's a poor lady."

"Then we can take her a present because poor people like presents."

"We'll send her a present if you want, Meaghan." Bill rose from the couch and went into the living room, snapping on the television before sitting down. Kathy followed him in.

"I don't like the idea of being made out to be a bad guy, Kathy," Bill said without looking away from the six o'clock news. "One word from you could have helped that little situation in there."

"Why didn't you just give her the same answer you gave Mother Fletcher? What did you tell her?"

"There are times, Kathy, when you don't give direct answers to questions. It's a way of dealing with people. You don't reject them, and you don't get yourself involved in a whole scene. Like this one, I might add."

"Would you mind giving *me* a direct answer? What did you tell her?"

"I told her yes, we'd come. But they know we don't come into that neighborhood when we're off duty," Bill answered. "And they're not that anxious to have us come, either."

"You said yes? That you'd come?" Kathy pulled her glasses from the top of her head and put them on. "That's your way of not answering a question directly?"

"I'll send her a present."

"That's awfully sweet of you, Mr. O'Brien." Kathy went back to the kitchen.

Bill turned up the television and watched as some senator complained about the military budget. If his wife had chosen this occasion to have one of her special "I simply don't understand" periods he wasn't going to fight her.

He also heard snatches of the conversation drifting from the kitchen. Meaghan was talking about getting a kitten and was trying to decide between a calico and a tabby. At any rate she seemed to have forgotten Mother Fletcher. He only hoped that Kathy would too.

And apparently she had. For that was the last O'Brien heard about visiting the old woman. That is, it was the last thing until just after eleven on Christmas morning. He was sitting in his favorite armchair, feeling especially regal in the smoking jacket that Kathy had given him, watching a college football game, when Kathy and Meaghan came into the room with their coats on.

"Going for a walk?" Bill asked, hoping he wouldn't be expected to leave his comfortable spot.

"We're going to Mother Fletcher's for dinner," Meaghan said brightly.

"You're not going to Mother Fletcher's, Kathy. And that's that!"

"Well, then I suggest you arrest me, Mr. O'Brien." The sunlight through the window caught the flare in Kathy's eyes. "Because that will be the only way you're going to prevent our going."

"I brought her a scarf." Meaghan held a small square package.

"What is this all about?" Bill felt his face getting red. "You don't even know this woman. Why do you have to drag Meaghan all the way to Harlem?"

"I'm not dragging her anywhere. I'm giving her the present of a visit to an old lady that even you like. Now, from what you say, all I have to do is go over to the neighborhood and ask anyone where she lives because they all know, right? Or would you like to drop us off?"

The silence of the long drive was broken only by an occasional observation from Meaghan. O'Brien took his wife slowly, carefully, through the worst streets he could find until he finally pulled up in front of Mother Fletcher's place.

"Well, well, well!" Mother Fletcher was wearing an ankle-length green dress with a white lace collar. She wore a red and gold pin shaped like a tree. "I thought I was going to be having Christmas dinner by myself this year." Bill shot a glance in Kathy's direction as they entered the small apartment. The smell of the ham in the oven filled the room.

"Mother Fletcher, this is my wife, Kathy, and this is Meaghan."

"Well, ain't she the prettiest little thing. Look just like her mama too. Sit on down in here while I see if I can't get something together for dinner. Did I wish you a Merry Christmas yet? Merry Christmas, children."

"Merry Christmas, and here's a present." Meaghan gave Mother Fletcher the package.

"Thank you, child," Mother Fletcher said.

"Daddy didn't want to come," Meaghan said, pulling off her coat.

"I just didn't want to put you out," Bill said quickly.

"Child, I don't blame you one bit," Mother Fletcher said. "You working here all week and then coming back on a holiday. But it's good for you to see we have holidays here too. You see the people in the street all wishing each other a Merry Christmas and dressed up in their churchgoing clothes. You see them in this frame and you get a different picture of them. Don't you think so, Officer?"

"Yeah, I guess you're right," Bill answered.

"You can take your coat off," Mother Fletcher said. "I'll put it in a safe place."

"Those plates are so lovely!" Kathy went to the kitchen table where three plates were set out. "Are they antiques?"

"Everything in this house is an antique, including me," Mother Fletcher said as she took another plate from the cabinet.

"It's a lovely setting and there sure are a lot of pots on the stove for you not to be expecting anyone."

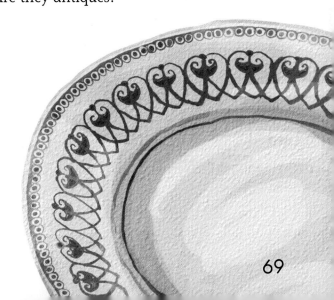

"Well, honey, let me tell you something. You don't survive, and that's what I been doing all these years, you don't survive sitting around expecting folks to act right." She opened the oven door, poked a fork in the ham and watched the clear juices run down its side, and then closed it. "'Cause the more you expect the more you get your heart broke up. But you got to be ready when they do act right because that's what makes the surviving worth surviving. That make any sense to you, honey?"

"It makes quite a bit of sense."

"That child of yours eat sweet potatoes?"

"Yes, she loves them," Kathy said. "Can I help you with anything?"

"You can help me with anything you have a mind to," Mother Fletcher said. "'Bout time you asked me too, old as I am."

"You're not as old as Santa Claus," volunteered Meaghan.

"Santa Claus?" Mother Fletcher put down the dish towel and turned her head to one side. "Child, I knew Santa Claus when he wasn't nothing but a little fellow. Let's see now. He wasn't any bigger than you when I knew him. Me and him used to play catch down near the schoolyard."

And Mother Fletcher went off into telling stories to Meaghan about how long she had known Santa Claus and how she used to have to lend him her handkerchief because his nose was always running.

And the Christmas dinner wasn't the best that the O'Briens would ever have but it was far from being the worst. But then, that's not what this story is about. This story is about how a policeman's young family brought a few hours of happiness to an old woman. Or perhaps it's about how an old woman taught a young family something about sharing. Or maybe, just maybe, it is about how a six-year-old girl found the only person in the world who played catch with Santa Claus when he was a little boy, even though she was a lot older than he was.

© Common Core State Standards

Literature 1. Cite textual evidence to support analysis of what the text says explicitly as well as inferences drawn from the text. **Also Literature 2., Writing 9.**

Envision It! Retell

Think Critically

1. Think about people you know who may be alone on holidays. Would you consider visiting them or inviting them to visit you on a holiday? Explain your answer. **Text to Self**

2. Mother Fletcher is a fictional character, but the author describes her in a way that makes her seem real. Find details from the story that bring her to life for the reader. **Think Like an Author**

3. The author reveals Officer O'Brien's character through the things he does. Find three examples of Officer O'Brien's actions that show his character, and explain how they do so. **Literary Elements**

4. Why did Mother Fletcher tell her stories about Santa Claus to Meaghan? What do you think Meaghan thought about the stories? **Inferring**

5. **Look Back and Write** At first, Officer O'Brien doesn't want to go to Mother Fletcher's for Christmas dinner. Write a paragraph from Officer O'Brien's point of view explaining how he feels after having dinner with his family at Mother Fletcher's house. Provide evidence to support your answer.

   Key Ideas and Details • Text Evidence

Walter Dean Myers

Walter Dean Myers was born in West Virginia but moved with his foster parents to Harlem when he was three years old. He grew up and went to school there, in New York City, before he joined the army. After that he earned a college degree while he worked at many different jobs. At night, though, he wrote, mainly for magazines. One day he came across a contest for black writers of children's books and decided to enter. That decision changed his life. He won the contest, and the book he submitted, *Where Does the Day Go?*, was soon published. From then on he never stopped writing. His work has earned Newbery Honors, the Coretta Scott King Award, and other prizes.

Other books by Walter Dean Myers: *Amistad* and *The Dream Bearer*

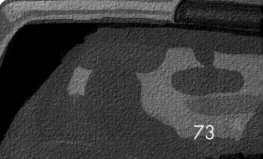

Use the Reading Log in the *Reader's and Writer's Notebook* to record your independent reading.

73

Common Core State Standards

Writing 4. Produce clear and coherent writing in which the development, organization, and style are appropriate to task, purpose, and audience. **Also Writing 9., Language 1.**

Let's Write It!

Key Features of a Thank-You Letter

- begins with a greeting
- expresses thanks
- includes personal details
- ends with a closing

READING STREET ONLINE GRAMMAR JAMMER
www.ReadingStreet.com

Expository

Thank-You Letter

A **thank-you letter** is a letter or note that expresses thanks. The student model on the next page is an example of a thank-you letter.

Writing Prompt *Mother Fletcher's Gift* is the story of friendship between people who might not ordinarily be connected. Think of characters in the story who learned or received something valuable from each other, and have one write a thank-you letter to the other.

Writer's Checklist

Remember, you should ...

☑ begin with a polite greeting.

☑ provide details that show what you are thankful for.

☑ write in complete sentences with subjects and predicates.

☑ end with a polite closing.

74

Thursday, December 26

Dear Mother Fletcher,

I want to thank you so much for your invitation to Christmas dinner. Meaghan, Bill, and I all had a wonderful time.

Your long green dress with the lace trim added to the Christmas spirit. So did your beautiful dishes. The ham was tasty and juicy, and the sweet potatoes were cooked to perfection.

Meaghan especially enjoyed your stories about Santa Claus. Her eyes sparkled the whole time you were speaking.

By the way, you were right when you said that it was good for Bill to come to Harlem on a holiday. We saw red and green wherever we looked. Everyone was dressed for church and full of Christmas spirit. He came to know Harlem and your neighbors in a new way. It was kind of you to share your Christmas day with us.

Yours truly,
Kathy

Genre
A **thank-you letter** begins with a greeting and a thank you.

Subjects and Predicates are used correctly.

Writing Trait Focus/Ideas Strong details support the ideas in the letter.

Conventions

Subjects and Predicates

Remember Every sentence must have a **subject** and a **predicate.** The subject is the word or group of words that tells who or what the sentence is about. The predicate tells something about the subject, such as what the subject is or does.

75

Social Studies in Reading

Genre
Expository Text

- Expository text informs readers about real people and places of the past or present.

- The purpose of expository text is to communicate information about the natural or social world.

- Expository texts present, in a straightforward manner, facts that support the topic.

- Read "The Harlem Renaissance" and look for information that explains why this historic period is still important today.

THE HARLEM RENAISSANCE

from *Cobblestone* magazine

IN THE 1920S AND EARLY 1930S, Harlem was the largest black urban community in the country. Many African Americans had moved there from the South in the two decades since 1900. Harlem was a community of families, homes, and businesses. It also was the spiritual center of the Harlem Renaissance, a 1920s artistic movement made up of black writers, poets, dancers, singers, actors, composers, and painters. A renaissance is a rebirth or rediscovery and is often a time when much artistic activity takes place. Black artists in the 1920s were interested not only in rediscovering their African roots and culture but also in understanding their place in American society.

The times—the Roaring Twenties—played a big role in giving these artists the opportunity to voice their black experiences. World War I had just ended, times were better economically for most people, including the black middle class, and people everywhere were eager to shed old ideas and accept new ones. Caught up in the

ZORA NEALE HURSTON

excitement of the times, black artists were eager to be heard, and many people listened.

The artists of the Harlem Renaissance were not a formal, organized group. They did not attend scheduled weekly meetings with set agendas or share a common political or philosophical belief. It was this growing black city within New York City, Harlem, and their common cultural experience that brought them together. Most of these artists lived in Harlem at one time or another and saw each other on the streets, in the library, and at parties, clubs, formal dinners, and readings. Many were friends. The Harlem artists also had strong relationships with their patrons, mostly whites who lived downtown. With their connections to publishing houses, art dealers, and the wealthy class, these patrons helped get African American art published, performed, and exhibited.

In the 1930s, when the economy collapsed and times got bad, the Harlem Renaissance lost its momentum. Money was no longer available to support the artists, and Harlem lost its focus as the center of the movement. But the creativity it inspired did not die. The spirit of the renaissance and the enormous body of art it produced have continued into the present to enrich those who enjoy it and to inspire new artists, both black and white.

LANGSTON HUGHES

Let's **Think** About...

Who were the real people of the Harlem Renaissance? What kinds of art did they create, and in what city is Harlem located?
Expository Text

Let's **Think** About...

Reading Across Texts Mother Fletcher says she lived in Harlem during its renaissance. Do you think her life would have been easier or more difficult back then?

Writing Across Texts Write a paragraph explaining your answer.

Let's Learn It!

READING STREET ONLINE
ONLINE STUDENT EDITION
www.ReadingStreet.com

Vocabulary

Greek and Latin Roots

Word Structure Many English words with Greek or Latin roots have prefixes or suffixes added to them. Recognizing roots and other word parts can help you decode new multi-syllable words. If you know the meaning of the root and the prefix or suffix, you can often figure out the meaning of a word.

Practice It! Look at the word *suburban*. What does the Latin root *urb* mean? Think of other words that use the same root. Can you guess the meaning? ("city") Now choose a vocabulary word that has a Greek or Latin root. Work with a partner to find other words with that root.

Fluency

Rate

As you read aloud, you will use different rates, or speeds, for different types of text. When you read descriptions, speak as you would normally speak. When you read dialogue, read the characters' words as they would speak them.

Practice It! With a partner, practice reading the conversation between Mother Fletcher and Officer O'Brien on page 61. Think about how each character might sound, and read the words as the characters would say them.

Listening and Speaking

Get Ready For High School

When you participate in planning a discussion, follow proper etiquette for conversation.

Talk Show

A talk show on television or radio discusses a specific topic and often allows listeners to call in with questions.

Practice It! Work with several classmates to prepare a talk show. Have the host interview other group members about the history of your neighborhood and community. Encourage your audience to "call in" with questions. Take turns listening and speaking.

Tips

Listening . . .

- Have a purpose for listening: to learn new things, to form an opinion, to solve problems, or for enjoyment.
- Pay attention and listen quietly.

Speaking . . .

- Speak clearly and distinctly.
- Speak at an appropriate pace.

Teamwork . . .

- Work together on the research.
- Take turns speaking.
- Listen carefully to "call-in" questions so that responses address the questions.

Common Core State Standards

Language 6. Acquire and use accurately grade-appropriate general academic and domain-specific words and phrases; gather vocabulary knowledge when considering a word or phrase important to comprehension or expression. **Also Speaking/Listening 1.c.**

Let's Talk About

Changes

- Describe how people safely meet strangers.

- Express opinions about the opportunities that await someone who moves to a new place.

- Ask questions about how change can help us grow.

READING STREET ONLINE
CONCEPT TALK VIDEO
www.ReadingStreet.com

Common Core State Standards

Literature 2. Determine a theme or central idea of a text and how it is conveyed through particular details; provide a summary of the text distinct from personal opinions or judgments. **Also Literature 1.**

Envision It! | Skill Strategy

Skill

Strategy

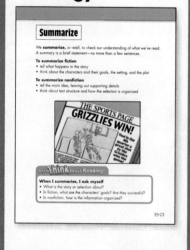

Comprehension Skill

Compare and Contrast

- When you compare and contrast, you tell how two or more things are alike and different.

- Clue words such as *like* or *as* show similarities. Clue words such as *but* or *unlike* show differences.

- You can also sum up differences and similarities between two things or people as in this example: *James is quiet while Juanita is outgoing, but they both like sports.*

- Make a graphic organizer like the one below to compare and contrast Marville and Abbey Creek as you read "This New Town."

Marville
Trait
Trait

Both
Trait
Trait

Abbey Creek
Trait
Trait

Comprehension Strategy

Summarize

Good readers understand text better when they summarize, or briefly state, the most important ideas in a selection. When you summarize something, use your own words, or paraphrase, and focus on main ideas rather than on details.

This New Town

It's been a year since we moved to Abbey Creek. I am still getting acquainted with my new town.

In Marville, we could play outside even after dusk. All summer long we'd play games in the street. There weren't many cars to be concerned about. Because there is so much traffic in Abbey Creek, we play in the yards instead of the street. The yards in Marville were really spacious. The yards here are like postage stamps.

In some ways, though, Abbey Creek is superior to Marville. The houses here are more interesting. Each one is unique. In Marville, the houses all looked similar. There are more places to visit here. There are convenience stores and comic book shops. Abbey Creek is like a carnival; Marville was like a golf course.

Despite the differences, the two towns have things in common. Both of them have outstanding schools. Each town's park district offers a lot of classes and sports. Abbey Creek has a terrific public library just like Marville did. And, like Marville, it has a lot of kids, although I'm not familiar with all of them yet.

Skill What does comparing the yards to postage stamps tell you about the yards?

Skill Compare the houses in the two towns. How are they different?

Strategy Summarize why Abbey Creek is superior to Marville. Then summarize how the two places are similar.

Your Turn!

 **Need a Review?** See the *Envision It! Handbook* for help with comparing and contrasting and summarizing.

 **Ready to Try It?** Use what you've learned about comparing and contrasting as you read *Viva New Jersey*.

Common Core State Standards
Language 4.a. Use context (e.g., the overall meaning of a sentence or paragraph; a word's position or function in a sentence) as a clue to the meaning of a word or phrase. **Also Language 4.**

Envision It! | Words to Know

corridors

groping

menacing

destination

mongrel

persisted

pleas

Vocabulary Strategy for
Unfamiliar Words

Context Clues Sometimes you can use context clues—the words and sentences around an unfamiliar word—to help you figure out the meaning of the word.

1. Read the words and sentences around the unfamiliar word. The author may give you a definition of the word, examples, or a relationship that can help you predict the word's meaning.

2. If not, say what the sentence means in your own words.

3. Predict a meaning for the unfamiliar word.

4. Try your predicted meaning in the sentence. Does it make sense?

Read "The Traveler." Use context clues to help you figure out the meanings of any unfamiliar words you find.

Words to Write Reread "The Traveler." Imagine you find an animal that needs to be rescued, and write about how you would rescue it. Use words from the Words to Know list as you write.

The Traveler

The dog I found standing in the yard was a hungry-looking mongrel. He was put together like a puzzle of many different breeds. Every rib stuck out. He might have been lost or even abandoned. I knew he had belonged to someone, for he was not one bit menacing. He wagged his tail politely and lowered his head to be petted. This dog had manners, and someone had taught them to him.

The feel of his ribs made me wince. I made for the kitchen. While I was groping in the cupboard for some bread, I thought I saw a movement. Sure enough, he had started trotting down the road. I tore back to the yard like a sprinter, hollering after him. He was deaf to my pleas that he return. Instead, he persisted in moving off at a brisk pace. It was as if he had a destination set in his mind. How far did he have to go, and how would he survive?

In the years since then, I have often wondered with a twinge of regret whether that dog made it home. I cannot forget his faithful path through the dusty corridors of that lost summer.

Your Turn!

Need a Review?
For help using context clues for unfamiliar words, see *Words!*

Ready to Try It?
Read *Viva New Jersey* on pp. 86–99.

Viva New Jersey

by Gloria Gonzalez
illustrated by Melodye Rosales

Genre

Realistic fiction stories have settings and characters that seem like real people though the stories are made up. As you read, notice the details in the story that give the feeling of reality.

86

Question of the Week

How do we learn to connect with others in a new place?

As far as dogs go, it wasn't much of a prize—a hairy mongrel with clumps of bubble gum wadded on its belly. Pieces of multicolored hard candies were matted in its fur. The leash around its neck was fashioned from a cloth belt, the kind usually seen attached to old bathrobes. The dog's paws were clogged with mud from yesterday's rain, and you could see where the animal had gnawed at the irritated skin around the swollen pads.

The dog was tied to an anemic tree high above the cliffs overlooking the Hudson River and the majestic New York City skyline.

Lucinda traveled the route each day on her way to the high school, along the New Jersey side of the river. The short walk saddened her, despite its panoramic vista of bridges and skyscrapers, for the river reminded her of the perilous journey six months earlier, when she and her family had escaped from Cuba in a makeshift boat with seven others.

They had spent two freezing nights adrift in the ocean, uncertain of their destination, till a U.S. Coast Guard cutter towed them to the shores of Key West.

From there they wound their way north, staying temporarily with friends in Miami and finally settling in West New York, New Jersey, the most densely populated town in the United States. Barely a square mile, high above the Palisades, the town boasted

a population of 47,000. Most of the community was housed in mammoth apartment buildings that seemed to reach into the clouds. The few private homes had cement lawns and paved driveways where there should have been backyards.

Lucinda longed for the spacious front porch where she'd sat at night with her friends while her grandmother bustled about the house, humming her Spanish songs. Lucinda would ride her bike to school and sometimes not see a soul for miles, just wildflowers amid a forest of greenery.

Now it was cement and cars and trucks and motorcycles and clanging fire engines that seemed to be in constant motion, shattering the air with their menacing roar.

Lucinda longed painfully for her grandmother. The old woman had refused to leave her house in Cuba, despite the family's pleas, so she had remained behind, promising to see them again one day.

The teenager, tall and slight of build with long dark hair that reached down her spine, was uncomfortable among her new classmates, most of whom she towered over. Even though the majority of them spoke Spanish and came from Cuba, Argentina, and Costa Rica, they were not like any of her friends back home. These "American" girls wore heavy makeup to school, dressed in jeans and high heels, and talked about rock singers and TV stars that she knew nothing of. They all seemed to be busy, rushing through the school corridors, huddling in laughing groups, mingling freely with boys, and chatting openly with teachers as if they were personal friends.

It was all too confusing.

Things weren't much better at home. Her parents had found jobs almost immediately and were often away from the tiny, cramped apartment. Her brother quickly made friends and was picked for the school baseball team, traveling to nearby towns to compete.

All Lucinda had were her memories—and now this dog, whom she untied from the tree. The animal was frightened and growled at her when she approached, but she spoke softly and offered a soothing hand, which he tried to attack. Lucinda persisted, and the dog, perhaps grateful to be freed from the mud puddles, allowed her to lead him away.

She didn't know what she was going to do with him now that she had him. Pets were not allowed in her building, and her family could be evicted. She couldn't worry about that now. Her main concern was to get him out of the cold.

Even though it was April and supposedly spring, the weather had yet to top fifty degrees. At night she slept under two blankets, wearing warm socks over her cold feet. Another night outdoors and the dog could freeze to death.

Lucinda reached her building and comforted the dog, "I'm not going to hurt you." She took off her jacket and wrapped it quickly around the animal, hoping to disguise it as a bundle under her arm. "Don't make any noise," she begged.

She waited till a woman with a baby stroller exited the building and quickly dashed inside, unseen. She opted not to take the elevator, fearful of running into someone, and instead lugged the dog and her schoolbag up the eight flights of stairs.

Lucinda quickly unlocked the apartment door and plopped the dog on her bed. The animal instantly shook its hair free and ran in circles atop her blanket.

"Don't get too comfortable," Lucinda cautioned. "You can't stay."

She dashed to the kitchen and returned moments later with bowl of water and a plate of leftover chicken and yellow rice.

The dog bolted from the bed and began attacking the food before she even placed it on the floor. The girl sat on the edge of the bed and watched contently as he devoured the meal.

"How long has it been since you've eaten?"

The dog swallowed the food hungrily, not bothering to chew, and quickly lapped up the water.

It was then, with the dog's head lowered to the bowl, that Lucinda spotted the small piece of paper wedged beneath the belt around its neck. She slid it out carefully and saw the word that someone had scrawled with a pencil.

"Chauncey. Is that your name?"

The dog leaped to her side and nuzzled its nose
against her arm.

"It's a crazy name, but I think I like it." She smiled. Outside the
window, eight stories below, two fire engines pierced the afternoon
with wailing sirens. Lucinda didn't seem to notice as she stroked the
animal gently.

Working quickly, before her parents were due to arrive, she
filled the bathtub with water and soap detergent and scrubbed
the animal clean. The dog didn't enjoy it—he kept trying to jump
out—so Lucinda began humming a Spanish song her grandmother
used to sing to her when she was little. It didn't work. Chauncey still
fought to get free.

Once the animal was bathed, Lucinda attacked the clumps of
hair with a scissor and picked out the sticky globs of candy.

"Look at that—you're white!" Lucinda discovered. While using
her brother's hair blower, she ran a quick comb through the fur,
which now was silvery and tan with faint traces of black. "You're
beautiful." The girl beamed.

The dog seemed to agree. It picked up its head proudly and flicked its long ears with pride.

Lucinda hugged him close. "I'll find you a good home. I promise," she told the animal.

Knowing that her parents would arrive any moment, Lucinda gathered up the dog, covering him with her coat, and carried him down nine flights to the basement. She crept quietly past the superintendent's apartment and deposited the animal in a tiny room behind the bank of washing machines.

The room, the size of a small closet, contained all the electrical levers that supplied power to the apartments and the elevator.

Chauncey looked about, confused. He jumped up as if he knew he was about to be abandoned again. His white hairy paw came dangerously close to hitting the protruding, red master switch near the door.

Lucinda knelt to the animal. "I'll be back. Promise."

She closed the door behind her, hoping the dog wouldn't bark, and hurried away. An outline of a plan was taking shape in her mind.

Ashley.

The girl sat in front of her in English and always went out of her way to say hi. She didn't seem to hang out with the other kids, and whenever they passed in the corridor, she was alone. But what really made her even more appealing was that she lived in a real house. Just a block away. Lucinda had seen her once going in. Maybe Ashley would take Chauncey.

Lucinda's parents arrived from work, and she quickly helped her mother prepare the scrumptious fried bananas. Her father had stopped at a restaurant on his way home and brought a *cantina* of food—white rice, black beans, avocado salad, and meat stew. Each food was placed in its own metal container and clipped together like a small pyramid. The local restaurant would have delivered the food to the house each day, if the family desired, but Lucinda's father always liked to stop by and check the menu. The restaurant also made fried bananas, but Lucinda's mother didn't think they were as tasty as her own. One of the nice surprises of moving to New Jersey was discovering that the Latin restaurants supplied *cantina* service.

"How was school today?" her mother asked.

"Okay," Lucinda replied.

The dinner conversation drifted, as it always did, to Mama's problems at work with the supervisor and Papa's frustration with his job. Every day he had to ride two buses and a subway to get to work, which he saw as wasted hours.

"You get an education, go to college," Lucinda's father sermonized for the thousandth time, "and you can work anywhere you like—even in your own house, if you want. Like a doctor! And if it is far away, you hire someone like me, with no education, to drive you."

Lucinda had grown up hearing the lecture. Perhaps she would have been a good student anyway, for she certainly took to it with enthusiasm. She had discovered books at a young age. School only heightened her love of reading, for its library supplied her with an endless source of material. She excelled in her studies and won top honors in English class. She was so proficient at learning the English language that she served as a tutor to kids in lower grades.

Despite her father's wishes, Lucinda had no intention of becoming a doctor or lawyer. She wasn't sure what she would

do—the future seemed far too distant to address it—but she knew somehow it would involve music and dance and magnificent costumes and glittering shoes and plumes in her hair.

They were talking about her brother's upcoming basketball game when suddenly all the lights in the apartment went out.

"*Qué pasó!*" her father exclaimed.

Agitated voices could be heard from the outside hallway. A neighbor banged on the door, shouting. "Call the fire department! Someone's trapped in the elevator!"

Groups of tenants mingled outside their apartments, some carrying candles and flashlights. The building had been pitched into darkness.

"We'll get you out!" someone shouted to the woman caught between floors.

Lucinda cried, "Chauncey!"

He must've hit the master switch. She could hear the distant wail of the fire engines and knew it was only a matter of minutes before they checked the room where the dog was hidden.

"I'll be right back!" Lucinda yelled to her mother as she raced out the door. Groping on to the banister, she felt her way down the flights of steps as people with candles hurried to escape.

The rescuers reached the basement before she did. Two firemen were huddled in the doorway checking the power supply. Lucinda looked frantically for the dog, but he was gone.

She raced out into the nippy night, through the throng of people crowded on the sidewalk, and searched for the dog. She was afraid to look in the street, expecting to see his lifeless body, the victim of a car.

Lucinda looked up at the sound of her name. Her mother was calling to her from the window.

"Come home! What are you doing?"

The girl shouted, "In a minute!" The crowd swelled about her as she quickly darted away.

Lucinda didn't plan it, but she found herself in front of Ashley's house minutes later. She was on the sidewalk, with the rest of

her neighbors, gazing up the block at the commotion in front of Lucinda's building.

"Hi," Lucinda stammered.

Ashley took a moment to place the face and then returned the smile. "Hi."

Lucinda looked about nervously, wondering if any of the adults belonged to Ashley's family. She didn't have a moment to waste.

"What happens," she blurted out, "when a dog runs away? Do the police catch it?"

The blond, chubby teenager, with light green eyes and glasses with pink frames, shrugged. "Probably. If they do, they only take it to the pound."

"What's that?" It sounded bad, whatever it was.

"A shelter. Where they keep animals. If nobody claims 'em, they kill 'em."

Lucinda started to cry. She couldn't help it. It came upon her suddenly. Greatly embarrassed, she turned quickly and hurried away.

"Wait up!" The blonde hurried after her. "Hey!"

Lucinda stopped, too ashamed to meet her eyes.

"Did you lose your dog?" Ashley's voice sounded concerned.

Lucinda nodded.

"Well, let's go find him," Ashley prodded.

They searched the surrounding neighborhood and checked underneath all the cars parked in the area in case he was hiding. They searched basements and rooftops. When all else failed, they walked to the park along the river, where Lucinda pointed out the tree where she had found him.

The girls decided to sit on a nearby bench in case Chauncey reappeared, though they realized there was little hope.

Lucinda knew her mother would be frantically worried.

"She probably has the police looking for me," she told Ashley.

"You've only been gone an hour."

"It's the first time I've left the house, except to go to school, since we moved here," she revealed.

It was a beautiful night, despite the cold tingling breeze that swept up from the river. The New York skyline was ablaze with golden windows silhouetted against dark, boxlike steel structures. You could make out the red traffic lights along the narrow streets. A long, thin barge sailed down the river like a rubbery snake.

Lucinda learned that Ashley's mother was a lawyer, often away from home for long periods, and her father operated a small business in New York's Chinatown, which kept him busy seven days a week. An only child, she spent her time studying and writing letters.

"Who do you write to?" Lucinda asked.

"My grandmother, mostly. She lives in Nevada. I spend the summers with her."

Lucinda told her how lucky she was to be able to see her grandmother. She felt dangerously close to tears again and quickly changed the subject. "I never see you with any friends in school. Why?"

Ashley shrugged. "Guess I'm not the friendly type. Most of the girls are only interested in boys and dates. I intend to be a famous writer one day, so there's a lot of books I have to read. Just so I know what's been done."

It made sense.

"What are you going to be?"

Lucinda admitted she had no ambition. No particular desire. But maybe, if she had her choice, if she could be anything she wanted, it would probably be a dancer.

"My grandmother used to take me to her friend's house who used to be a famous ballerina in Cuba. She'd let me try on her costumes, and she'd play the records and teach me the steps. It hurt my feet something awful. Hers used to bleed when she first started, but she said it got easier after the first year."

Ashley told her, "You have the body for it. I bet you'd make a wonderful dancer."

When it became apparent that Chauncey would never return, the girls walked home together.

Despite all that had happened, Lucinda found herself sad to have the evening end. For the first time since leaving her homeland, she felt somewhat at peace with herself. She now had someone to talk to. Someone who understood. Someone who carried her own pain.

"Wanna have lunch tomorrow?" Ashley asked her. "I usually run home and eat in front of the television. I'm a great cook. My first book is going to be filled with exotic recipes of all the countries I plan to visit. And if you want," she gushed excitedly, "after school we can go to the library. You can get out a book on how to be a ballerina."

Lucinda agreed immediately, "That would be wonderful!"

The girls parted on the sidewalk, and Lucinda raced home where her irate father and weeping mother confronted her angrily.

"Where have you been! I was only going to wait five more minutes and then I was calling the police! Where were you?"

Before she could stammer a reply, the lights went out.

"Not again!" her mother shrieked.

Lucinda's heart throbbed with excitement.

Chauncey was back!

She ran out of the apartment, unmindful of the darkness, with her mother's screams in the air: "Come back here!"

This time Lucinda made it to the basement before the firemen, and she led her pal safely out the building. She reached Ashley's doorstep just as the first fire engine turned the corner.

98

Envision It! | Retell

Think Critically

1. At the beginning of the story, Lucinda longs for her spacious front porch in Cuba. What is something you long for that you had when you were younger? **Text to Self**

2. The author leaves the story a bit open-ended. What effect does this kind of ending have on you as a reader? **Think Like an Author**

3. In what ways are Ashley and Lucinda different from each other? In what ways are they similar? Make a list of these similarities and differences. **Compare and Contrast**

4. Summarize what happens in the time between the power failure in the building where Lucinda's family lives and the point when Lucinda arrives at Ashley's house. **Summarize**

5. **Look Back and Write** Lucinda's father wants her to get an education to become a doctor or a lawyer. Look back at pages 94 and 98 to find what Lucinda wants to do instead. Then write sentences that summarize her wishes. Provide evidence to support your answer.
Key Ideas and Details • Text Evidence

Meet the Author

GLORIA GONZALEZ

Gloria Gonzalez, the daughter of a Cuban mother and Spanish father, was born in New York City. From the age of five, she knew that she would become a writer. She became an investigative newspaper reporter and freelance writer before she turned to writing plays and then fiction. She lived for many years in West New York, New Jersey, where her story *Viva New Jersey* takes place. Though she is probably best known as a playwright, Ms. Gonzalez has also written novels for young people and for adults. Her play *Curtains* was named one of the best short plays of 1976. In 1991 she moved to Nevada to concentrate on writing novels.

Other books about people and dogs: *A Girl's Best Friend* and *Wanted . . . Mud Blossom*

Use the Reading Log in the *Reader's and Writer's Notebook* to record your independent reading.

Common Core State Standards
Writing 4. Produce clear and coherent writing in which the development, organization, and style are appropriate to task, purpose, and audience.
Also Language 1., 3.

Let's Write It!

Key Features of a Poem

- uses verse to communicate ideas

- may use poetic techniques, such as rhyme or sound patterns

- includes carefully chosen words to create a strong effect

READING STREET ONLINE
GRAMMAR JAMMER
www.ReadingStreet.com

Poem

A **poem** is a composition arranged in lines. The lines often have a distinct pattern of beats, or rhythm. The student model on the next page is an example of a poem.

Writing Prompt *Viva New Jersey* begins with the memorable day when Lucinda finds her dog. Write a poem about a memorable day in your life.

Writer's Checklist

Remember, you should . . .

☑ arrange your composition in lines of verse.

☑ choose powerful sensory words.

☑ think about how you can make your reader feel strong emotions.

☑ include poetic techniques.

My Race

The skate trail loomed large up ahead.
I took the starting place.
Screaming fear filled my heart with dread:
Could I finish out this race?

Wells of sweat dripped from my brow.
My hands, they shook and quaked.
I couldn't say just when or how,
I had a choice to make.

I heard the starting whistle blow.
I dashed across the line.
My heart, it leapt out of my chest,
I hoped I'd do fine.

I zipped from ramp to curve to ramp.
And when the race was done,
I felt just like a champ — though someone else had won!

Genre
This **poem** is arranged in lines with clear, regular rhythm.

Writing Trait
The writer's **word choice** includes powerful verbs and adjectives.

Independent and Dependent Clauses are used correctly.

Conventions

Independent and Dependent Clauses

Remember An **independent clause** has a subject and a verb and can stand alone as a complete sentence. A **dependent clause** has a subject and a verb but does not express a complete thought; it cannot stand alone as a complete sentence.

Common Core State Standards

Writing 6. Use technology, including the Internet, to produce and publish writing as well as to interact and collaborate with others; demonstrate sufficient command of keyboarding skills to type a minimum of three pages in a single sitting. **Also Informational Text 10.**

21st Century Skills
INTERNET GUY

E-mail is even better than texting. You can share documents for a school project. E-mail skills help to get you ready for the world of work. They're useful!

- Electronic mail, also known as e-mail, is a message sent over the Internet from one user to another.

- E-mail lets you communicate with people all over the world.

- The "To" box shows to whom a message is going. You can send a message to more than one person at a time.

- An e-mail message looks like the body of a regular letter.

- Read "Visiting Another Country." Think of the steps you must follow to send an e-mail.

Visiting Another Country

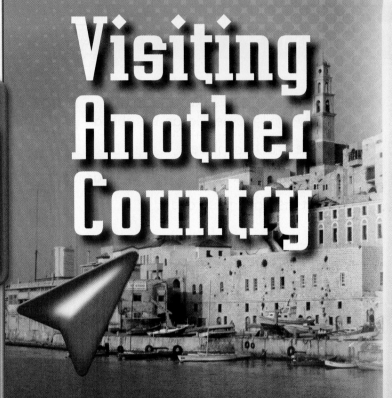

Elizabeth got scared when her parents told her they were going to Israel for the summer. She thought, *I'll be just like Lucinda in* Viva New Jersey. *I won't have any friends and I won't know what to do.* Elizabeth wanted to know more about Israel. With her parents' permission, Elizabeth surfed the Internet and found a great Web site about travel for kids. At the site, she found a link for contacting people there and sent an e-mail.

The e-mail address of the person to whom you are writing goes here.

| Send | Attach | Address |

To:	Receiver's e-mail address goes here
Cc:	
Subject:	Visiting Israel

Dear Sir or Madam:

My parents just told me that we're visiting Israel for the summer. They were both very young when they moved from Israel to the United States. Can you help me find information on what a kid can do in Israel? Thank you very much.

Elizabeth

| Write | Reply | Send | Forward | Delete |

Elizabeth received this reply.

Dear Elizabeth,

The first reaction some people have when they think of Israel is that it may not be very exciting for kids. Israel has religious importance for many of the people who visit, but there are also many other things for kids to see and do. Click on the links at our Web site to find breathtaking sights, activities, and books to read. And have a great trip!

Web Site Editor

Common Core State Standards
Language 4.a. Use context (e.g., the overall meaning of a sentence or paragraph; a word's position or function in a sentence) as a clue to the meaning of a word or phrase. **Also Speaking/Listening 5., Language 4.**

Let's Learn It!

READING STREET ONLINE
ONLINE STUDENT EDITION
www.ReadingStreet.com

Vocabulary

Unfamiliar Words

Context Clues Remember that you can use nearby words and phrases to figure out the meanings of unfamiliar words. You can also predict a meaning for an unfamiliar word and then try the meaning to see if it makes sense in the sentence.

Practice It! Select a book from your classroom or media center that you have not read. Read several paragraphs from the beginning of the book. Choose two or three words you do not understand. Use context clues to figure out what each unfamiliar word means.

Fluency

Expression

Use different tones of voice to show different emotions as you read. Your voice should rise and fall—or get higher and lower—in ways that make sense for the story. If you are speaking words that characters are saying, say them as the characters would.

Practice It! With a partner, practice reading aloud from page 96 of *Viva New Jersey*. Read with expression to show how Lucinda and Ashley feel. Take turns reading and offering each other feedback.

106

Listening and Speaking

When you write an advertisement, use words that get people's attention.

Advertisement

An advertisement is an announcement that promotes a product, service, or event in order to sell it to people. With catchy language and often vivid graphics, advertisers persuade customers to buy a product or service or do something an advertiser wants.

Practice It! With a partner, create an advertisement for volunteering at an animal shelter. Include basic information about the shelter, its types and numbers of animals, and the kinds of things kids can do to help. Add visuals and then present your ad to the class.

Tips

Listening . . .

- Interpret the ad's message.
- Ask questions to clarify the ad's purpose.

Speaking . . .

- Make eye contact with your audience to communicate your ideas and message.
- Use clear, direct language.

Teamwork . . .

- Be able to tell why some ads are more convincing than others.
- Listen to others' opinions and combine ideas into one ad.

Common Core State Standards

Language 6. Acquire and use accurately grade-appropriate general academic and domain-specific words and phrases; gather vocabulary knowledge when considering a word or phrase important to comprehension or expression. **Also Speaking/Listening 1.d.**

Oral Vocabulary

Let's Talk About

Ecosystems

- Share what you know about the rain forest.

- Express opinions about why it's important to preserve nature.

- Describe areas where nature might be threatened.

READING STREET ONLINE
CONCEPT TALK VIDEO
www.ReadingStreet.com

You've learned

0 3 0

Amazing Words
so far this year!

109

Common Core State Standards

Informational Text 8. Trace and evaluate the argument and specific claims in a text, distinguishing claims that are supported by reasons and evidence from claims that are not. **Also Informational Text 1.**

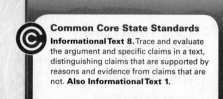

Skill

Strategy

Comprehension Skill

Fact and Opinion

- A statement that can be proved true or false is called a fact.

- A statement that tells a person's thoughts, feelings, or ideas is called an opinion. Opinions cannot be proved true or false.

- Opinions may be either valid or faulty. Valid opinions are supported by facts or are stated by experts. Faulty opinions are not supported by facts, experts, or logic; they might be based on a false statement of fact.

- Use a graphic organizer like the one below as you read "Give the Oceans a Break!"

Statement of Opinion	Support	Valid or Faulty
Statement	Facts or Expert Knowledge	Valid
Statement	None	Faulty

Comprehension Strategy

Important Ideas

Good readers pay close attention to the important ideas in a piece of writing. Important ideas are sometimes set off in a different typeface or are found in graphics that show the essential ideas and supporting details. Finding important ideas helps readers understand what an author is writing about.

Give the Oceans a Break!

Why do humans harm the oceans when oceans are so important to them?

The oceans provide humans with many important things, such as fish. Overall, humans really like fish. Each year millions of tons of ocean fish are caught and eaten by humans.

The oceans are also a source of energy. Millions of barrels of oil are pumped from the oceans each day. Energy from oceans is important because if we didn't have it, we would not have electricity.

The most important thing humans get from the oceans is minerals. My friend Tom, who lives near the ocean, says, "The ocean gives us sand, gravel, and sometimes even gold and silver."

But humans have really harmed the oceans. Many areas of the oceans have been heavily polluted by raw sewage, garbage, and toxic chemicals. In other areas, the fertilizers and pesticides that humans use enter the oceans and make it harder for sea animals to survive.

Overfishing has also hurt sea life. The populations of many sea creatures have declined over the years because of humans' fishing. I think all ocean fishing should be illegal.

I think it's time we took better care of our oceans.

Skill Is this statement a fact, a valid opinion, or a faulty opinion? Why?

Strategy In your own words, what is the important idea in this paragraph?

Skill How can you tell whether this opinion is faulty or valid?

Your Turn!

Need a Review? See the *Envision It! Handbook* for help with fact and opinion and important ideas.

Ready to Try It? Use what you've learned about fact and opinion as you read *Saving the Rain Forests*.

Common Core State Standards

Language 4.a. Use context (e.g., the overall meaning of a sentence or paragraph; a word's position or function in a sentence) as a clue to the meaning of a word or phrase. **Also Language 3.**

Envision It! | Words to Know

erosion

evaporates

tropics

basin	exported
charities	industrial
equator	recycled

READING STREET ONLINE
VOCABULARY ACTIVITIES
www.ReadingStreet.com

Vocabulary Strategy for

🎯 Word Endings *-ed, -s*

Word Structure The endings *-ed* and *-s* may be added to verbs. The ending *-s* may also be added to nouns. It is often possible to use word endings to help you figure out the meanings of words.

1. Cover the ending and read the base word. Keep in mind that the spelling of a word sometimes changes when endings are added.

2. Reread the sentence and determine what part of speech the word is. (The ending *-s* may signal a plural noun or a present-tense, singular verb.)

3. Do you know the meaning of the verb or noun? If not, look for clues in the sentence.

4. Decide what meaning you think the word has and check to see if it makes sense in the sentence.

As you read "The Amazing Amazon," look for words that end in *-ed* or *-s*. Use the endings and the way the words are used to help you figure out their meanings.

Words to Write Reread "The Amazing Amazon." Look at the photo and write a description of what you see. Use words from the Words to Know list.

The Amazing Amazon

The basin of the Amazon River in South America is the area covered by the Amazon River and the rivers that flow into it. It is an area of Brazil that holds amazing wealth. Its riches lie in its vast forests. This area is part of the tropics, the land near the equator. The forests of the Amazon Basin are thought to hold millions of species of plants and animals. Many organisms can live there because of the warmth and heavy rainfall.

It rains every day in the tropical forest. Then the hot sun evaporates water from the soil and trees and other plants. This water vapor goes into the air, becomes clouds, and falls again as rain. Water is thus recycled and kept in the region. It is believed that many valuable medicines and other products can be made from the plants and animals that live there.

However, people who live in the region want to live well. They want Brazil to become an industrial nation. Many thousands of square miles of forest are being cut down every year to make way for industry. Some wood is exported, but much is burned. The tropical soil is thin, and soon erosion carries it away. Then the bare land is poor. The people often need the help of charities to help them find ways to exist without destroying their forests.

Your Turn!

 Need a Review?
For additional help with word endings, see *Words!*

 Ready to Try It?
Read *Saving the Rain Forests* on pp. 114–127.

Why is it important to care about nature?

Genre

Expository text gives information about real people, places, and events. Note the features in this selection that show that what you're reading about is real.

114

Saving
the
Rain Forests

by Sally Morgan

What Is a Rain Forest?

A rain forest is a special kind of forest that grows in warm, wet places. The trees are tall and grow close together. There are three main types of rain forest.

TROPICAL FORESTS

Tropical rain forests grow near the equator (an imaginary line around the middle of Earth). The climate is hot and rain falls nearly every day. The rain forest trees are evergreen trees—they have leaves year-round.

The largest area of rain forest is the Amazon rain forest, in the huge Amazon River basin in South America. There are also tropical rain forests in Central Africa, Southeast Asia, and Australia.

Lush vegetation in a tropical rain forest

CLOUD FORESTS

Rain forests that cover mountains in tropical regions are called cloud forests because they are up in the clouds. The air is cooler higher up a mountain, and there is more moisture in the air. Trees in cloud forests are shorter than those in tropical forests, and they are deciduous—they drop their leaves once a year.

TEMPERATE FORESTS

Temperate rain forests grow farther from the equator, where the climate is cooler. Here there are distinct seasons, when some parts of the year are cool and others warm. Many of the trees are conifer trees, which have needlelike leaves that drop gradually all through the year. The trees are covered in mosses and lichens. There are temperate rain forests in Australia, New Zealand, North America, and parts of South America.

ECO THOUGHT

In the tropics, more than one billion people depend on the water that falls on rain forests. They need it for drinking, cooking, and watering crops.

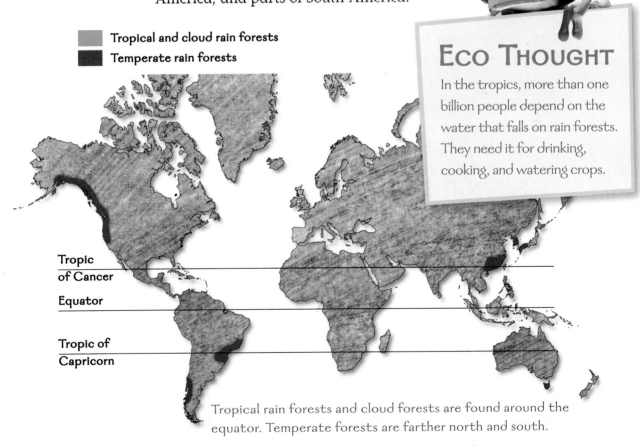

Tropical and cloud rain forests
Temperate rain forests

Tropic of Cancer

Equator

Tropic of Capricorn

Tropical rain forests and cloud forests are found around the equator. Temperate forests are farther north and south.

Rain Forests at Risk

In the last few years, huge fires in the rain forests of Brazil and Indonesia have hit the news. On television, we have seen dramatic pictures of the fires and the damage they have caused. Forest fires are common, so why should they worry us?

This rare bird, called an iiwi, resides in the rain forests of Hawaii.

MILLIONS OF PLANTS AND ANIMALS

We should worry because forests are important. Scientists think that about ten million different species (types) of plants and animals live on Earth. The rain forests are home to nearly two-thirds of these. Some animals live among the leaves, others on tree trunks, and some on the forest floor. Because of this, scientists say rain forests have a high biodiversity (variety of living things).

WATER AND CLIMATE

We should also save rain forests because they release so much water into the air that they affect the climate of the tropics. Plant roots draw up water from the ground. A lot of the water evaporates (turns to vapor, or tiny droplets) from the surface of the leaves and mixes with the air. This helps form rain clouds.

ECO THOUGHT

In a patch of rain forest 4 miles (6.7 kilometers) square, there can be 1,500 species of flowering plants, 400 species of birds, 150 species of butterflies, 100 species of reptiles, and 60 species of amphibians.

GASES IN THE AIR

Leaves use the energy of sunlight to join water and carbon dioxide gas from the air to make food. As they do this, they give off the gas oxygen.

Most living things, including trees, need oxygen to convert food material into energy for their bodies. Removing rain forests cuts down the amount of oxygen in the air, threatening the lives of many plants and animals.

How a Tree Takes Up and Loses Water

Water vapor
from leaves

Flow of water

As fallen leaves
rot, nutrients
return to the soil.

Water travels up from
the roots through the
stem to the leaves.

119

Disappearing Forests

As the world's population gets larger, more food and building materials are needed. Half the world's rain forests have been destroyed to provide timber or farmland. It will take centuries for them to grow back.

LAND FOR FARMING

In Central and South America, land that was once forest is now pasture for cattle. In many countries, the best farmland outside the forest is all owned by rich people. Poorer farmers need somewhere to live, so they clear forestland for farms. They grow crops and use wood as fuel. In many parts of the world, wood is the only fuel available for cooking and for heating water.

An Indonesian farmer is clearing brush after cutting trees in this rain forest area.

TROPICAL WOODS

Tropical wood is used a lot in building. In Southeast Asia and Africa, logging for timber is the main reason for clearing the forests. Timber companies build roads into the forests so they can bring in machinery to cut down the trees and pull out the logs. The logs are sent by road, or floated down rivers, to ports. From the ports, they are exported all over the world and used to make tables and other furniture.

BIG BUSINESS

Huge areas of rain forests are burned to clear land. On much of this land, cash crops (crops grown for sale) such as coffee, bananas, and rubber are grown instead of fruit and vegetables for local people.

Mining, industrial development, and the building of large dams all damage the rain forests too. Even tourism is threatening some of the more popular rain forests.

These young rubber trees in West Africa will be planted in land that was once rain forest.

121

Washed Away

In parts of the tropics (regions of the world near the equator), there are heavy downpours of rain almost every day. About 6 inches (15 centimeters) of rain can fall in just a few hours. New York might get that much rain in a month.

A HUGE SPONGE

The rain forest is like a huge sponge. The plants soak up most of the rainwater. This evaporates from the leaves, creating mist and low clouds.

    The water in the clouds falls back onto the forest as rain. The water is recycled over and over again. Some of the water drains into streams and rivers. The rain forests release this water slowly, so the rivers never run dry.

Cascade in Hana Rain Forest

SOIL EROSION

If the trees are cleared away, there are no roots to hold the soil. Rain washes it away. This is called soil erosion. Soil washes into streams and rivers and chokes them with mud. Aquatic (water) plants and animals that need clear and clean water die.

LESS RAIN

With fewer trees, rainwater drains away quickly. At first, farmers have more water for their crops. But then, less water evaporates, so less falls as rain. The climate of the rain forest changes. Instead of reliable rainfall, there may be droughts.

Erosion in Papua New Guinea's Star Mountains caused by mining and heavy tropical rainfall

A Normal Tropical Rain Forest

Water drains from the forest soil into rivers.

Tropical Rain Forest with Soil Erosion

Without the trees, rain washes away the soil. Mud clogs up the rivers.

Rich Resources

Rain forests are rich in materials used in industry. These are called resources. Wood, such as teak and mahogany, is used in building and to make furniture. The rocks beneath the forests may contain oil and metals, such as gold, silver, and zinc.

LOGGING

Many rain forests produce hardwood, which is tough and long lasting. It is ideal for building and making furniture such as tables. Unfortunately, the best trees are scattered through the forest. In reaching them, loggers damage other trees and the soil, making it hard for young trees to grow.

VALUABLE TIMBER

Most hardwood is sold and transported to other countries. There, it is usually sold again for hundreds of times more than the local people were paid for it. Often, this valuable wood is wasted when it is used to make throw-away objects such as packing crates and chopsticks.

Huge numbers of logs are floated away from a tropical rain forest on a river in Borneo.

This mine in Guinea-Bissau, Africa, is an important source of money, but it has damaged the rain forest.

MINING

Huge areas of forest are cleared so that mining companies can reach the rock that contains oil and valuable metals. Sometimes they remove whole hillsides.

Digging quarries produces a lot of waste material, and this is usually dumped on nearby land. Water running off this waste and from the quarries may be polluted and can harm the aquatic life of streams and rivers.

In Colombia, South America, local people extract gold from a hillside in the rain forest.

New Finds

Scientists believe that they have only found about one-tenth of the animals and plants in the world's rain forests. New species (kinds) are being discovered every day. Many forest plants could be the source of new medicines or foods.

NEW MEDICINES

About a quarter of all modern drugs came originally from rain forests. The forest people discovered most of these long ago. They use plants to treat headaches, fevers, cuts, snakebites, toothaches, and skin infections.

Scientists have tested only a hundredth of the rain forest plants to see if they can be used in medicine. It is important to test more, because they may help to cure many diseases.

EXOTIC FOODS

Crops such as rice, coffee, bananas, and peanuts all came first from rain forests. There may be around 75,000 types of edible plants in the world, but we eat only a few hundred of them. Our diets could be far more varied and healthy if we used more rain forest plants.

MAKING DISCOVERIES

Scientists are discovering useful rain forest plants all the time. There are fruits containing more vitamin C than oranges, and substances 300 times sweeter than sugar. One tree produces a kind of oil that can be used in diesel engines. Some plants contain insecticides (substances that kill insect pests).

No one is sure how many useful plants there may be. But if the forests disappear, we will never know.

A scientist studies a weed growing in a rain forest in Hawaii.

What Can We Do?

The future of the rain forests is important to everyone. People and governments need to work together to make sure this precious resource is used well.

THE EARTH SUMMIT

In 1992, there was a meeting in Brazil called the Earth Summit. Politicians and experts from 150 countries discussed biodiversity, the importance of rain forests, and global warming. They drew up a biodiversity action plan—they agreed to list the plants and animals found in their countries, to set up more nature reserves and national parks, and to manage forests in a sustainable way.

RAIN FOREST CHARITIES

Some charities raise money to work with rain forest peoples. Others set up nature reserves to protect wildlife. We can help to protect the rain forests by supporting these charities.

The challenge for the future is finding ways for people to live in rain forests, find sufficient food in them, earn a living from them, and look after them, all at the same time.

In Uganda, Africa, children help grow new trees to plant in the rain forest.

Common Core State Standards

Informational Text 1. Cite textual evidence to support analysis of what the text says explicitly as well as inferences drawn from the text. **Also Informational Text 2., 8.**

Envision It! | Retell

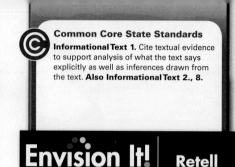

Think Critically

1. How might the disappearance of rain forests affect your life? **Text to Self**

2. How do the photos and diagrams help convey the author's message? Choose three examples that could be used effectively in a speech about the need to preserve rain forests. **Think Like an Author**

3. The author states, "many rain forests produce hardwood, which is tough and long lasting." Is this statement a fact or an opinion? How do you know? **Fact and Opinion**

4. This article has a purpose: to make you aware of a problem. What is the problem? What is the evidence? What can you do about the problem? **Important Ideas**

5. **Look Back and Write** The Earth Summit meeting's action plan included three ideas to help solve the rain forest problem. Look on page 127; then write the three ideas in your own words.

   Key Ideas and Details • Text Evidence

Meet the Author

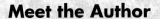

Sally Morgan

Sally Morgan was once the head of a biology department at a high school. Today she is a writer and has more than fifty books on science to her credit. She has written on a wide variety of subjects ranging from plants and animals to water, sound, and light. Her special interests are conservation, genetic engineering, and health.

Other books by Sally Morgan: *The Ozone Hole* and *Acid Rain*

THE OZONE HOLE
Sally Morgan

ACID RAIN
Sally Morgan

Use the Reading Log in the *Reader's and Writer's Notebook* to record your independent reading.

Reading Log

Common Core State Standards
Writing 9. Draw evidence from literary or informational texts to support analysis, reflection, and research.
Also Writing 1.b., Language 1.

Let's Write It!

Key Features of a Problem-Solution Essay

- follows a problem-solution text structure
- may persuade readers
- opinion supported by facts

READING STREET ONLINE
GRAMMAR JAMMER
www.ReadingStreet.com

Expository

Problem-Solution Essay

A **problem-solution essay** addresses a problem in our world and offers a solution to it. The student model on the next page is an example of a problem-solution essay.

Writing Prompt *Saving the Rain Forests* describes a problem and then suggests a solution. Think about a problem that concerns you. Now write a problem-solution essay describing the problem and suggesting a solution.

Writer's Checklist

Remember, you should . . .

✓ describe a problem.

✓ present a well-supported solution.

✓ use cue words to signal important information, such as *for example,* *moreover,* and *in conclusion.*

✓ know your audience and purpose for writing.

Curbing the Habits of Litterbugs

Yesterday I did an experiment. I brought a garbage bag with me to school, and I picked up all of the litter I found along the way. When I got to school, the bag was almost full! I realized that littering is a big problem, while also discovering a related problem.

While I was walking to school, I did not pass any garbage cans or recycling bins. How can we expect people not to litter if we don't give them anywhere to put their trash?

I think there should be a public garbage can and recycling bin on every street corner. They could be colorful and well marked, so that everyone knows what can be recycled and what belongs in the garbage. This way, when people have garbage, they will have a place to put it.

We should also put up eye-catching signs near the bins and cans to remind people to use them.

This solution will help make our neighborhood a cleaner and nicer place to live.

Compound and complex sentences are used correctly.

Writing Trait Focus/Ideas The writer provides support for his or her ideas.

Genre A **problem-solution essay** offers a solution to a problem.

Conventions

Compound and Complex Sentences

Remember A **compound sentence** contains two or more simple sentences joined by a comma and a conjunction, such as *and* or *but*. A **complex sentence** has an independent clause and one or more dependent clauses introduced by a conjunction, such as *if* or *since*.

Common Core State Standards
Informational Text 6. Determine an
author's point of view or purpose in a text
and explain how it is conveyed in the text.
Also Informational Text 2.

Science in Reading

Genre
Persuasive Text

- Persuasive text tries to convince the reader to do something or think about something in a particular way by establishing the truth or falsity of an idea.

- The author of a persuasive text has a distinct viewpoint and position.

- Persuasive text can give surprising information to the reader.

- Read the persuasive article "Drip, Dry?" As you read, look for elements that make this selection a persuasive text. What is the author's position? How does he support his views?

by Sean Price
from *Science World* magazine

Drip, Dry?

Is it possible that America's water sources could one day be tapped out?

Across much of the United States, the days of carefree water use are long gone. Take for instance Denver's Water World: The theme park sells cold soft drinks, but those who want ice in theirs have to ask for it. Why the hassle? Park officials discovered that giving ice only on request saves about 30,000 gallons of water each year—enough to fill two backyard swimming pools.

Such water-stingy behavior seems unusual to most Americans, who are used to cheap, plentiful H_2O. But more and more people are finding that the 341 billion gallons that the nation uses daily can no longer be taken for granted. Overuse, *drought* (below-normal rainfall and snowfall), water-wasting technology, and pollution are sapping the supply. Meanwhile, demand for water continues to surge.

WATER WORLD

How could a liquid that covers two-thirds of Earth be in short supply? There are two main reasons, says Peter Gleick, a water expert at the research group Pacific Institute. First, 97 percent of the world's water is saltwater—useless for drinking or nurturing crops unless expensive desalination techniques are used to purify it. Second, much of the remaining freshwater is either in an unusable form, like glaciers, or unevenly distributed due to geography and *climate* (average weather in an area over time). "The fact that there's a lot of water in the Great Lakes doesn't help people in Arizona," Gleick says.

Today, rivers, lakes, and underground *aquifers* (rocks that contain water) are equipped to supply freshwater to the country's 295 million people. But the population is expected to double by about the 2080s. "As populations grow, you're going to run into a limit to your resources," says Steve Vandas, a hydrologist with the U.S. Geological Survey.

SUSTAINING SUPPLIES

To keep up with demand, U.S. waterways must stay clean. Just decades ago, waterways were so polluted with chemicals that one actually caught on fire. Thanks to tough antipollution laws like the Clean Water Act of 1972, many factories stopped treating rivers and lakes like garbage dumps. Robbi Savage, president of World Water Monitoring Day, says some of the most pervasive pollution now comes from household chemicals such as oil and pesticides.

Reducing household pollutants can help. But we also need to use less water, says Gleick. "We can grow food, get rid of waste, and [run factories] with less water—without harming our quality of life," he says. "We're not always using the smartest tools to do the job. We still waste tremendous amounts of water." *Read on to learn what's tapping your freshwater supply.*

Let's **Think** About...

What point of view is the author trying to explain and support in this article?
Persuasive Text

DOWN AND OUT

In 1999, the Western states entered their worst drought in 500 years. Water reservoirs along the Colorado River have since dropped to half their normal levels. That's critical for the 25 million people in seven states who rely on the river's water. However, the drought has inspired millions of people to switch to using water-saving toilets and washing machines. The efforts have worked so well in Denver that water consumption rates currently are at their lowest levels in thirty years.

133

POTENT POLLUTION

Water pollution threats come from many sources, including animal manure and chemicals. For instance, underground gasoline tanks have been leaking methyl tertiary butyl ether (MTBE) into groundwater in 49 states. MTBE makes gasoline burn cleaner, but it can cause cancer when consumed. Additionally, chemicals such as nitrogen and phosphorus found in fertilizers and factory pollution regularly wash into the Mississippi River. The pollutants deprive fish of oxygen. The result: a 7,000-square-mile "dead zone" around the river's mouth.

HIGH AND DRY

Explosive population growth around Atlanta, Georgia, is outstripping the water supply in the Southeast. This has triggered a legal fight among three states. Georgia wants to pump more water from the Chattahoochee River. Two downstream states—Alabama and Florida—argue that the extra water removal will leave them high and dry.

WATER HAZARD

Burning fossil fuels, such as coal and oil, emits air pollutants. U.S. autos produce 8.2 million tons of nitrogen oxide a year. This, along with sulfur dioxide and other pollutants, makes acid rain. *Precipitation*—rain, snow, hail, or sleet—mixes with the poisons and slowly kills plants and fish.

Let's **Think** About...

How do the illustrations on this page reinforce important points the author is making in the text?
Persuasive Text

WARM WARNINGS

Scientists believe that air pollution magnifies Earth's natural greenhouse effect, causing *global warming* (average increase in Earth's temperature). In California's Sierra Nevada, winter precipitation that once came down as snow now falls as rain. The snow used to melt gradually, delivering water to thirsty Californians during near-rainless summers. Now, the water runs into waterways at once, leaving less for the dry months. This year, rain fell in bucketfuls, washing out to sea.

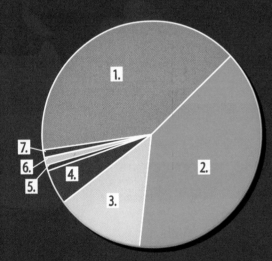

1. Irrigation: 40%

2. Thermoelectric power: 39%

3. Drinking and home use: 13%

4. Industry: 5%

5. Livestock: 1%

6. Commercial: 1%

7. Mining: 1%

Source: U.S. Geological Survey

HOW IS WATER USED IN THE UNITED STATES?

A. What percentage of water is used for drinking and home use?

B. What steps could you take to stem the flow in your house?

Let's **Think** About...

Reading Across Texts The authors of *Saving the Rain Forests* and "Drip, Dry?" have strong positions they want to promote. What environmental message does each author try to persuade you to heed?

Writing Across Texts Tell which message you felt was more compelling and why.

135

Common Core State Standards
Language 4.a. Use context (e.g., the overall meaning of a sentence or paragraph; a word's position or function in a sentence) as a clue to the meaning of a word or phrase. **Also Informational Text 10., Speaking/Listening 1.a.**

Let's Learn It!

READING STREET ONLINE
ONLINE STUDENT EDITION
www.ReadingStreet.com

Vocabulary

Word Endings -ed, -s

Word Structure Remember that endings such as -ed and -s can help you figure out the meanings of words. For example, the ending -s may signal either a plural noun or a singular, present-tense verb. The way a word is used in a sentence will help you to know its meaning.

Practice It! Look back at *Saving the Rain Forests* and choose one word that ends with -ed and one that ends with -s. Quickly determine the meaning of each word, and then exchange your words and definitions with a partner.

Fluency

Appropriate Phrasing

When you read aloud, group related words together so that they sound the way they would in natural speech. Follow the cues of punctuation as you read, pausing at commas or stopping at the end-of-sentence marks.

Practice It! With a partner, practice reading aloud page 121 from *Saving the Rain Forests*. As you read, pause for commas and stop for periods. Give your partner feedback on his or her phrasing.

136

Listening and Speaking

When you participate in a discussion, ask relevant questions to clarify each speaker's purpose.

Panel Discussion

In a panel discussion, a group of experts guided by a moderator share ideas and information about a specific topic.

Practice It! Work with a group of four to present a panel discussion about soil erosion in the tropics. Assign roles, with one student acting as moderator and the others as experts on the topic. Use information from *Saving the Rain Forests* in your discussion, especially pages 122–123.

Tips

Listening . . .

- Determine the speakers' main and supporting ideas.
- Take notes as you listen.

Speaking . . .

- Speak loudly enough to be heard and enunciate clearly.
- Organize information before you begin and stick to your topic.

Teamwork . . .

- Consider suggestions from other group members.
- Limit your speaking to the agreed-upon time limit.

137

Let's Talk About

Loyalty

- Describe how animals can form bonds with people.

- Suggest what being loyal means.

- Share examples of loyalty.

READING STREET ONLINE
CONCEPT TALK VIDEO
www.ReadingStreet.com

Common Core State Standards

Literature 1. Cite textual evidence to support analysis of what the text says explicitly as well as inferences drawn from the text.

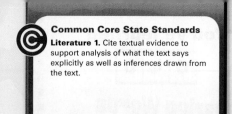

Skill

Strategy

Comprehension Skill

Fact and Opinion

- A statement of fact can be proved true or false by reading, observing, or asking an expert.

- A statement of opinion is a judgment or belief. It cannot be proved true or false, but it can be supported by facts and logic.

- Sometimes one statement expresses both a fact and an opinion.

- Use a graphic organizer like the one below to identify statements of fact and statements of opinion in "Dogs Versus Cats."

Statement	Fact? How Can It Be Checked?	Opinion? What Are Clue Words?

Comprehension Strategy

Questioning

You will better understand what you are reading if you ask questions about important text information before, during, and after you read. Record questions as you develop them. Make a note when you find information that answers your questions.

DOGS Versus CATS

Doug and Rose heard Biscuit barking frantically as they walked up the path. His friendly face looked out eagerly from the front window. As they entered, Biscuit bounded toward them, his tail a blur. He raced from Doug to Rose and then around in circles.

Skill Which sentence in this paragraph states an opinion?

Mittens slept curled up on the sofa. Rose sat beside her and stroked her fur. Mittens purred loudly. Then she stood up, stretched, and walked away. "Dogs are much better pets than cats," said Doug, scratching Biscuit's ears. Biscuit licked his hand.

Strategy What question could a reader ask at this point?

"No, they aren't!" said Rose.

Doug said, "Biscuit always runs to meet us. Mittens stays where she is. If we go to her, sometimes she lets us pet her and sometimes she doesn't. Biscuit follows us everywhere and always wants to please us."

Skill Find a fact and an opinion in this paragraph.

"Dogs can be pests. Biscuit always wants attention," said Rose. "He barks at every person or dog that passes by."

"It's better to have a pet that thinks I am wonderful and that is always there for me," said Doug.

"It's better to have a pet that is quiet, independent, and leaves me alone sometimes," said Rose.

"I guess it all depends on what you prefer in a pet," said Doug. "They're both good choices."

Your Turn!

⏸ **Need a Review?** See the *Envision It! Handbook* for help with fact and opinion and questioning.

▶ **Ready to Try It?** Use what you've learned about fact and opinion as you read *Hachiko: The True Story of a Loyal Dog.*

Envision It! | Words to Know

morsel

ruff

stooped

fixed

furious

nudge

quietly

vigil

Vocabulary Strategy for

🎯 Suffixes *-ly, -ous*

Word Structure When you are reading and come across a word you don't know, check to see if the word has a suffix at its end. Suffixes add meaning. For example, *-ly* means "a characteristic of," as in *honestly,* and *-ous* means "having much" or "full of," as in *adventurous.* The meaning of the suffix combines with the meaning of the base word.

Choose one of the Words to Know and follow these steps.

1. Cover the suffix and identify the base form of the word.

2. If you know this word, think about its meaning.

3. Look at the suffix and decide what extra meaning it adds.

4. Combine the meanings from steps 2 and 3.

5. Use this meaning in the sentence. Does it make sense?

Read "Jack to the Rescue." Look for words that end with the suffixes *-ly* and *-ous.* Analyze the base words and the suffixes to figure out meaning.

Words to Write Reread "Jack to the Rescue." Think about a time when you observed a scene in a public place. Imagine you are waiting in that place and describe what you see. Use as many words from the Words to Know list as you can.

Jack to the Rescue

I sat in the park watching the ducks feed. The ducks made a furious noise as people fed morsels to them. Just then, a little boy ran down the path. He looked about three. A duck waddled into the pond. The little boy boldly started to follow him.

As I jumped up to stop him, a Husky raced to the boy. The dog stepped between the boy and the pond. "Jack!" cried the boy, grabbing Jack's ruff.

Jack used his nose to nudge the boy away from the pond. He kept nudging until the boy toddled to a sandbox filled with children that was just past the pond.

The boy played happily in the sandbox. Jack sat quietly, never taking his eyes off the child.

Suddenly I heard a woman in a quavering voice call, "Has anyone seen my son? He disappeared when I went over to pick up his toys." She was stooped over with fear.

Jack barked, but he did not take his eyes off the boy. The woman rushed over to the sandbox and ran to the boy. Her reaction was to hug him and then lead him away.

Once Jack's vigil was over, he came over to me. He fixed his eyes on my sandwich. I gave him the whole thing. I realized that he had earned it. Then he ran off to be with his family.

Need a Review? For help using suffixes, see *Words!*

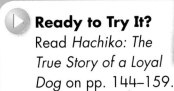
Ready to Try It?
Read *Hachiko: The True Story of a Loyal Dog* on pp. 144–159.

忠犬八千公

Hachiko

The True Story of a Loyal Dog

by Pamela S. Turner

illustrated by Yan Nascimbene

Genre

Historical fiction is realistic fiction that takes place in the past. It is a combination of imagination and fact, for fictional characters are placed in a historically factual setting. See how fictional characters make the true story of Hachiko come alive.

There is a statue of my old friend at the entrance to Shibuya Station. His bronze feet are bright and shiny, polished by thousands of friendly hands. There is a sign that says, simply, "Loyal dog Hachiko." I close my eyes and remember the day we met, so long ago.

Question of the Week
What is the bond between animals and humans?

When I was six years old, my family moved to a little house in Tokyo near the Shibuya train station. At first the trains frightened me. But after a while, I grew to enjoy their power and the furious noises they made. One day I begged Mama to take me to meet Papa as he came home on the afternoon train. She laughed and said, "Kentaro, you have become big and brave, just like a samurai!" Together we walked to the station.

It was spring, and the day was clear and cold. There were tiny carts all around the station, selling snacks, newspapers, and hundreds of other things to the crowds of people rushing by. Ladies in kimonos walked carefully, trying to keep their white *tabi* socks away from the grime of the streets. Businessmen strode about, hurrying home or to catch another train. Mama and I had stopped near the station entrance when I noticed the dog.

He was sitting quietly, all alone, by a newspaper stand. He had thick, cream-colored fur, small pointed ears, and a broad, bushy tail that curved up over his back. I wondered if the dog was a stray, but he was wearing a nice leather harness and looked healthy and strong.

His brown eyes were fixed on the station entrance.

Just then, Papa appeared. He was chatting with an older man. The dog bounded over to the man, his entire body wiggling and quivering with delight. His eyes shone, and his mouth curled up into something that looked, to me, just like a smile.

"Ah, Kentaro! You see, Dr. Ueno, you are not the only one who has someone to welcome him," said Papa. He introduced us to the older man. "Dr. Ueno works with me at Tokyo Imperial University."

"What is your dog's name?" I asked timidly. The dog was beautiful, but his sharp face reminded me of a wolf's. I grabbed Mama's kimono and stepped behind her, just in case.

"Don't be afraid," said Dr. Ueno kindly. "This is Hachiko. He is big, but still a puppy. He walks me to the station every morning and waits for me to come home every afternoon. I think Hachiko stores up all his joy, all day long, and then lets it all out at once!"

Hachiko stood wagging his tail next to Dr. Ueno. I reached to touch him, and he bounced forward and sniffed my face. I yelped and jumped back behind Mama.

They all laughed. "Oh, Kentaro, don't worry—he just wants to get to know you," said Dr. Ueno. "Dogs can tell a lot about people just by smelling them. Why, Hachiko probably knows what you ate for lunch!"

I sniffed my hand, but it didn't smell like rice balls to me. I reached out and touched Hachiko gently on the shoulder. "His fur is so thick and soft," I said. "Like a bear's."

"Dogs like Hachiko once hunted bears in the north, where it is very cold and snowy," said Dr. Ueno, kneeling down next to me and rubbing Hachiko's ears.

From that day on, I went to the train station almost every afternoon. But I no longer went to see the trains. I went to see Hachiko. He was always there, waiting near the newspaper stand. I often saved a morsel from my lunch and hid it in one of my pockets.

Hachiko would sniff me all over, wagging his tail, until he found a sticky bit of fish or soybean cake. Then he would nudge me with his nose, as if to say, "Give me my prize!" When it was cold, I would bury my face in the thick ruff of creamy fur around his neck.

One day in May, I was waiting at the station with Hachiko. The moment I saw Papa, I knew something was wrong. He was alone, and he walked hunched over, staring sadly at the gray pavement under his feet.

"What's the matter, Papa?" I asked him anxiously, standing with one hand on Hachiko's broad head. He sighed. "Kentaro, let's go home." Hachiko's bright brown eyes followed us as we walked away, but he stayed behind, waiting for Dr. Ueno.

When we got home, Papa told us that Dr. Ueno had died that morning at the university. I was stunned. "But what will happen to Hachiko?" I asked, blinking hard to keep the tears back. "What will he do?"

"I don't know," said Papa. "Perhaps Dr. Ueno's relatives will take him in."

"What about tonight?" I asked. "Can we go see if he is all right?"

Papa was very sad and tired, but he walked with me back to the Shibuya Station. Hachiko was curled up by the newspaper stand. He wagged his tail when he saw us. Papa and I gave him water in an old chipped bowl and some food. Hachiko ate and drank, but he kept looking up toward the station entrance for Dr. Ueno. Papa and I left even sadder than we had come.

The next day, I went back to check on Hachiko, but he was not there. Papa told me that Hachiko had been taken several miles away to live with some of Dr. Ueno's relatives. "But I'll never see him again!" I cried. "Why can't he live with us?"

"We don't have room for a dog," protested Papa. "And Hachiko really belongs to Dr. Ueno's relatives, now that Dr. Ueno is dead. Hachiko is better off having a home than sitting in a train station."

But Hachiko had other ideas. A few days later he was back at Shibuya Station, patiently waiting, his brown eyes fixed on the entrance. Hachiko had run back to his old home, and from there to Shibuya Station.

Mama and Papa let me take food and water to Hachiko every day. Mama grumbled a bit about the food, saying we couldn't afford to feed a big bear like Hachiko, but she always seemed to cook more rice than we could eat.

Other people at the station took an interest in Hachiko. Men and women who rode Papa and Dr. Ueno's train stopped by to scratch his ears and say a few kind words. One day I saw an old man filling Hachiko's water bowl as Hachiko licked his hand. The old man's hair was streaked with gray, and he was stooped, as if he had spent most of his life bent over the ground. But his eyes were as sharp and bright as Hachiko's.

"Are you young Kentaro?" the old man asked. I nodded. "I am Mr. Kobayashi. I was Dr. Ueno's gardener.

"Dr. Ueno told me that you and Hachiko often wait for the afternoon train together."

"Do you still take care of the house where Dr. Ueno lived?" I asked.

"Yes," said Mr. Kobayashi. "Hachiko comes back to the house every night to sleep on the porch. But in the morning, he walks to the station just like he did with Dr. Ueno. When the last train leaves the station, he returns home."

We were both silent. Then I asked, "Do you think Hachiko knows that Dr. Ueno died?"

Mr. Kobayashi said thoughtfully, "I don't know, Kentaro. Perhaps he still hopes that Dr. Ueno will return someday. Or perhaps he knows Dr. Ueno is dead, but he waits at the station to honor his master's memory."

As the years passed and Hachiko got older, he became very stiff and could barely walk to Shibuya Station. But still he went, every day. People began collecting money to build a statue of Hachiko at the station. Papa, Mama, and I all gave money, and we were very happy when the statue was placed next to the spot where Hachiko had waited for so many years.

One chilly morning I woke to the sound of Mama crying. "What's wrong?" I asked as I stumbled into the kitchen. Papa sat silently at the table, and Mama turned her tear-stained face to me. "Hachiko died last night at Shibuya Station," she choked. "Still waiting for Dr. Ueno."

I was seventeen, and too big to cry. But I went into the other room and did not come out for a long time.

Later that day we all went to the station. To our great surprise, Hachiko's spot near the newspaper stand was covered in flowers placed there by his many friends.

Old Mr. Kobayashi was there. He shuffled over to me and put a hand on my shoulder.

"Hachiko didn't come back to the house last night," he said quietly. "I walked to the station and found him. I think his spirit is with Dr. Ueno's, don't you?"

"Yes," I whispered.

The big bronze statue of Hachiko is a very famous meeting place. Shibuya Station is enormous now, and hundreds of thousands of people travel through it every day. People always say to each other, "Let's meet at Hachiko." Today Hachiko is a place where friends and family long separated come together again.

The Story Behind the Story

Some years ago, my family moved to Tokyo, and we rented a home not far from Shibuya Station. Everyone, it seemed, knew that Hachiko's statue was the place to meet at the huge train station. No matter what time of day or night I visited Shibuya, I would always see someone standing near the large bronze dog, with eyes searching the crowd.

My Japanese friends told me Hachiko's story. Hachiko was born in northern Japan in November of 1923, and a few months later he was sent to Dr. Ueno in Tokyo. When Dr. Ueno died on May 21, 1925, they had been together for just over a year.

In October 1932, a newspaper reporter wrote a story about Hachiko. The headline read: "A Faithful Dog Awaits the Return of Master Dead for Seven Years." People began traveling to Shibuya from all over Japan, just to pet loyal Hachiko.

Hachiko's vigil at Shibuya Station lasted almost ten years. He died March 7, 1935. One year earlier, a bronze statue of Hachiko had been placed near the entrance to Shibuya Station, right next to the spot where he always waited for Dr. Ueno. There is an old photo of the real Hachiko next to the bronze one, surrounded by a crowd of people. Hachiko seems to be wondering what all the fuss is about.

During World War II, the Japanese military was desperately short of metals. Many statues, including Hachiko's, were melted down. But Hachiko was not forgotten. In 1947, a few years after the war ended, the son of the original sculptor made a new statue of Hachiko. It stands there still.

Every spring, there is a special Hachiko festival at Shibuya Station. It is always held on April 8, one month after Hachiko's death anniversary, when Tokyo's cherry trees are in full bloom. The Shibuya mayor, police chief, and stationmaster are always there. A Shinto priest performs a ceremony, and Hachiko's friends come to admire the beautiful wreaths of flowers that are displayed around his statue.

I thought Hachiko's story was lovely, both sad and wonderful, and I wanted to share it. Kentaro was invented for this story, but I am sure many children who lived near Shibuya Station knew and loved Hachiko.

Common Core State Standards
Writing 9. Draw evidence from literary or informational texts to support analysis, reflection, and research. **Also Literature 1.**

Envision It! | Retell

Think Critically

1. Think about dogs you have known or heard about. How do they show loyalty to their owners? If their owners were to die or disappear, would you expect any of these dogs to behave as Hachiko did? Explain your answer.
   Text to Self

2. Hachiko is a real character, and many of the events in the story really happened. Why do you think the author chose to write this with a fictional main character, rather than as nonfiction?
   Think Like an Author

3. Find a statement of fact and a statement of opinion on page 154. How did the gardener know the facts he was stating were true?
   Fact and Opinion

4. What questions might a reader ask after reading page 157? Where might you go to find answers to more questions about Hachiko?
   Questioning

5. **Look Back and Write** Look back at page 154 where Mr. Kobayashi expresses two possible opinions about why Hachiko waits every day at the station. Which explanation seems more likely? Write your answer as a debate that uses "pro" and "con" arguments.
   Key Ideas and Details • Text Evidence

Pamela S. Turner

When she was four years old, in southern California, Pamela Turner got her first library card. Her first memory of what she wanted to be is a children's author. But her life took her to other places first. With her husband, and then also with their three children, Ms. Turner lived in many different countries, from Kenya to South Africa to the Philippines and Japan. It was the story of Hachiko, which she heard in Japan, that led her to write her first book. The Turners now live in northern California, where Ms. Turner writes many science and nature articles for adults and children. She has a dog and a rabbit and likes to scuba dive, snow ski, and, of course, read.

Other books by Pamela S. Turner:
Gorilla Doctors: Saving Endangered Great Apes and *LIFE on Earth—and Beyond*

Use the Reading Log in the *Reader's and Writer's Notebook* to record your independent reading.

Common Core State Standards
Writing 4. Produce clear and coherent writing in which the development, organization, and style are appropriate to task, purpose, and audience. **Also Writing 3.a., 3.b., Language 1.**

Let's Write It!

Key Features of a Journal Entry

- tells about an event, experience, or observation
- is written in first person
- shares the feelings and thoughts of the writer

READING STREET ONLINE
GRAMMAR JAMMER
www.ReadingStreet.com

Journal Entry

A **journal entry** is an entry in a journal or daily log. It may focus on the writer's daily experiences, but it can also discuss an event or personal observation. The student model on the next page is an example of a journal entry.

Writing Prompt Write a journal entry about a time you were inspired by someone else's story.

Writer's Checklist

Remember, you should . . .

☑ write about a time you were inspired by someone else.

☑ include details about the person's story and why it inspired you.

☑ organize information into paragraphs.

☑ stick to the subject.

January 11, 20__

Today I was inspired by the story of Elizabeth Smith Miller. She lived at a time when women were expected to wear uncomfortable corsets and skirts. She rebelled and made a comfortable dress worn over loose-fitting pants.

The outfit let Elizabeth garden and move around much more easily. Soon enough, other women started wearing the outfit too! One was Amelia Bloomer; the pants became known as bloomers after Amelia's last name. These women wore bloomers even though people made fun of them.

The pictures we looked at of bloomers did look pretty funny, but the women also looked very comfortable.

This makes me think I should design my own clothing. I could make something that is super comfortable, but that doesn't look funny. I could use the material that my pajama pants are made of, since they are soft and warm. Maybe I could even make a skirt to wear over the pants. I should ask if Mom or Dad can take me to the fabric store soon!

Jennifer

Writing Trait Organization
The journal entry is organized into paragraphs that relate to the main subject.

Common and proper nouns are used correctly.

Genre
A **journal entry** reveals the personal thoughts of the writer.

Conventions

Common and Proper Nouns

Remember A **common noun** can name any person, place, or thing. Examples include *boy* and *city*. A **proper noun** names a specific place or thing, such as *José* or *Dallas.*

163

Science in Reading

Genre
Narrative Nonfiction

- Narrative nonfiction vividly recounts a true event or series of events.

- The accounts of narrative nonfiction may be considered factual stories.

- These factual stories may be long or they may be short, interesting anecdotes.

- Narrative nonfiction is often, but not always, arranged in chronological order, or the order in which events happened.

- Magazine and newspaper articles are often narrative nonfiction.

- Read "They've Got Personality" and look for ways that it is narrative nonfiction.

They've Got Personality

from *National Geographic WORLD*
by Aline Alexander Newman

"Personality is what makes a person (or an animal) unique as an individual," says Samuel D. Gosling, a psychologist at the University of Texas at Austin. Animal personality has become a hot new topic with scientists who study animals.

WORLD asked wildlife experts to share their four favorite stories about the personalities of memorable animals. Here are the tales of a few characters they've come across.

1 A bossy gray parrot rules the roost.

Let's **Think** About...

What are Max the parrot's human-like personality traits that help readers relate to him?
Narrative Nonfiction

Who's the Boss?

Patricia Simonet's African gray parrot Max gets his kicks by giving orders. One time when Max was home alone in Incline Village, Nevada, a visitor knocked at the door. "Come on in," the parrot shouted. And the man did!

Whenever Simonet's other pet bird begins squawking, Max yells at him, "Pierre, be quiet!" Peace is restored.

Even the cat obeys Max. "Oh, Valentine!" Max calls in a singsong voice that practically beckons. The cat comes running to Max's cage. Max tosses a corn kernel onto the floor. Then the game begins. As the playful feline "soccer" player kicks and chases the kernel all around the room, "coach" Max sits on his perch watching, completely entertained.

Let's **Think** About...

How does the author use sensory language on this page to create imagery about the animals' personalities? **Narrative Nonfiction**

Do Not Disturb!

Ursula, a giant Pacific octopus who lived at the Seattle Aquarium in Washington State, had excellent aim. The trouble was her choice of targets. Every night this crabby sea creature blasted water out through the breathing tube on the side of her head, completely drenching the researcher whose job it was to check Ursula's tank. "This woman actually felt picked on," says biologist Roland Anderson. "Ursula never soaked anyone else, only this researcher." The cold shower was obviously intentional, since an octopus can spray in any direction it wants to. And Ursula turned an angry red every time she did it.

What prompted these nightly temper tantrums? Nobody knows for sure. But Anderson suspects that the researcher's flashlight beam may once have irritated the sleeping giant. From then on, Ursula carried a grudge.

2 An armed octopus gets revenge.

Friends "R" Us

Jenny, an abandoned circus elephant, lumbered into the barn at her home at The Elephant Sanctuary in Hohenwald, Tennessee. Then she stopped and stared. A new arrival, Shirley, stood in a stall. Jenny rumbled hello. But Shirley, who had spent many years in a zoo with no elephant companions, didn't reply.

3 Elephants: friends forever!

166

Jenny trumpeted louder. She paced. She even tried to climb over the barrier that separated the two elephants. Still nothing. Jenny poked and prodded the newcomer with her trunk. Finally Shirley lifted her head. "Her eyes got huge and she started to trumpet," says Carol Buckley, cofounder of the sanctuary. "Both elephants began screaming and bellowing excitedly."

Jenny and Shirley had been barnmates twenty-five years earlier. After more than two decades apart, they recognized each other! Now they share everything. They're never apart and often stand touching. The mutual devotion of the animals amazes Buckley, who says she's never seen such togetherness. It's true that elephants never forget—especially their friends!

Smile, Please

Nibble. Nibble. The gray seal yanked and chewed on the scuba diver's swim fins. Feeling the tug, underwater photographer Brian Skerry spun around. But quick as a flash, the seal flipped backward and disappeared.

4 A seal poses politely.

Many of these underwater acrobats glide around between the rocks in the Gulf of Maine off the coast of Acadia National Park. But they almost always stay out of sight.

This young seal was much braver than most. Moments after their first encounter, the animal returned. "His flippers came together and he kind of posed," says Skerry. "It was almost as if he were saying 'OK, I've had my fun. Now you can take my picture.'"

Let's **Think** About...

Which of the Five W's does the author of this selection use in each of these four short anecdotes? **Narrative Nonfiction**

Let's **Think** About...

Reading Across Texts Hachiko and the four animals in this article all have definite personalities. What word would you use to describe each animal?

Writing Across Texts Make a list of the five animals and the main personality traits for each animal.

167

Common Core State Standards
Language 4.a. Use context (e.g., the overall meaning of a sentence or paragraph; a word's position or function in a sentence) as a clue to the meaning of a word or phrase. **Also Informational Text 10., Speaking/Listening 1.a., Language 4.b.**

Let's Learn It!

READING STREET ONLINE
ONLINE STUDENT EDITION
www.ReadingStreet.com

Vocabulary

Suffixes -ly, -ous

Word Structure When you add the suffix *-ly* to a word, the new word tells how something is done. When you add *-ly* to the word *quick*, it shows that something is done very fast.

Practice It! Take the word *friendly*. What does the base word *friend* mean? Use the meaning of the suffix *-ly* and the meaning of the base word to figure out the word's meaning. Now try words that end in *-ous*, which means "having much" or "full of," as in *nervous, numerous, famous,* or *glamorous*.

Fluency

Accuracy

When you are reading aloud and come to a word you do not recognize, stop and try to figure out its meaning from context clues. Then go back to reading at your original pace. Sometimes it is important to read more slowly in order to be accurate.

Practice It! With a partner, practice reading page 158 from *Hachiko: The True Story of a Loyal Dog*. Take turns and read it until both of you can read the four paragraphs without any errors.

Listening and Speaking

When you are part of an oral presentation, organize your part carefully.

Book Review

A book review aims to tell would-be readers a little about a particular book so that they know whether or not they want to read the book. It summarizes the book and may include opinions backed by examples.

Practice It! With a small group, choose another book that tells about a loyal animal. Divide the book equally. Have each group member read and summarize his or her part, comparing the new book's loyal animal to the story of Hachiko. Present your reports to the class.

Tips

Listening . . .

- Face the speakers.
- Take notes on what they say.
- Draw conclusions about the books.

Speaking . . .

- Follow the order you agreed on.
- Speak loudly enough to be heard.
- Answer questions completely.

Teamwork . . .

- Prepare your part of the book report and try to rehearse as a group before you appear in front of the class.
- Listen quietly to others' reports.

Common Core State Standards
Literature 5. Analyze how a particular sentence, chapter, scene, or stanza fits into the overall structure of a text and contributes to the development of the theme, setting, or plot. **Also Literature 4., 10.**

Poetry

- Poetry is written in lines. Poems have words to make us see, feel, and think about everyday things in a different way.

- Poems sometimes include rhyming words and a regular meter, or beat, to reinforce meaning.

- **Free verse poems** don't have regular rhymes or meter. They may not even use capital letters or punctuation.

- **Analogies** such as metaphors and similes often create vivid images.

- Look for sensory details that create images you can see, hear, smell, and even taste in these free verse poems.

Song to Mothers

by Pat Mora

Your laugh is a green song,
canción verde,
that branches
through our house,
its yellow blooms smelling
like warm honey.
Your laugh peels apples
and stirs their cinnamon bubblings,
then opens a book and pulls me
onto your lap.
At night, your laugh kisses
us soft as a petal, smooths my pillow
and covers me, a soft leafy blanket,
green and yellow.
I snuggle into your laugh,
your canción verde
and dream of growing
into my own green song.

Louisa Jones Sings
a Praise to Caesar
by Emanuel di Pasquale

Caesar is my king.
He is my guard dog
and barks at anything—
at visitors and strangers,
always trying to protect
Mom and me from danger.
For his reward
He gets the weirdest
breakfast, ice cream.
He loves me,
and when I play with him
or bring him fresh water,
he flaps his ears
and wags his tail
and even tries to sing.

Let's **Think** About...

What three
elements make
"Song to Mothers"
a free verse poem?
Find two metaphors
and one simile.

Let's **Think** About...

These two poems
tell about a much-
loved mother and
a much-loved dog.
Which speaks more
directly to you?
Why?

Those Winter Sundays

by Robert Hayden

Sundays too my father got up early
and put his clothes on in the blueblack cold,
then with cracked hands that ached
from labor in the weekday weather made
banked fires blaze. No one ever thanked him.

I'd wake and hear the cold splintering, breaking.
When the rooms were warm, he'd call,
and slowly I would rise and dress,
fearing the chronic angers of that house,

speaking indifferently to him,
who had driven out the cold
and polished my good shoes as well.
What did I know, what did I know
of love's austere and lonely offices?

Grandma

by Ralph Fletcher

On the first warm morning
she's kneeling in the dirt,
smiling and humming
like she does making bread.

Grandma's planting tulip bulbs
that are almost the same color
as her own worn knuckles.
Watch how her hands work

the dark mounds of soil
in that dirty confusion
of bulb and knuckle,
knuckle and bulb.

Space and Time

Why might things far away and long ago be important to us now?

Let's **Think** About Reading!

connect to
SCIENCE

The Universe EXPOSITORY TEXT

Why is it important to know about the universe?

Paired Selection
Creating a World Like Ours EXPOSITORY TEXT

The Emperor's Silent Army EXPOSITORY TEXT

What can we learn about the past by examining its relics?

connect to
SOCIAL STUDIES

Paired Selection
The Taj Mahal NARRATIVE NONFICTION

Stones, Bones, and Petroglyphs EXPOSITORY TEXT

Why is it important to learn about America's past?

connect to
SOCIAL STUDIES

Paired Selection
Adobe Homes WEB SITES

Good-bye to the Moon SCIENCE FICTION

How can a focus on the future help us imagine new possibilities?

connect to
SCIENCE

Paired Selection
Zoo SCIENCE FICTION

Egypt EXPOSITORY TEXT

Why is it important to understand ancient civilizations?

connect to
SOCIAL STUDIES

Paired Selection
The Rosetta Stone EXPOSITORY TEXT

Common Core State Standards

Language 6. Acquire and use accurately grade-appropriate general academic and domain-specific words and phrases; gather vocabulary knowledge when considering a word or phrase important to comprehension or expression. **Also Speaking/Listening 1., 1.c.**

Oral Vocabulary

Let's Talk About

Outer Space

- Share what you know about outer space.

- Ask questions about why people are interested in the universe.

- Express opinions about the importance of learning more about the universe.

READING STREET ONLINE
CONCEPT TALK VIDEO
www.ReadingStreet.com

Common Core State Standards
Informational Text 1. Cite textual evidence to support analysis of what the text says explicitly as well as inferences drawn from the text. **Also Informational Text 2.**

Envision It! Skill Strategy

Skill

Strategy

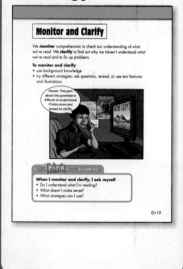

READING STREET ONLINE
ENVISION IT! ANIMATIONS
www.ReadingStreet.com

Comprehension Skill

Main Idea and Details

- To find the topic of a paragraph or selection, ask yourself, "What is this text about?"

- To find the main idea, ask yourself, "What is the most important idea about the topic?" Often it is in the first sentence of a key paragraph.

- Once you find the main idea, look for supporting details that explain or tell about the main idea.

- As you read "The Telescope," use two graphic organizers like the one below, one for "Optical Telescopes" and the other for "Radio Telescopes," to help you determine the main idea and supporting details about each telescope.

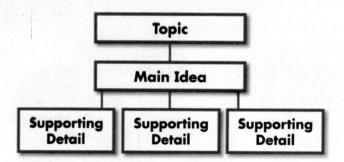

Comprehension Strategy

Monitor and Clarify

When you are reading, it's important to know when you understand something and when you don't. If you are confused, you can use text features such as headings to clarify information. You can also look back and reread, either silently or aloud.

The Telescope

For thousands of years humans studied the sky using only their eyes. Today, however, astronomers have a much more powerful tool to use: the telescope. There are two kinds of telescopes: optical and radio.

Optical Telescopes

Optical telescopes work by collecting light. The larger the aperture, or opening, of the telescope, the more powerful it is. The largest optical telescope in the world is in Russia. It has an opening 236 inches wide. Most of the world's large, powerful optical telescopes are in buildings called observatories. These are usually high on mountains, away from cities and lights. Some, such as the Hubble Space Telescope, are in space.

Radio Telescopes

Radio telescopes collect long energy waves from far-away objects in space through a "dish," a curved object that looks like a bowl. The world's largest radio telescope, in Germany, is almost 300 feet wide! The most powerful radio telescope, though, is in New Mexico. Scientists use it to study the solar system and other galaxies.

Without telescopes, we would know very little about the amazing objects in the sky.

Strategy Text features such as headings can help you find topics. What is the topic of this paragraph?

Skill Which of the following sentences best states the main idea of the section "Optical Telescopes"?
a) Optical telescopes work by collecting light.
b) The largest optical telescope is in Russia.
c) Most large optical telescopes are in observatories.

Skill What is the main idea of the section "Radio Telescopes"?

Your Turn!

⏸ **Need a Review?** See the *Envision It! Handbook* for help with main idea and details and monitoring and clarifying.

Let's Think About...

▶ **Ready to Try It?** Use what you've learned about main idea and details as you read *The Universe*.

THE UNIVERSE

Common Core State Standards

Language 4.b. Use common, grade-appropriate Greek or Latin affixes and roots as clues to the meaning of a word (e.g., *audience, auditory, audible*). **Also Language 4.a.**

Envision It! | Words to Know

astronomers

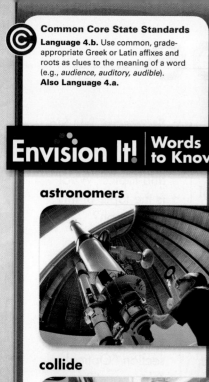

collide

galaxy

collapse

compact

particles

Vocabulary Strategy for
Greek and Latin Roots

Word Structure When you find a word you do not recognize, see if you can find a familiar root in it. Greek and Latin roots, or basic original parts of words, are used in many English words. For example, the Latin root *sol* means "sun." The Greek root *astr-* means "star." The root *astr-* is used to build the words *astronaut, astrology,* and *astronomer.*

Choose one of the Words to Know and follow these steps:

1. If the word has a prefix or suffix, cover it.

2. Do you recognize the root? Does the root make a base word you know?

3. If so, see if the meaning of this base word is similar to a meaning that would make sense for the word.

4. Add the meaning(s) of the prefix and/or suffix and predict the meaning of the word.

5. See if your meaning makes sense in the sentence. Use a dictionary if you need to.

Read "The Birth and Death of Stars." Look for Greek and Latin roots to help you figure out the meanings of words. You may also use the glossary to help you figure out the meanings of this week's Words to Know.

Words to Write Reread "The Birth and Death of Stars." Use what you know about astronomy to write a story set in outer space. Include words from the Words to Know list.

180

The Birth and Death of Stars

For thousands of years, astronomers have gazed up into space and wondered. We are beginning to understand our galaxy, the huge cluster of stars in our corner of the universe. How do we think our sun and the planets of our solar system came to be?

One idea says that they formed from an enormous spinning cloud of gas and dust. The spinning pulled most of the matter in the cloud toward the center. However, smaller whirlpools also formed in the cloud. Some matter also collected in the whirlpools. The dust particles grew closer together and began to collide with each other. As they were pressed together, the balls of matter became more compact. The matter in the center formed the sun. The matter in the whirlpools formed the planets.

The sun, at the heart of our solar system, is a star. All stars have a life cycle of many billions of years. Some stars end as a cold piece of matter—a sort of space junk. Others may explode and then collapse into a black hole. We will not get to see how our sun dies. That ending is billions of years away.

Your Turn!

⏸ **Need a Review?** For help using word structure and understanding Greek and Latin roots, see *Words!*

Let's Think About...

▷ **Ready to Try It?** Read *The Universe* on pp. 182–193.

THE UNIVERSE

by Seymour Simon

Question of the Week
Why is it important to know about the universe?

Let's **Think** About **Reading!**

From Earth we can look into space and study the universe with telescopes and other instruments. The moon is Earth's nearest neighbor in space, only about a quarter of a million miles away. That's very close in space, almost next door. Still, it's very far away compared to the distance between places on Earth's surface. You'd have to travel around the Earth ten times in order to match the distance from the Earth to the moon. The sun, the closest star to us, is over four hundred times farther away from us than the moon is—about ninety-three million miles.

The nearest star after our sun is much farther away than that. But measuring the distance between stars and planets in miles is like measuring the distance around the world in inches. We measure the distance to the stars in light-years: the distance that light travels in one year, which is close to six *trillion* miles. A spaceship speeding at ten miles per second would still take more than seventy thousand years to get to Alpha Centauri, the nearest star after the sun—a distance of 4.3 light-years, or twenty-five trillion miles.

For many years, our solar system was the only one we had ever seen. But in recent years, scientists using new instruments began to observe what looked like other solar systems in the making. These are two images (right) of gas-and-dust disks forming around young stars. The disks range in size from about two to eight times the diameter of our solar system. The glow in the center of each disk is a newly formed star, about one million years old.

The disks do not mean, for certain, that planets will form. But the building blocks for planets are there. Now that they know so many young stars have planetary disks, scientists feel more optimistic about the possibility of locating other solar systems.

Let's **Think** About...

How does the author's image of measuring the Earth in inches help to show how vast the universe is?
Visualize

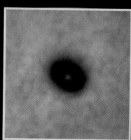

Let's **Think** About...

Is all of the information given so far getting confusing? You can stop to re-read the first page.

Monitor and Clarify

Let's Think About...

How do the author's descriptions of nebulas help you to "see" them for yourself? **Visualize**

186

Finding individual planets is more challenging than finding planetary disks, because a single planet is much smaller and more compact than a whole solar system in the making. Still, we have discovered more planets around distant stars than in our own solar system.

All stars are born within nebulas, which are eerie, dark clouds of hydrogen gas and dust. Stars are not born singly but in groups or clusters. Usually each star grows at a different speed, and most clusters finally drift apart. Some of the young stars are ten thousand times brighter than our sun is now.

This photo of the Eagle Nebula——also called M-16—— was taken by the Hubble Space Telescope in 1995. The Eagle Nebula is in a nearby star-forming region of the Milky Way galaxy. It is about seven thousand light-years away from Earth. The new stars are the bright lights inside the finger-like bulges at the top of the nebula. Each "fingertip" is tens of billions of miles across——larger than our entire solar system.

When stars get older, they cool off, swell up one hundred times larger, and turn red. These aging stars are called red giants. The red giants become very active, blowing off violent gusts of hot gas from their surfaces into space. When a red giant has shed its outer layers, the hot core within the star makes the surrounding cloud of gases glow. This cloud is called a planetary nebula because early astronomers thought its shape and color looked like a planet.

Planetary nebulas come in a variety of shapes: from narrow jets of exploding gases to peanut-shaped clouds to bright globes surrounding stars.

Let's Think About...

What are nebulas, how are they related to stars, and what are red giants?
Summarize

187

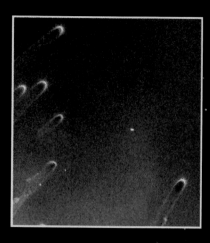

What look like spaceships from a science fiction movie are really the result of a dying star's final outbursts. These mysterious "space pods" (right) are gigantic tadpole-shaped clumps of gas, each several billion miles across, twice the size of our solar system. The comet-like tails fan out around the central star like the spokes on a wheel.

No one knows what will happen to the pods. Perhaps they will expand and disappear within a few hundred thousand years. Or perhaps the dust particles inside each gas ball will collide and stick together. Planets the size of Earth, but frigid and icy, might form over time. Thousands of these icy worlds might escape the dead star and roam the dark space between the stars forever.

Let's Think About...

How do these descriptions evoke other images you may have of outer space?
Visualize

Our sun is just one of about two hundred billion stars in the Milky Way galaxy, a vast spiral of stars about one hundred thousand light-years across. Viewed from the side, it looks like a lens, with a thick bright center of stars and flattened edges. All the stars we see in the night sky are in our galaxy. Other galaxies are much too distant for us to see their individual stars.

Our solar system is about thirty thousand light-years away from the center of the Milky Way. The central galaxy is much more crowded than our lonely part of space. In one star cluster near the center of the Milky Way, there are one hundred thousand stars in one cubic light-year. But in our remote corner of the galaxy, there are no stars within four light-years of our solar system.

This is a radio photo of a star called Sagittarius A*, near the center of the Milky Way. Hidden someplace within this photo, there might be an enormous black hole marking the true center of our galaxy.

Let's **Think** About...

What are the most important facts about the Milky Way and its place in our solar system? **Summarize**

Scientists class galaxies by their shape. There are four main types of galaxies: spirals, ellipticals, barred spirals, and irregular-shaped galaxies. Spirals are disk-shaped, with older stars in the center and newer stars in the arms. Ellipticals are the most common and are shaped like balls or eggs. They contain mostly old stars. Barred spirals are spirals whose central stars form a bar. Irregulars are the rarest and do not fit any known pattern.

Many galaxies in space are so distant that their light fades out before it reaches the Earth, and they can only be seen with radio telescopes. This radio image of a large elliptical galaxy called Fornax A is in the center of a distant cluster of galaxies. The central bright white region shines with the light of more than ten billion stars. Fornax A is so huge that it is swallowing nearby galaxies. The small spiral galaxy just above Fornax A may soon be captured.

Scientists think that there are at least one hundred billion galaxies in the universe, and each galaxy contains about one hundred billion stars. There are more stars in the universe than there are grains of sand on all the beaches in the world.

With a high-powered telescope, scientists discovered fifteen hundred galaxies in different stages of their lives. From Earth, some of these galaxies are as faint as a flashlight on the moon would be.

Looking at distant galaxies in the universe with a telescope is like using a time machine to peer into the past. Light from the dimmest galaxies has taken ten billion years to reach us.

Let's Think About...

How might jotting down the most important facts about galaxies help you to understand them?
Monitor and Clarify

Among the strangest objects in the universe are black holes. A black hole is a region of space where matter is squeezed together so tightly and the pull of its gravity is so powerful that nothing can escape from it, not even light. It is impossible to see a black hole, but we can see vast amounts of matter being sucked into the hole, never to return. Black holes seem to come in two sizes: small and super-large. The small ones are formed when stars collapse and are only a few miles in diameter. Most we cannot detect.

Scientists think that the super-large black holes are probably at the center of most galaxies. This drawing shows a spiral of dust and gases eight hundred light-years wide being sucked into a giant black hole in the center of a nearby galaxy. The black hole contains more than one billion times the amount of matter in our sun, all packed tightly together.

These discoveries have led to new mysteries: Does every galaxy have a black hole at its center? If there's a black hole in a galaxy, does that mean that all the stars in the galaxy will eventually disappear inside it? What starts a black hole, and does it ever end?

Quasars are as mysterious as black holes. Before stars vanish into a black hole, they give off energy in a burst of light and radio waves. This outpouring of energy is called a quasar. About the size of our solar system, quasars contain the mass of more than a million suns. Yet they pour out one hundred to one thousand times as much light as an entire galaxy of one hundred billion stars.

Does life exist on Earth-like planets in distant solar systems? Will the universe expand forever or finally stop and then collapse into a gigantic black hole? Searching for answers about the universe is

Let's  About...

How can rereading the information about black holes make it easier to understand them?
⊙ Monitor and Clarify

192

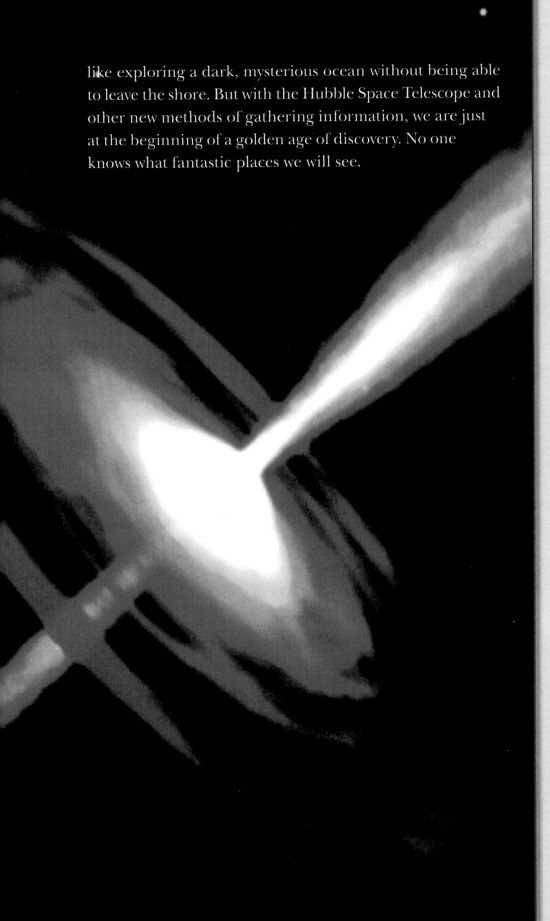

like exploring a dark, mysterious ocean without being able to leave the shore. But with the Hubble Space Telescope and other new methods of gathering information, we are just at the beginning of a golden age of discovery. No one knows what fantastic places we will see.

Common Core State Standards
Informational Text 1. Cite textual evidence to support analysis of what the text says explicitly as well as inferences drawn from the text. **Also Informational Text 2., Writing 9.**

Envision It! | Retell

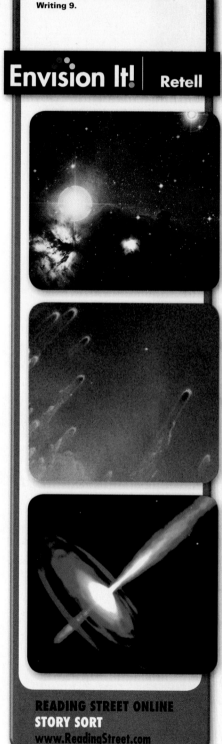

Think Critically

1. Why is it important for us to look into space and study the universe? **Text to World**

2. Vast sizes and distances are almost impossible to comprehend, but Seymour Simon comes to the rescue. Find sentences he wrote to help readers comprehend the vastness of the universe. **Think Like an Author**

3. The main idea of the information in the first paragraph of page 191 is that there are different types of galaxies. What details from the paragraph support that statement? **Main Idea and Details**

4. How do the pictures on pages 188 and 189 help you better understand what you've read? **Monitor and Clarify**

5. **Look Back and Write** What is the relationship between a quasar and a black hole? Look back at page 192 to help you write an answer. Then write why that relationship may be of special interest to astronomers. Provide evidence to support your answer. **Key Ideas and Details • Text Evidence**

SEYMOUR SIMON

Seymour Simon is a popular, award-winning writer of science books for young people. He is praised not only for his clear, interesting writing but also for his attention to the latest research. You can count on a book by Seymour Simon to be accurate and reliable. Mr. Simon grew up in the Bronx in New York and often visited the local science museums. He graduated from the City College of New York and taught science in that city for 23 years. Since he retired, he has published more than 200 books. Many are about space, but he has also written books about animals, the weather, the human body, and icebergs. "I try to write the way I talk," he says. He admits that he will probably never give up teaching—"not as long as I keep writing." He lives in the Hudson Valley of New York State.

Other books by Seymour Simon: *The On-Line Spaceman and Other Cases* and *Destination: Space*

Use the Reading Log in the *Reader's and Writer's Notebook* to record your independent reading.

Common Core State Standards
Writing 4. Produce clear and coherent writing in which the development, organization, and style are appropriate to task, purpose, and audience.
Also Writing 1.a., Language 1.

Let's Write It!

Key Features of a Movie Review

- gives an opinion of a movie

- includes a plot summary without revealing ending

- shares the writer's thoughts and opinions

READING STREET ONLINE
GRAMMAR JAMMER
www.ReadingStreet.com

Movie Review

A **movie review** gives an opinion about a movie, using facts, details, and examples from the movie to support the writer's argument. The student model on the next page is an example of a movie review.

Writing Prompt Think about a movie you have seen that takes place in outer space. Write a review of it. Be sure to include details from the movie that support your opinion and a brief explanation of the plot.

Writer's Checklist

Remember, you should . . .

☑ provide a brief summary of the plot.

☑ state your opinion about the movie.

☑ allow your personal voice to come through in writing.

☑ use a friendly tone that appeals to readers' emotions.

Space Game Makes Bad Movie

Titanium Moon was one of the most exciting video games to hit the stores last year. When people found out there would be a movie based on the game, they couldn't wait to see it. Hopefully, they'll wait until they read this review, because the movie does not live up to the game.

Titanium Moon is set in the future, on a planet deep in outer space. It is about a brother and sister who are private investigators. They're hired by two elderly women to recover a valuable model of the planet's moon, but it turns out the model has a dangerous weapon hidden inside.

Parts of the movie are high-quality. The futuristic cities on the planet really look like they are in outer space, and they are also believable. The actors who play the brother and sister are great. But even with lots of action, including two space battles, the story was boring. I won't reveal the surprise ending, but I feel that it did not make any sense.

Overall, it turns out that Titanium Moon works as a game, but it's a dud on the movie screen.

Writing Trait Voice
The writer's friendly tone is appropriate for this review.

Genre
A **movie review** gives an evaluation of a movie.

Regular and irregular plural nouns are used correctly.

Conventions

Regular and Irregular Plural Nouns

Remember A **plural noun** names more than one person, place, or thing. To form the plural of most regular nouns, add -s. To form the plural of most singular nouns ending with s, z, sh, x, or ch, add -es. You can memorize how to form **irregular plural nouns,** which change spelling, such as child/children and goose/geese.

197

Science in Reading

Creating a World Like Ours
by Jan Young

Genre
Expository Text

- Expository text provides information about a person, place, thing, or event.

- Expository text sometimes includes graphics such as photographs and charts.

- Read "Creating a World Like Ours" and look for facts that the author has presented about making a colony for humans on Mars.

Science fiction author Ray Bradbury wrote stories about people colonizing the planet Mars. At that time, during the 1940s, Bradbury's idea was seen as pure fantasy.

But today, NASA scientists talk of one day building a real colony for humans on Mars. What makes them think this could actually happen?

Of all the planets in our solar system, Mars is most like Earth. The climate is generally colder, but during the Martian summer, temperatures can reach as high as 80 degrees Fahrenheit. Earth and Mars also have similar landforms and terrains. Both have mountains, canyons, and plains. Mars does not have a supply of fresh water, which is vital for plant and animal life. But scientists have ideas for solving that problem.

The first step is to warm up Mars. This would be done by adding so-called greenhouse gases to the atmosphere, such as carbon dioxide and chlorofluorocarbons.

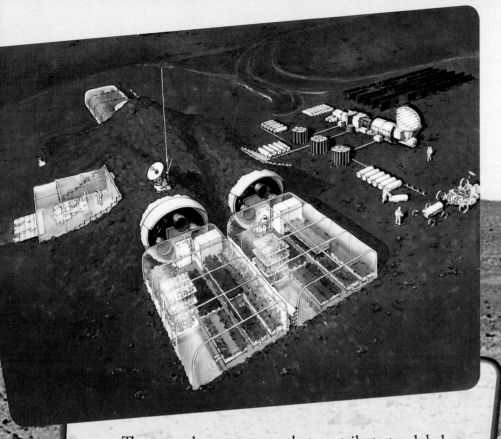

These are the same gases that contribute to global warming on Earth. They would trap more heat from the sun in Mars's atmosphere, and that would raise that planet's surface temperature. The warmer temperatures would in turn melt Mars's polar ice caps, producing additional warming and creating a source of fresh water.

Once the Martian climate changed enough to support vegetation, trees could be planted. These trees would thrive on the carbon dioxide and produce additional oxygen to make the air more breathable.

Thus, scientists believe we could eventually create an environment on Mars where people could live and thrive. This process is called *terraforming*. Although terraforming Mars would take centuries to complete, conditions there could eventually become similar to those on Earth, and the planet could be colonized. That would turn Ray Bradbury's fantasy into a reality.

Let's Think About...

What is the author's explanation of how Mars might be colonized?
Expository Text

Let's Think About...

Reading Across Texts Do the authors of *The Universe* and "Creating a World Like Ours" seem negative or positive about the future of our solar system? Make a list of words or phrases used that demonstrate the negative or positive attitude of each author.

Writing Across Texts Write a paragraph explaining whether you feel negatively or positively about the future of our solar system and why you feel as you do.

Common Core State Standards
Language 4.b. Use common, grade-appropriate Greek or Latin affixes and roots as clues to the meaning of a word (e.g., *audience, auditory, audible*).
Also Informational Text 7., Speaking/Listening 1.a., Language 4.a.

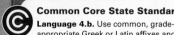

Let's Learn It!

Vocabulary

Greek and Latin Roots

Remember to look for a familiar root when you find a word you do not understand. Greek and Latin roots are used in many English words. If the word has a prefix or a suffix, remember to cover it as you work to understand the root.

Practice It! Read the sentences below. Find the root as you work to figure out the meanings of *discredited* and *ungrateful*.

- The dog's growling *discredited* its reputation as a friendly animal.

- Even though its family had brought it new toys and treats, the cat seemed *ungrateful*.

Fluency

Rate

As you read aloud, use different rates or speeds for different material. When you read scientific descriptions such as those in *The Universe*, for example, it is wise to slow down so that complicated ideas can be better understood.

Practice It! With a partner, practice reading aloud page 189 of *The Universe*. Why is it important for you to read aloud this passage more slowly than you might read aloud a work of fiction?

Listening and Speaking

When you analyze media, ask specific questions and be aware of any use of propaganda.

Analyze Media

When you analyze media, watch for propaganda—information that is biased or inaccurate in order to influence public opinion. Also identify the intended audience, the purpose, and what you learned.

Practice It! In a small group, discuss a television show or film you have seen that focuses on outer space or a topic related to outer space. Examine the intended audience, the purpose of the show or film, if it was successful, and what you learned from it. Then present your findings to the class.

Tips

Listening . . .

- Listen attentively to each speaker.
- Take notes on what he or she says.
- Ask relevant questions.

Speaking . . .

- Speak clearly and distinctly.
- Wait your turn or raise your hand before you speak.

Teamwork . . .

- Listen to everyone's ideas before you take a position on the TV show or film you are analyzing.
- Take turns.

Common Core State Standards

Language 6. Acquire and use accurately grade-appropriate general academic and domain-specific words and phrases; gather vocabulary knowledge when considering a word or phrase important to comprehension or expression. **Also Speaking/Listening 1., 1.c.**

Oral Vocabulary

Let's Talk About

Archaeology

- Share what you know about archaeology.

- Describe an earlier time period.

- Ask questions about why archaeology is important today.

READING STREET ONLINE
CONCEPT TALK VIDEO
www.ReadingStreet.com

You've learned
060
Amazing Words
so far this year!

Common Core State Standards
Informational Text 2. Determine a central idea of a text and how it is conveyed through particular details; provide a summary of the text distinct from personal opinions or judgments. **Also Informational Text 1.**

Envision It! | Skill Strategy

Skill

Strategy

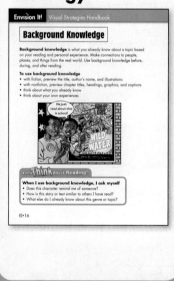

Comprehension Skill

◎ Main Idea and Details

- The topic of a selection can usually be stated in a few words.

- The main idea is the most important idea about the topic. It is often stated at or near the beginning of a selection.

- Supporting details tell more about the main idea.

- As you read, look for details that link back to the main idea.

- Use a graphic organizer like the one below as you read "Artifacts."

Comprehension Strategy

◎ Background Knowledge

Background knowledge is what you already know about a topic, either on your own or from your reading. Good readers connect that knowledge to whatever they read in order to understand better and remember more.

ARTIFACTS

The continent of Asia has some of the oldest civilizations on Earth. Evidence of how early people in that area lived is studied by archaeologists. Archaeologists are scientists who study past human cultures. They look at artifacts that have been uncovered.

What is an artifact? Any object made by a human and then later discovered by an archaeologist is called an artifact. Artifacts tell scientists about the culture of an ancient civilization. These artifacts are often buried for centuries and have to be carefully excavated during a dig.

How are artifacts found? In order not to harm artifacts, members of an excavation team follow certain procedures. They might first use special radar to look below ground. Then special instruments help move away layers of soil. All of the results must be documented. The entire process often takes years, as was the case with China's terra cotta soldiers.

What do artifacts tell? Some artifacts have been able to tell archaeologists what people in an ancient civilization ate or what they did for entertainment. Most often artifacts reveal the materials, skills, and technology that ancient people used.

Strategy Read the title and bold headings. What are some things you already know about artifacts?

Skill What is the main idea of this section?

Skill What supporting detail from this paragraph could you add to your graphic organizer?

Your Turn!

 Need a Review? See the *Envision It! Handbook* for help with main idea and details and background knowledge.

Ready to Try It? Use what you've learned about main idea and details as you read *The Emperor's Silent Army*.

Common Core State Standards

Language 1. Demonstrate command of the conventions of standard English grammar and usage when writing or speaking.

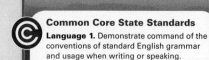

Envision It! | Words to Know

excavated

pottery

terra cotta

approximately

divine

mechanical

restore

superstitious

watchful

Vocabulary Strategy for

🎯 Suffixes *-al, -ful,* and *-ly*

Word Structure When you are reading and come across a word you don't know, check to see if the word has a suffix, or word part added to the end of the word. Suffixes add meaning. For example, *-al* means "of" or "like"; *-ful* means "full of" or "showing"; and *-ly* means "in a way" or "of or from." The suffixes *-al* and *-ful* change a noun into an adjective; *-ly* changes an adjective into an adverb.

Choose one of the Words to Know and follow these steps.

1. Cover the suffix and see if you recognize the base word.

2. If you know this word, think about its meaning.

3. Look at the suffix. Think about its meaning and how it changes the meaning of the base word.

4. Decide what meaning makes sense for the word.

Read "Discovering Artifacts." Use suffixes and word structure to help you figure out the meanings of any unfamiliar words you find.

Words to Write Reread "Discovering Artifacts." Write a description of what you imagine you might see during a trip to a natural history museum. Use as many words from the Words to Know list as you can.

Discovering Artifacts

Last week we went to visit a museum that has approximately two thousand artifacts from ancient China. Most of the things we saw were made by humans thousands of years ago. How cool is that!

We started the day by watching a video about how archaeologists carefully uncover pottery. They use mechanical equipment and dig into the ground. Somehow they manage not to break the excavated objects. Some pottery in the video reminded me of the terra cotta flowerpots at my grandmother's house. The film ended with a look at how specialists work to restore any damaged pieces.

After the film, we walked around to see several displays. I kept a watchful eye for something about the first emperor of China. I had read that he considered himself to be divine and the ruler of everyone. The museum did not have anything from the emperor's mausoleum, but I did read an interesting description about the superstitious fears many people used to have about the emperor's terra cotta army.

Your Turn!

❚❚ Need a Review?
For additional help with suffixes, see *Words!*

▶ Ready to Try It?
Read *The Emperor's Silent Army* on pp. 208–223.

JANE O'CONNOR

The Emperor's Silent Army

Genre

Expository texts explain what certain things are and how they came to be. As you read, notice how the author explains this hidden army.

208

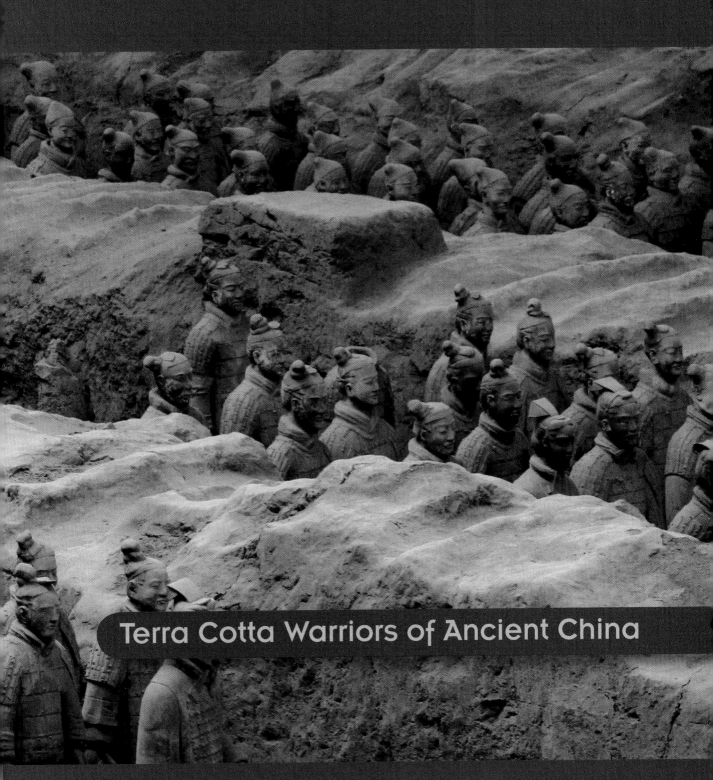

Terra Cotta Warriors of Ancient China

Question of the Week

What can we learn about the past by examining its relics?

A Strange Discovery

It's just an ordinary day in early spring, or so three farmers think as they trudge across a field in northern China. They are looking for a good place to dig a well. There has been a drought, and they must find water or risk losing their crops later in the year.

The farmers choose a spot near a grove of persimmon trees. Down they dig, five feet, ten feet. Still no water. They decide to keep on digging a little deeper. All of a sudden, one of the farmers feels his shovel strike against something hard. Is it a rock? It's difficult to see at the bottom of the dark hole, so the farmer kneels down for a closer look. No, it isn't a rock. It seems to be clay, and not raw clay but clay that has been baked and made into something. But what?

Now, more carefully, the men dig around the something. Perhaps it is a pot or a vase. However, what slowly reveals itself is the pottery head of a man who stares back at them, open-eyed and amazingly real looking. The farmers have never seen anything like it before. But they do remember stories that some of the old people in

▲ The 2,000-year-old terra cotta figures were discovered in the countryside of northern China.

▼ The terra cotta army was discovered when well-diggers found the head of a "pottery man" like this one. No photographs were taken that day.

210

their village have told, stories of a "pottery man" found many years ago not far from where they are now. The villagers had been scared that the pottery man would bring bad luck so they broke it to bits, which were then reburied and forgotten.

The three well-diggers are not so superstitious. They report their discovery to a local official. Soon a group of archaeologists arrives to search the area more closely. Maybe they will find pieces of a clay body to go with the clay head.

In fact, they find much more.

During the weeks and months that follow, the archaeologists dig out more pottery men, which are now called by a more dignified term—terra cotta figurines. The figurines are soldiers. That much is clear. But they come from a time long ago, when Chinese warriors wore knee-length robes, armor made from small iron "fish scales," and elaborate topknot hairdos. All of the soldiers are life-size or a little bigger and weigh as much as four hundred pounds. They stand at attention as if waiting for the charge into battle. The only thing missing is their weapons. And those are found too— hundreds of real bronze swords, daggers, and battle-axes as well as thousands of scattered arrowheads—all so perfectly made that, after cleaning, their ancient tips are still sharp enough to split a hair!

▲ These soldiers' hands are clenched as if still holding their bronze weapons.

Today, after nearly thirty years of work, terra cotta soldiers are still being uncovered and restored. What the well-diggers stumbled upon, purely by accident, has turned out to be among the largest and most incredible archaeological discoveries of modern times. Along with the Great Pyramids in Egypt, the buried army is now considered one of the true wonders of the ancient world. Spread out over several acres near the city of Xian, the soldiers number not in the tens or hundreds but in the thousands! Probably 7,500 total. Until 1974, nobody knew that right below the people of northern China an enormous underground army had been standing guard, silently and watchfully, for more than 2,200 years. Who put them there?

One man.

Known as the fierce tiger of Qin, the divine Son of Heaven, he was the first emperor of China.

◄ Although more than seven thousand strong, the terra cotta army is small compared to the emperor's real army.

213

The Quest for Immortality

Before the time of Qin Shi Huang (pronounced chin shir-hwong), who lived from 259 to 210 B.C., there was no China. Instead, there were seven separate kingdoms, each with its own language, currency, and ruler. For hundreds of years they had been fighting one another. The kingdom of Qin was the fiercest; soldiers received their pay only after they had presented their generals with the cut-off heads of enemy warriors. By 221 B.C. the ruler of the Qin kingdom had "eaten up his neighbors like a silkworm devouring a leaf," according to an ancient historian. The name China comes from Qin.

The king of Qin now ruled over an immense empire—around one million square miles that stretched north and west to the Gobi Desert, south to present-day Vietnam, and east to the Yellow Sea. To the people of the time, this was the entire civilized world. Not for another hundred years would the Chinese know that empires existed beyond their boundaries. To the ruler of Qin, being called king was no longer grand enough. He wanted a title that no one else had ever had before. What he chose was Qin Shi Huang. This means "first emperor, God in Heaven and Almighty of the Universe" all rolled into one.

But no title, however superhuman it sounded, could protect him from what he feared most—dying. More than anything, the emperor

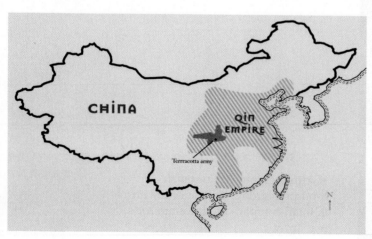

◄ The map shows the Qin kingdom and the Qin empire in stripes. The dot indicates where the terra cotta army was found.

wanted to live forever. According to legend, a magic elixir had granted eternal life to the people of the mythical Eastern Islands. Over the years, the emperor sent expeditions out to sea in search of the islands and the magic potion. But each time they came back empty-handed.

If he couldn't live forever, then Qin Shi Huang was determined to live as long as possible. He ate powdered jade and drank mercury in the belief that they would prolong his life. In fact, these "medicines" were poison and may have caused the emperor to fall sick and die while on a tour of the easternmost outposts of his empire. He was forty-nine years old.

If word of Qin Shi Huang's death got out while he was away from the capital there might be a revolt. So his ministers kept the news a secret. With the emperor's body inside his chariot, the entire party traveled back to the capital city. Meals were brought into the emperor's chariot; daily reports on affairs of state were delivered as usual—all to keep up the appearance that the emperor was alive and well. However, it was summer, and a terrible smell began to come from the chariot. But the clever ministers found a way to account for the stench. A cart was loaded with smelly salted fish and made to precede the chariot, overpowering and masking any foul odors coming from the dead emperor. And so Qin Shi Huang returned to the capital for burial.

▲ This painting from the seventeenth century shows the first emperor carried on a covered litter called a palanquin.

▼ This is a modern stone engraving of the first emperor of China.

215

The tomb of Qin Shi Huang had been under construction for more than thirty years. It was begun when he was a young boy of thirteen and was still not finished when he died. Even incomplete, the emperor's tomb was enormous, larger than his largest palace. According to legend, it had a domed ceiling inlaid with clusters of pearls to represent the sun, moon, and stars. Below was a gigantic relief map of the world, made from bronze. Bronze hills and mountains rose up from the floor, with rivers of mercury flowing into a mercury sea. Along the banks of the rivers were models of the emperor's palaces and cities, all exact replicas of the real ones.

In ancient times, the Chinese believed that life after death was not so different from life on earth. The soul of a dead person could continue to enjoy all the pleasures of everyday life. So people who were rich enough constructed elaborate underground tombs filled with silk robes, jewelry and precious stones, furniture, games, boats, chariots—everything the dead person could possibly need or want.

Qin Shi Huang knew that grave robbers would try their best to loot the treasures in his tomb. So he had machines put inside the tomb that produced the rumble of thunder to scare off intruders, and mechanical crossbows at the entrance were set to fire arrows automatically should anyone dare trespass. The emperor also made certain that the workers who carried his coffin in to its final resting place never revealed its exact whereabouts. As the men worked their way back through the tunnels to the tomb's entrance, a stone door came crashing down, and they were left to die, sealed inside the tomb along with the body of the emperor.

Even all these measures, however, were not enough to satisfy the emperor. And so, less than a mile from the tomb, in underground trenches, the terra cotta warriors were stationed. Just as flesh-and-blood troops had protected him during his lifetime, the terra cotta troops were there to protect their ruler against any enemy for all eternity.

Buried Soldiers

Qin Shi Huang became emperor because of his stunning victories on the battlefield. His army was said to be a million strong. In every respect except for number, the terra cotta army is a faithful replica of the real one.

So far terra cotta troops have been found in three separate pits, all close to one another. A fourth pit was discovered, but it was empty. The entire army faces east. The Qin kingdom, the emperor's homeland, was in the northwest. The other kingdoms that had been conquered and had become part of his empire lay to the east. So Qin Shi Huang feared that any enemy uprising would come from that direction.

The first pit is by far the biggest, more than two football fields long, with approximately six thousand soldiers and horses. About one thousand have already been excavated and restored. None of the soldiers in the army wears a helmet or carries a shield, proof of the Qin soldier's fearlessness. But the archers stationed in the front lines don't wear any armor either. They needed to be able to move freely in order to fire their arrows with accuracy. And so these frontline sharpshooters, who were the first targets of an approaching enemy, also had the least protection.

Following the vanguard are eleven long columns of foot soldiers

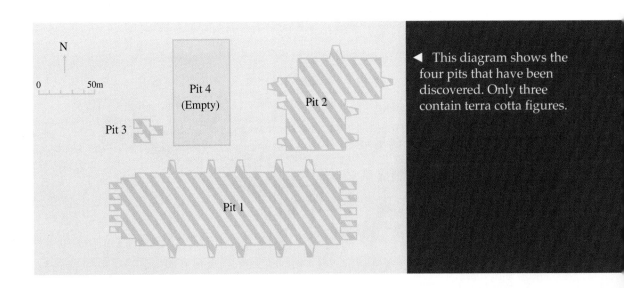

◄ This diagram shows the four pits that have been discovered. Only three contain terra cotta figures.

and lower-ranking officers, the main body of the army, who once carried spears, battle-axes, and halberds. The soldiers are prepared for an attack from any direction; those in the extreme right and extreme left columns face out, not forward, so that they can block enemy charges from either side. Last of all comes the rear guard, three rows of soldiers with their backs to the rest of the army, ready to stop an attack from behind.

Stationed at various points among the foot soldiers are about fifty charioteers who drove wooden chariots. Each charioteer has a team of four horses and is dressed in full-length armor. In some carts, a general rides beside the charioteer, ready to beat a drum to signal a charge or ring a bell to call for a retreat.

The long rectangular arrangement of soldiers in Pit 1 follows a real battle formation used to defeat real enemies in ancient times. It is called a sword formation, with the frontline archers representing the tip of the sword, the chariots and the columns

▲ In Pit 1, three rows of unarmored soldiers are followed by the main body of the army.

▲ This drawing shows what a wooden chariot would have looked like.

◀ The actual chariots rotted away long before the discovery of the terra cotta army.

of foot soldiers forming the blade, and the rear guard the handle.

Pit 2 is far smaller than Pit 1. With an estimated 900 warriors of all different ranks, Pit 2 serves as a powerful back-up force to help the larger army in Pit 1. There are also almost 500 horses—about 350 chariot horses and more than 100 cavalry horses.

The terra cotta horses are Mongolian ponies, not very big, but muscular and full of power. With their flaring nostrils, bared teeth, and bulging eyes, the chariot horses all look as if they are straining to gallop across a battlefield. The mane of each horse is trimmed short and its tail braided. That is so it won't get caught in the harness.

By the time of the first emperor, soldiers on horseback were replacing war chariots. It was hard for even the most experienced drivers to manage a chariot over bumpy, rock-strewn ground. Cavalrymen could move much more swiftly and easily. Their horses had fancy saddles decorated with rows of nail heads and tassels, but no stirrups—they hadn't come into use yet.

Pit 3, by far the smallest, contains fewer than seventy war-riors and only one team of horses. Archaeologists think that Pit 3 represents army headquarters. That's because the soldiers are not arranged in an attack formation.

Instead, they face one another in a U shape, as if they are busy consulting among themselves. Although the officers at command central would not engage in hand-to-hand combat, the fate of the thousands of troops in Pit 1 and Pit 2 rests in their hands.

Altogether, the three pits of warriors and horses make up an unstoppable army. All the warriors are stationed strategically, exactly as they would have been on a real battlefield. For example, rows of kneeling soldiers with crossbows alternate with rows of standing archers. This way, while one row is firing, the other row has time to reload their bows. The crossbow was by far the most powerful weapon of the time. The Chinese were using crossbows as early as 400 B.C. In Europe, however, crossbows didn't come into use for at least another 1,300 years.

In earlier times in ancient China, real soldiers and horses were killed and buried alongside their dead ruler. But by the time of Qin Shi Huang this horrible custom was no longer so common. Instead, clay or wooden figurines were substituted for human sacrifices. Once the figures were buried underground, it was believed that they would come to life magically and protect the dead emperor both from real attackers hoping to ransack his tomb and from any evil spirits wanting to harm his immortal soul.

Interestingly, there is not a single word about the buried army in any records from ancient times. Why was this? Was the creation of the clay soldiers simply not worthy of mention? Or was the emperor making sure that nobody knew about his ultimate secret weapon?

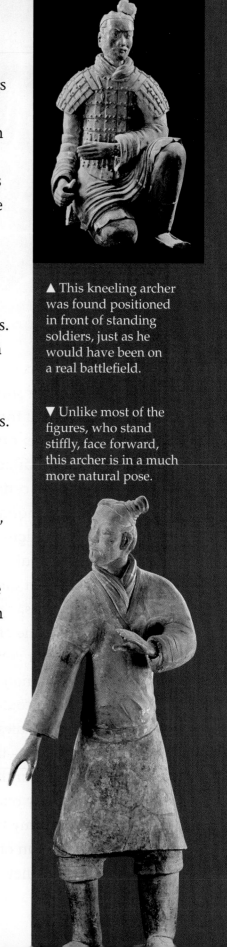

▲ This kneeling archer was found positioned in front of standing soldiers, just as he would have been on a real battlefield.

▼ Unlike most of the figures, who stand stiffly, face forward, this archer is in a much more natural pose.

The Faces of Ancient China

About two thousand soldiers have been unearthed, yet, amazingly, so far no two are the same. The army includes men of all different ages, from different parts of China, with different temperaments. A young soldier looks both excited and nervous; an older officer, perhaps a veteran of many wars, appears tired, resigned. Some soldiers seem lost in thought, possibly dreaming of their return home; others look proud and confident. Although from a distance the figures appear almost identical, like giant-size toy soldiers, each is a distinct work of art.

Did real-life models pose for the figures? Probably not. But hundreds of craftsmen from all over the empire spent more than ten years in workshops set up near the pits creating the warriors. It is likely that they made the faces of the soldiers look like the faces of people that they knew from home.

The uniforms of the terra cotta figures are exact copies in clay of what real soldiers of the day wore. The soldier's uniform tells his rank in the army. The lowest-ranking soldiers are bareheaded and wear heavy knee-length tunics but no armor. Often their legs are wrapped in cloth shin guards for protection.

▲ At the time of the first emperor, Chinese men wore their waist-length hair in a variety of braids and buns.

◀ The expressions on the soldiers' faces make the figures look real.

The generals' uniforms are the most elegant. Their caps sometimes sport a pheasant feather; their fancy shoes curl up at the toes; and their fine armor is made from small iron fish scales. Tassels on their armor are also a mark of their high rank.

The terra cotta soldiers are now the ghostly grayish color of baked clay, clay that came from nearby Mount Li. Originally the soldiers were all brightly colored. Tiny bits of paint can still be seen on many of the figures and are proof that uniforms came in a blaze of colors—purple, blue, green, yellow, red, and orange. The colors of each soldier's uniform indicated not only which part of the army he belonged to—cavalry or infantry, for example—but also what his particular rank was. The terra cotta horses were fully painted, too, in brown with pink ears, nostrils, and mouths. Unfortunately, when figures are dug out of the ground, most of the paint on them peels off and sticks to the surrounding earth. Also, when exposed to air, the paint tends to crumble into dust.

Today groups of artisans in workshops near the three pits make replicas of the soldiers, following the techniques used 2,200 years ago. Their work helps archaeologists learn more about how the original figures were created. Even though the workers today have the advantages of modern kilns that register temperatures exactly, no copies have ever come out as hard or as lustrous as the ancient originals. (The workers of today are also not under the same kind of pressure as the emperor's potters—if they made a mistake, they were killed!)

◀ The colored computer image shows how this general would have looked originally.

Who were the potters who made the original soldiers? For the most part, they have remained anonymous. In ancient times, being a craftsman was considered lowly work. However, some soldiers are signed, probably by the master potter in charge of a workshop. The signature is like a stamp of approval, a sign of quality control.

Of course, the creators of the terra cotta warriors never intended their work to be seen by anyone other than the emperor. That is a strange notion for twenty-first-century minds to accept. Artists today want their work to be seen, enjoyed, admired. But as soon as the emperor's army was completed, it was buried. Pits were dug twenty feet deep. Green-tiled floors were laid down. Dirt walls were constructed, creating tunnels in which the soldiers and horses and chariots were placed. A wooden roof was built overhead, and then ten feet of dirt was shoveled on top of the army. It was supposed to remain undisturbed for all eternity, but it did not turn out that way. How surprised Qin sculptors would be by the crowds from all over the world who come to see their creations!

Common Core State Standards

Informational Text 1. Cite textual evidence to support analysis of what the text says explicitly as well as inferences drawn from the text. Also Informational Text 2., Writing 9.

Envision It! Retell

Think Critically

1. What judgment would you make about a modern-day leader who built and then buried an army of terra cotta soldiers? **Text to Self**

2. The selection begins, "It's just an ordinary day in early spring, or so three farmers think. . . ." Why do you think the author starts this way instead of first explaining what the terra cotta warriors are? **Think Like an Author**

3. Look back at pages 215 and 216. In your own words, what is most important about Qin Shi Huang's death, his trip back to the capital, and his plans for his tomb and its silent guards? **Main Idea and Details**

4. Before reading *The Emperor's Silent Army,* how did what you know about ancient China, the making of terra cotta objects, or archaeology help you to better understand the selection? **Background Knowledge**

5. **Look Back and Write** What do the terra cotta warriors tell us about the craftsmen of ancient China? Look back at pages 221–223 and write your response. Provide evidence to support your answer.

   Key Ideas and Details • Text Evidence

Meet the Author

Jane O'Connor

Jane O'Connor saw the terra cotta soldiers while she was on vacation in China in 2000. When she learned that no books about them existed for younger readers, she decided to write one, which became *The Emperor's Silent Army*.

Ms. O'Connor has written more than thirty books for children, most of them fiction, as well as award-winning nonfiction books for older readers. She has also written books with her husband, Jim O'Connor, and she wrote one with her older son, Robert—when he was in sixth grade. Her younger son, Teddy, wrote his first book in 2001. Ms. O'Connor was born in New York City and lives there with her husband and two sons.

Other books by Jane O'Connor:
Henri Matisse: Drawing with Scissors and *Mary Cassatt: Family Pictures*

Use the Reading Log in the *Reader's and Writer's Notebook* to record your independent reading.

225

Common Core State Standards

Writing 3. Write narratives to develop real or imagined experiences or events using effective technique, relevant descriptive details, and well-structured event sequences. **Also Writing 4.**

Let's Write It!

Key Features of a Mystery

- plot revolves around unexplained events

- may have elements of suspense or terror

- signs or clues help reveal the mystery

READING STREET ONLINE
GRAMMAR JAMMER
www.ReadingStreet.com

Narrative

Mystery

A **mystery** is a story about a puzzling problem or question one or more characters try to solve. The student model on the next page is an example of a mystery.

Writing Prompt The origin of the ancient terra cotta army was a mystery when first discovered in China. Write your own mystery. Explain what the mystery is; then use clues to reveal what happened, how it happened, and why.

Writer's Checklist

Remember, you should . . .

✓ introduce the question or problem that needs to be solved.

✓ create a suspenseful plot with mysterious events and ideas.

✓ have the character or characters follow clues to solve the puzzle.

✓ build the plot to a climax, in which the mystery is solved.

The Disappearing Bicycle

Juanita walked outside and closed the front door before realizing something was horribly wrong. Her bicycle, which had been locked to the front porch railing less than an hour earlier, was missing. Juanita would have to walk to soccer practice in the rain.

But who stole Juanita's bicycle? Only two other people knew the combination to the lock — Ron, her brother, and Julia, her sister. Could one of them have taken the bike, or could someone else have guessed the combination?

As Juanita started walking, she thought about who might take her bicycle. Julia had her driver's license, and was usually allowed to drive their mother's car. Ron did not drive, but said earlier that he was staying home for the day. Was Ron telling the truth?

Just then, Ron rode by, on Juanita's bike.

"Sorry, Juanita!" He yelled, and leaped off to offer her the bike. "I had to return my books to the library before it closed!"

Writing Trait Focus/Ideas
The setting helps introduce suspense.

Possessive nouns are used correctly.

Genre
A **mystery** tells a story about unexplained events.

Conventions

Possessive Nouns

Remember A **possessive noun** tells who or what has something. To form most **singular possessive nouns,** add an apostrophe (') and the letter s. (John's jacket) For **plural possessive nouns** ending in -s, add an apostrophe ('). (The bushes' leaves)

227

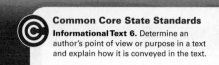
Common Core State Standards
Informational Text 6. Determine an author's point of view or purpose in a text and explain how it is conveyed in the text.

The Taj Mahal

by Barbara Sturges

Sweet Dreams and Sorrow

Genre
Narrative Nonfiction

- Narrative nonfiction tells of a true event or a series of events in story form.

- A narrative often tells its story in chronological order, as in a newspaper or magazine article. It may be a current event or a historical event.

- Biographies and autobiographies are forms of narrative nonfiction.

- Narrative nonfiction may use description in order to tell about something better.

- Read "The Taj Mahal: Sweet Dreams and Sorrow" and see how it is an example of narrative nonfiction.

Could a young boy and girl, upon seeing each other for the very first time, fall instantly and forever in love? This sweet dream came true hundreds of years ago in Agra, India. But this true story is as tragic as it is joyful.

Reflecting pool of the Taj Mahal

The boy was Prince Khurram, favored son of Emperor Jahangir, and the girl was Mumtaz Mahal, whose name meant Chosen One of the Palace. They were married in 1612. By then, Prince Khurram had become the emperor. Now he was known as Shah Jahan: King of the World.

Shah Jahan and Queen Mumtaz Mahal lived happily and had many children. But in 1631, the queen's life came to a sudden end. Their love story was not at an end though. With her dying breath, the queen made a final request. She asked the Shah to build her a memorial more beautiful than the world had ever seen.

And so he did. Shah Jahan ordered the building of the Taj Mahal, a monument so vast that it took 20,000 workers and 1,000 elephants almost 20 years to build. It is said that the Taj was "designed by giants and finished by jewelers." The white marble structure is inlaid with sapphires, diamonds, turquoise, and jade; it was topped off with a golden dome that soars high into the sky. Queen Mumtaz Mahal was buried there, in the most bejeweled and imposing of all the world's mausoleums.

Eventually, the Emperor was deposed by one of his sons, Aurangzeb. After seizing power, Aurangzeb had his father cruelly imprisoned. For the rest of his days, Shah Jahan could only gaze longingly out a window across a river at the distant jeweled tomb of his wife.

Today the Taj Mahal is known as one of the world's great wonders. Inside the tomb's central chamber are the final resting places of both Shah Jahan and Mumtaz Mahal. Each year millions of tourists visit this monument of an emperor to his beloved queen.

Let's Think About...

What description on this page tells you that the Taj Mahal is a real place? **Narrative Nonfiction**

Let's Think About...

Reading Across Texts The Taj Mahal and the terra cotta soldiers may be considered two wonders of the ancient world. Why do you think they are such great wonders?

Writing Across Texts Based on what you read about the Taj Mahal and the terra cotta soldiers, which do you think is more impressive? Write a paragraph that explains why.

Common Core State Standards

Language 1. Demonstrate command of the conventions of standard English grammar and usage when writing or speaking. **Also Speaking/Listening 1.b., 1.c.**

Let's Learn It!

READING STREET ONLINE
ONLINE STUDENT EDITION
www.ReadingStreet.com

Vocabulary

Suffixes -al, -ful, and -ly

Word Structure Remember that suffixes add additional meanings to words. The suffixes -al and -ful change nouns to adjectives. The nouns *mechanic* and *meaning,* for example, become the adjectives *mechanical* and *meaningful.* The suffix -ly changes an adjective to an adverb, as *quick* is changed to the adverb *quickly.*

Practice It! Choose several words that end in -al, -ful, or -ly from *The Emperor's Silent Army* and "The Taj Mahal: Sweet Dreams and Sorrow." Make a chart to divide each word into its base word and the suffix. Add your definition of each word. Then use a dictionary to confirm each word's meaning.

Fluency

Accuracy

Remember that it is important to read words accurately so that you understand their meanings. Take time before you read to skim the text, looking for unfamiliar words you can sound out. Keep a dictionary or glossary handy.

Practice It! With a partner, take turns reading aloud the first two paragraphs on page 214 of *The Emperor's Silent Army.* How can you read so that the difficult information is easier to understand?

Listening and Speaking

When giving an oral presentation, speak clearly and confidently.

Talk Show

A talk show has a host or hosts and one or more guests who present a given topic and may also address questions called in by listeners or viewers. Either the guests or the hosts may answer a caller's question.

Practice It! Prepare a talk show about *The Emperor's Silent Army.* A host or two will present as guests the farmers who unearthed the terra cotta figures. The guests appear so that they can tell about their chance discovery.

Tips

Listening . . .

- Listen attentively to each speaker.
- Take notes on important points.
- Ask informed questions.

Speaking . . .

- Speak clearly and to the point.
- Speak at an appropriate pace.

Teamwork . . .

- Choose different roles fairly.
- Be sure no one has already asked your question.
- Listen carefully so that responses to "call-in" questions really answer the questions.

Common Core State Standards

Language 6. Acquire and use accurately grade-appropriate general academic and domain-specific words and phrases; gather vocabulary knowledge when considering a word or phrase important to comprehension or expression. **Also Speaking/Listening 1., 1.c.**

Oral Vocabulary

Let's Talk About

Clues from the Earth

- Describe a place where archaeologists work.

- Ask questions about how archaeologists work.

- Share ideas about how the past helps us today.

READING STREET ONLINE
CONCEPT TALK VIDEO
www.ReadingStreet.com

233

Envision It! | Skill Strategy

Skill

Strategy

Comprehension Skill

Graphic Sources

- Graphic sources such as maps, photographs, and time lines show information visually.

- As you read, compare information in a graphic source with information in the text.

- Use a Venn diagram like the one below to organize details about two very different groups of early Native American people.

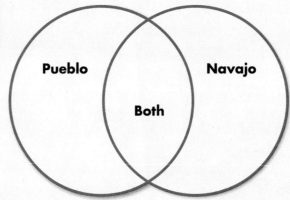

Pueblo   Navajo

Both

Comprehension Strategy

Text Structure

Good readers use the structure of an article to help them understand what they read. Before reading, preview the selection. Look at the title, headings, and captions to get an idea of what the selection will be about and how it is organized. Headings sometimes outline an article.

234

In One Place or On the Move

Group of Early People	Pueblo	Navajo
Way of Life	permanent settlements	nomadic
How They Got Food	farmed, raised turkeys, hunted, gathered	hunted, gathered
Foods	turkey, corn, squash, beans, sunflower seeds, game, wild plants	deer, elk, rabbits, birds, snakes, wild plants such as mesquite and cactus
Homes	permanent buildings, like apartments	temporary huts with covered poles

Skill Based on this graphic source, what do you think this article will be about?

Skill Use the chart to answer this question: How did the Navajo get their food?

Strategy What will this section be about? How can you tell?

Very early Native Americans in the Southwest lived in two different ways. Some, like the Pueblo, lived in one place. Others, like the Navajo, were nomadic and moved from place to place.

Different Lifestyles

Pueblo people lived in connected buildings made of stone or adobe brick. The buildings were something like apartments. They could be as high as five levels. The Pueblo also built special buildings where people gathered for meetings and ceremonies.

Nomadic people, such as the Navajo, would settle in one spot for a time. There they built huts with frames made of logs and poles. The frames were covered with mud, sod, and bark. When the Navajo moved on, they left their huts and built new ones in the next place.

STONES, BONES, AND PETROGLYPHS

Your Turn!

Need a Review? See the *Envision It! Handbook* for help with graphic sources and text structure.

Ready to Try It? Use what you've learned about graphic sources as you read *Stones, Bones, and Petroglyphs.*

Common Core State Standards
Language 4.d. Verify the preliminary determination of the meaning of a word or phrase (e.g., by checking the inferred meaning in context or in a dictionary). **Also Language 4.a.**

Envision It! | Words to Know

alcoves

obsidian

pueblo

decades

prehistoric

trowels

READING STREET ONLINE
VOCABULARY ACTIVITIES
www.ReadingStreet.com

Vocabulary Strategy for
🎯 Unknown Words

Dictionary/Glossary When you are reading and come across a word you do not know, first try to use context clues to figure out its meaning. If that doesn't work, look up the word in a dictionary or glossary.

Choose one of the Words to Know and follow these steps.

1. Look in the back of your book for the glossary.

2. Find the entry for the word. The entries in both glossaries and dictionaries are in alphabetical order.

3. Use the pronunciation key to pronounce the word.

4. Read all of the meanings given for the word. If you want more information, look in a dictionary.

5. Choose the meaning that makes sense in your sentence.

Read "A Door into the Past." Use context clues before you consult a dictionary or the glossary to determine the meanings of unknown words.

Words to Write Reread "A Door into the Past." Think of a building or location that is part of your community's history. Do some research to find out the facts about it. Then write about this place, using as many words from the Words to Know list as you can.

A Door into the Past

"Today we are going to my secret fishing spot," said Grandpa.

"I don't like to fish," I complained.

Grandpa winked. "If you can sacrifice one day with your friends, you'll learn that the fishing spot is not my only secret."

After a hike we headed down a long, steep slope. "My fishing spot is at the bottom," said Grandpa.

Halfway down, he picked up an arrowhead made of obsidian. He pointed to an alcove cut into a cliff face. I saw a grinding stone on the ground with a few corncobs next to it.

"How did you know about this place?" I asked.

"It's on the way to my fishing spot. I've been coming here for decades," he said. "I think I'm the only one who knows it's here. I knew you were interested in archaeology, so it was time to show you. What prehistoric people lived here, do you think?"

"The early Pueblo," I said. "They lived in alcoves before they began building pueblos near a kiva."

"That was my guess too," said Grandpa. "All these years, I have wanted to share this with just the right person."

Then he opened his fishing pack. Inside were two trowels wrapped in cloth. "Someday we will do more exploring here. But now, let's fish!"

Your Turn!

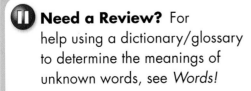
Need a Review? For help using a dictionary/glossary to determine the meanings of unknown words, see *Words!*

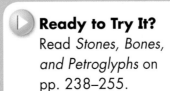
Ready to Try It? Read *Stones, Bones, and Petroglyphs* on pp. 238–255.

237

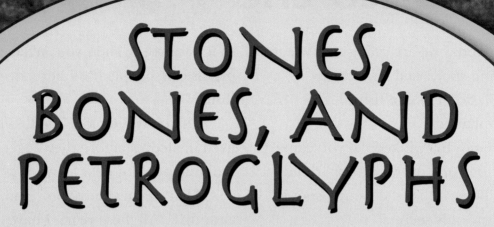

STONES, BONES, AND PETROGLYPHS

DIGGING INTO SOUTHWEST ARCHAEOLOGY

by Susan E. Goodman
photographs by Michael J. Doolittle

Question of the Week
Why is it important to learn about America's past?

Genre

Expository text gives information about the real world. Look for facts and information about archaeologists and what they do.

AN ULTIMATE FIELD TRIP

A long time ago...

After a hot day in his cornfield, the man drops his digging stick and slowly lowers himself over the canyon's edge. Clinging to the wall with his hands, he uses his foot to feel for the holes his people have pecked into the stone. Carefully, he inches down to the village built right into the cliff....

For more than a thousand years, Pueblo people lived on mesas, or canyon tops, in a part of the American Southwest called the Four Corners, where Colorado, New Mexico, Utah, and Arizona meet. Suddenly, around A.D. 1200, these people moved into giant alcoves that nature had cut into the middle of the canyon walls. They created their Stone Age apartment buildings by chipping out one stone block after another. To make the mud that held these blocks in place, they carried water hundreds of feet from a spring on the canyon floor. All that work and they used these buildings for just a few decades.

By the year 1300, every Pueblo man, woman, and child had left the Four Corners area. Their fire pits held only ashes. Their fields fed only birds and animals. Their cities stood empty and silent.

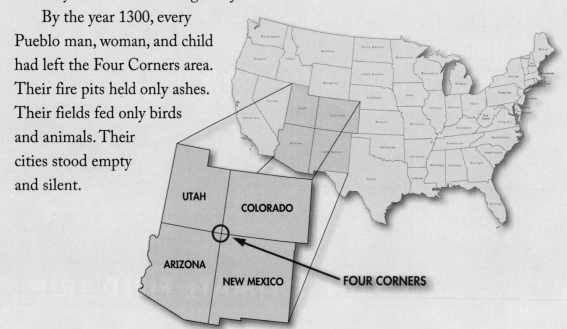

UTAH
COLORADO
ARIZONA
NEW MEXICO
FOUR CORNERS

The Hannibal kids and their advisers.

We know where these people went. They moved south into what is now New Mexico and Arizona. But why did they leave the land they had lived in for more than one thousand years?

This is just one question archaeologists at Crow Canyon Archaeological Center in Colorado are trying to answer. Archaeologists study people of the past, and these archaeologists are working to understand who these Puebloans were and how they lived. They excavate, or dig, in ruins to help build a picture of this ancient world.

Now the archaeologists have help. A group of eighth-graders from Hannibal Middle School in Hannibal, Missouri, came to Crow Canyon to learn what these scientists already know.

And to help them find new answers.

Ancient Puebloans used ladders they could pull up instead of stairs to enter their homes and keep out intruders as well.

241

CHAPTER 2

Gooping Up and Setting Off

"Everybody got their hats and sunscreen?" Sara asked. Sara Kelly and Ken Lanik were two Crow Canyon educators guiding the Hannibal kids through their adventure with archaeology. The kids were getting ready to tour the ruins in Woods Canyon, where they'd be excavating later that week.

"Don't forget your water bottles," Sara added. "Newcomers have a hard time remembering how much they need to drink around here."

The land around Four Corners doesn't have sand dunes, but it is like a desert, with plants and trees that can live without much water. Its climate is so dry that sweat evaporates before it can bead up on your skin. That's great for archaeology because a dry climate helps baskets, bones, even buildings last for hundreds of years.

The kids piled into vans and drove past dry grasslands and deep canyons. They saw pinyon pines, cactus, and sagebrush wherever nature chose the landscape, and green fields where farmers watered their crops. If the kids had scratched around one of those sagebrush fields, they might have found a spear point or stone tool. For more than a thousand years, ancient Pueblo people had lived all over this land.

"We used to call these people the Anasazi," Ken explained. "But the Navajo gave them that name, which means enemy of our people. So you can understand why their current relatives don't like it. Since we don't know what they named themselves, we call them the ancestral Puebloans."

"Everyone out for Woods Canyon," said Sara as the vans rolled to a stop. "Grab your water bottles and let's go."

A few minutes down the path, Ben B. stopped and stared at the ground. "I found something," he called out.

"Congratulations," said Sara. "We call these pottery pieces *potsherds*. You'll see artifacts as you walk along," said Sara. "It's okay to pick something up to look at it, but mark its place with your foot so you can return it to the right spot. Archaeologists get a lot of information from an item's location."

"Could it really make much difference if you moved it?" asked Ben B.

"Sure. Villages two hundred years apart in age can be built just one hundred feet from each other," answered Ken. "It can be confusing if you put something from a newer settlement into the older one."

"And, don't forget, taking artifacts from public lands like Woods Canyon is against the law," Sara added. "Just think about it this way. You can learn a lot from these artifacts because they're still here. If you picked them all up, there wouldn't be any left for your kids or their kids to enjoy."

"Anyway, archaeology is more than finding neat stuff. It's finding out about the people who left all that neat stuff," added Pat Mahlia, the teacher who came with them from Hannibal.

As the kids scrambled into the canyon, Sara pointed to some rocks that used to be a tower. Imagining that pile of rubble as a tall building was hard. In fact, the kids walked past many mounds and piles without even noticing them. It takes training to see what used to be.

"Look carefully," said Sara as they all gathered on a cliff. "That spot used to be an underground circular room called a *kiva*. Over there on that cliff is where people built their homes."

The kids took a moment to study the canyon. Some noticed how deep it was. Others listened to the wind. Still others tried to imagine the people living there 750 years ago.

These structures were home to some Pueblo people seven hundred years ago.

As long as ten thousand years ago, people roamed the Four Corners. They gathered wild seeds and cactus fruits and used spears to hunt animals that are now extinct, such as the wooly mammoth.

By the year A.D. 1, people in the Four Corners were growing corn and squash and living on the mesa tops in circular houses built with logs and mud. They still hunted, but with bows and arrows. By A.D. 550, they planted beans along with their corn and squash. They stored these foods in baskets and cooked them in clay pots.

As time went on, people clustered their homes together in rows of connected rooms. In front, they built kivas for the village to share. They traded with other groups for red pottery and cotton and shell beads that came from what is now Mexico.

Over the years, villages grew larger. Some had buildings four stories high. Large plazas built on kiva roofs provided a place to work and visit. By 1150, tens of thousands of people lived in the area.

About 1200, villages moved from mesas to alcoves in the middle of cliffs. These new stone cities had towers and kivas and hundreds of rooms. There, people traded and made beautiful pots and weavings and jewelry.

By 1300, the villages were empty of voices and laughter. The people were gone.

Four Corners Time Line

1200 B.C. AND BEFORE
nomadic hunter-gatherers

A.D. 1–500
earliest pit houses,
early agriculture,
earthen ("adobe") buildings

500–750
advanced agriculture,
early villages

750–900
stone buildings

900–1150
stone villages, roads,
population 30,000
(1064–1066 – volcano erupts)
(1130–1180 – 30-year drought)

1200
cliff dwellings
(1276–1299 – 23-year drought)

1300
area abandoned

CHAPTER 3

The Facts About Artifacts

Before the kids dug them up, they needed to know more about artifacts. The first thing they learned is that an artifact is something made or used by people. A rock in a river most likely isn't an artifact. But it becomes one as soon as it's placed with others in a ring around a fire or shaped into an axe head.

Artifacts tell the story of how people live. The kids got a clearer picture of the ancient Pueblo world by looking at the things its people had used.

"You'll hear this all week long," Sara said. "It's not what you find, it's what you find *out*. Archaeology isn't just finding stuff, it's finding out what it means. A pot can be near some corncobs and the remains of a fire or in a kiva surrounded by turquoise—the same pot, but totally different uses that tell us different things."

Sometimes looking at the way an object was damaged provided a clue of how it was used. When Joe realized he was holding a piece of bone, he asked Sara why it was black.

"It's burned," she said. "Why would you burn bone?"

"Sacrifice?" Joe said.

"That's a good guess. Could there be another reason?"

"Food?"

"That's right, cooking," said Sara. "This bone was left over from someone's dinner."

The wear on the front ladle's handle reveals that its owner was right-handed.

Later Joe looked at the painted design on a piece of pottery. "That's a pitchfork, so we know that they farmed," he concluded.

"Let's think this one out," said Ken. "What do we use pitchforks for?"

"Hay."

"And why do farmers pitch hay?"

"To feed animals."

"Have we seen any bones from cows and horses, the type of animals that eat hay?" asked Ken.

"No," Joe admitted. "Then why did they make a design that looked like a pitchfork?"

"Well, that does look like a pitchfork to us," said Ken. "One problem archaeologists have is we're looking at another culture with ideas formed by our own. We're influenced by the things we know and the things we believe. We can't be certain these people were thinking the same way."

Luckily, scientists have another way to learn about the ancient Pueblo world. The people who left the Four Corners in the late 1200s joined up with other Pueblo groups. What some people see as archaeology is family history for many of today's Pueblo tribes. Understanding how current Pueblo people live can provide a window into the past. By looking at how today's Hopi and Zuni people weave, for example, researchers learned that the loops on kiva walls held looms.

Forgetting pots and hammer stones for a moment, Bill wondered what future scientists would say about the artifacts in his bedroom. "People from seven hundred years ago look so primitive to us," he said. "Future archaeologists might think the same about us. Still, I think they'd be amazed by my stereo."

"We're trying to figure out how many people lived in Woods Canyon and how they related to other people nearby," said Ken. "We need to find artifacts to answer these questions. So your work is really necessary."

Sometimes artifacts can be mysterious. The kids thought these things might be (clockwise from lower left) a hat, a helmet, a shoehorn, an incense burner, and a bedpan. They are really a basket, a broken pot, a scraping tool, a spear-thrower, and a ladle.

Will future archaeologists wonder whether this Frisbee is a toy or a plate? What will they think about these other mysterious artifacts?

CHAPTER 4

Digging Into The Past

The kids were ready to dig. They had studied all kinds of artifacts, from necklaces to cooking pots. They now knew that important clues could be easily overlooked. What first seemed like a regular rock with one smooth side, for example, could really be a grinding stone that had been flattened by crushing corn.

Back in the lab, the kids had also learned how to dig archaeologist style. They had marked off an area and carefully used trowels to skim off thin layers of dirt. This dirt went into buckets to be screened or sifted for tiny treasures like nuggets of charcoal and pottery beads. If the kids had found a larger artifact, they removed all the dirt around it first. Once they saw that nothing else was nearby, they could pick it up.

In the canyon, the kids split into groups and followed different archaeologists to test pits around the site. In archaeologist Mark Varien's group, one boy said he had thought the whole village would be excavated. Mark explained that just uncovering small sections leaves untouched areas for future scientists to make new discoveries with better technology.

"This is harder than I expected," Tyler said, scraping at dirt that had been packed down for seven hundred years.

"It is hard," said Ben K. "It's worth it though. I found a potsherd and a fragment of animal bone."

Meanwhile, in archaeologist Melissa Churchill's area, kids were digging in a midden, or trash heap. Ancient garbage is an archaeologist's treasure chest. Think of how much someone could learn about your life from the pizza box, ripped jeans, and old telephone bill in your trash can. Broken pottery and tools and worn-out clothing help archaeologists learn about daily life in ancient times.

CHAPTER 5

Trying Out The Old Ways

Digging up artifacts isn't the only way archaeologists learn about the past. Learning about past cultures includes knowing how they did things. That's why archaeologists at Crow Canyon built a pithouse, the type of home the ancestral Puebloans made around A.D. 700. Kids helped the archaeologists make their pithouse by using ancient building techniques. After a lot of tired muscles and sore backs, they had even more reason to appreciate prehistoric people.

"Imagine using a stick and a basket to remove three feet of dirt," said Sara to the kids as they sat inside the pithouse. "Think about cutting down all the trees you'd need to build this thing. It takes about an hour just to cut through an inch of trunk with a stone axe.

"And it took several truckloads of willow to weave between beams to make the walls," she continued. "That's a lot of armloads when you don't have a pickup."

Testing old methods provides many insights about how and why things were done. Archaeologists used to think, for example, that ancient people burned the tops of wooden beams to cut them. Once they tried it themselves, scientists realized that charred beams keep out termites.

The fancy name for trying out ancient ways is *experimental archaeology*. Doing a little experimental archaeology themselves, the kids performed some daily chores of the ancient Pueblo world.

"It made me realize how hard they worked," said Erin.

And it made other kids realize how hard the work was.

GRINDING CORN

Talk about Stone Age. Women used *manos*, hand-sized stones, to grind dried corn on *metates*, stone slabs. Eventually the flour was cooked into flat breads or mush. Unfortunately, these foods had an added ingredient. Tiny bits of stone broke off and mixed in with the corn. After years of chewing this food, many people's teeth were ground to stubs.

"It's harder than I thought to get it small," said Ben K. after he tried grinding his share of corn.

"I was surprised to find there was really a pattern to using a mano and metate," said Jacob. "I ate some—bland but not half bad."

Lindsey disagreed. "It looks like school chalk," she said, "and it tasted like school chalk."

STARTING FIRES

Start by making a nest of shredded juniper bark or cattail fluff. Twirl a stick on a little board until friction heats things up. Poof, you've got fire.

"Sara made it look easy," said Joe, "but when me and Phillip tried to start one, we couldn't even get smoke."

250

MAKING POTTERY

Sara demonstrated how ancient Puebloans formed coils into a bowl. Then she used a piece of gourd to scrape them smooth. The kids started making their own pots and bowls and ladles.

"My pot sorta looks like Mr. Potato Head without eyes or a mouth," said Erin. "But I think the Pueblo would be impressed if they saw us trying to learn their ways."

"I bet they didn't use a knife to cut off the tops of their mugs," said Brooke, as she reached for one herself.

"They certainly didn't use steel ones," answered Sara, "but they had blades made from obsidian that were even sharper. Sometimes we're so proud of our own technology, we are blind to how advanced ancient cultures actually were."

Bill learned to appreciate a potter's skill when he tried to paint a traditional design on his pot with a brush made from yucca leaves. "Oops," he said as he made a mistake. "I guess I'll make a stripe instead."

251

CHAPTER 6

Visiting The Past

"I find myself looking for potsherds everywhere," said Brett, "even in this parking lot."

Brett's parking lot was at Mesa Verde National Park, where the kids were spending the last day of their trip. Mesa Verde is a park created to preserve the works of prehistoric people. The location was a good choice. Mesa Verde has more than four thousand archaeological sites, including six hundred cliff dwellings.

Visiting Mesa Verde was a perfect ending to the kids' week at Crow Canyon. It summed up much of what they learned about ancestral Puebloans. Fully excavated ruins helped them more clearly picture how villages were laid out. And after a week of study, they could look at a ruin and say, "There's the kiva" or "These rooms were used for storage."

Mesa Verde was like a time machine where the kids could visit a pithouse built in A.D. 500, a rectangular village from A.D. 950, and, finally, thirteenth-century cliff dwellings. Moving from one to the other, the kids could see how society and people's individual lives changed over time.

"As they got more experience, they got smarter," said Bill. "You can see how they made their houses better through the years."

"I think the ones in later years had it easier," said Amanda. "The earlier ones had to come up with all the ideas that the later people could improve on."

"Today was my favorite event of our Colorado trip. I think I liked it because I got to see actual sites that were fully excavated." JOE

It was those "later people" who built the last ruin on the kids' schedule. With only thirty-five rooms, Balcony House wasn't the park's largest cliff dwelling, but it was one of the most exciting. Tucked under an overhanging cliff and six hundred feet above the canyon floor, Balcony House was a great example of how ancient Puebloans kept defense in mind when they built their final homes in this region. Back then, people could only enter Balcony House through a long tunnel carved into the rock. A hand-and-toe-hold trail led to the mesa top above. Whether they were afraid of others or not, the residents of Balcony House made it very hard to get in and out of their home.

The kids got in thanks to modern ladders and railings. To some, that seemed hard enough. But every kid agreed the climb was worth it. They admired the wall that kept them and ancient Puebloans from falling over the steep cliff. They peeked into rooms and thought of sleeping on beds of juniper bark and animal skins. They looked at kiva walls blackened by smoke and imagined spending cold winters by a fire.

"This house may not look like your house, but these people were like us," said Dawn O'Sickey, the park ranger who led their tour. "No, they didn't have computers or vans. Yes, they spent long days planting and finding their food. But they also found time to do things they enjoyed.

"These buildings aren't just stone," Dawn continued. "They were people's homes. Babies cried here. Two-year-olds broke their parents' best pots. Older children whined, 'Do I have to grind corn now?' Young men and women were drawn to each other and made families. And became grandparents who passed stories on to new children.

"These people lived their lives with what they had and tried to do better—just like people today. We may never understand exactly why they built T-shaped doorways or why they left this area. But since we understand what it means to be human, we know the most important thing about them."

Thinking over his week, Bill agreed with Dawn. "My favorite part is that you realize that the Puebloans were human beings, not just things that are dead and gone."

"I have realized how important every little artifact is," said Jeannie. "Each artifact can tell or complete a story. Before this week, I probably could have cared less who bothered what [artifact], but now I do."

"This was a good experience," said Christy. "I was glad I could help aid science. I think being an archaeologist would be a fun job."

"I thought it was going to be just like a bunch of school days strung together," said Jeannie, "but I want to come back."

WHY DID THEY LEAVE?

What if the population had been growing for years, using up local resources? And what if drought meant there were not only fewer natural resources but fewer crops as well? And what if this shortage of food and water created tension between neighbors? And what if people, under all this stress, heard about a better, easier life in the south?

We may never know exactly why these ancient Puebloans left their homeland, but, after their week at Crow Canyon, the kids had their own ideas. "I like the theory about how their food was getting used up," said Bill. "We see that today, people moving someplace better when they run out of resources."

"I don't know," said Amanda, "I think it's still a big mystery."

255

Envision It! | Retell

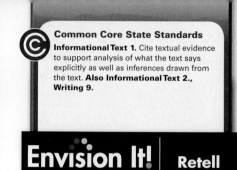

WHY DID THEY LEAVE?

READING STREET ONLINE
STORY SORT
www.ReadingStreet.com

Think Critically

1. Think about how we learn about early people from the artifacts they leave behind. Think about an object that belongs to your family. If it were found a thousand years from now, what would it tell people about your lives? Explain your answer. **Text to Self**

2. Why does the author use dialogue in this nonfiction text? Refer to a few lines of dialogue and explain how they support your answer. **Think Like an Author**

3. Reread page 240. How does the map of the Four Corners help you better understand the text? **Graphic Sources**

4. Reread the title in Chapter 5. What is the chapter about? Which "old ways" were tried out? **Text Structure**

5. **Look Back and Write** The Pueblo left the regions where they had lived for centuries. Look back at page 255 to find the answer to the question *Why did they leave?* In your own words, write the answer that makes sense to Bill. Write whether you agree or disagree, based on your reading of the selection. Provide evidence to support your answer.

   Key Ideas and Details • Text Evidence

SUSAN E. GOODMAN

Do you think being a writer might be boring? Well, it hasn't been for Susan E. Goodman. Ms. Goodman's writing adventures include spending a night in an underwater hotel and swimming with dolphins. She has met many interesting people along the way. "I visited a guy who makes models of dinosaurs for museums and a zookeeper in charge of elephants. It's great to talk to experts; their enthusiasm is catching." Her advice to would-be writers? "Read a lot—then read some more. Think a lot—then think some more. And imagine a lot—and then imagine some more." Besides books, Ms. Goodman has written about seven hundred magazine articles. She has two sons and lives in Boston.

Other books by Susan E. Goodman: *Ultimate Field Trip 1: Adventures in the Amazon Rain Forest* and *Ultimate Field Trip 5: Blasting Off to Space Academy*

Use the Reading Log in the *Reader's and Writer's Notebook* to record your independent reading.

Common Core State Standards
Writing 4. Produce clear and coherent writing in which the development, organization, and style are appropriate to task, purpose, and audience. **Also Language 1.**

Narrative

Poem

A **poem** is a written work arranged in lines. The lines have rhythm, or a regular pattern of stressed and unstressed syllables. The student model on the next page is an example of a poem.

Writing Prompt In *Stones, Bones, and Petroglyphs*, a group of students learns about ancestral Puebloans in the southwestern United States. Think about an ancient civilization you've studied. Now write a poem about it.

Let's Write It!

Key Features of a Poem

- words arranged in lines, or groups of lines called stanzas

- lines have rhythm

- words may rhyme

READING STREET ONLINE
GRAMMAR JAMMER
www.ReadingStreet.com

Writer's Checklist

Remember, you should . . .

☑ write a poem about some aspect of ancient civilization.

☑ arrange your poem in lines.

☑ use complete sentences.

☑ create a regular rhythm in the lines.

Pompeii

To many people Pompeii **was** home.
This ancient city **was ruled** by Rome.

Until the day Vesuvius **erupted**—
the volcano **spewed** ash uninterrupted.

Some people **ran**, some people **fled**.
Others, unaware, **napped** in their bed.

We've since **discovered** the people of Pompeii,
who **were covered** by ash on that fateful day.

Action and linking verbs are used correctly.

Genre
A **poem** is arranged in lines.

Writing Trait Sentences
Words are arranged to create rhythm.

Conventions

Action and Linking Verbs

Remember Action verbs show action and tell what the subject does. **Linking verbs** connect the subject of a sentence with a predicate. The following words can be linking verbs: *am, are, is, was, were. Become, seem,* and *appear* can also be linking verbs.

21st Century Skills
INTERNET GUY

Do you want to find information at a **Web site** quickly? Type Control + F. Then type the information you are looking for. Hit Return. A great trick!

- Web sites contain information about a topic or topics and have links to other information.

- Every Web site has a home page, which is like the table of contents in a book.

- Move around the home page by clicking on links to different Web pages. It may take several tries to find one that's useful to you.

- Links are printed in a different color or are underlined.

- Read "Adobe Homes" and think about how a Web site can present much new information.

Adobe Homes

Sometimes people who design a home look to the past for inspiration. After reading about the Pueblo people, you might want to learn how their homes have influenced modern-day architects in the Southwest.

First you might go to a Web page like the one pictured here. Notice that the information on this page does *not* help you learn more about your topic: how their homes have influenced modern day architects in the Southwest.

File   Edit   Vie

http://www.url.here

Southwest Homes

Styles of Southwest Homes

1. Pueblo style: flat roof with wood beams.

2. Territorial style: flat roof with roof details around top of building. Most windows have white painted wood.

3. Northern New Mexico: metal pitched roof with gables around the windows.

Links to Homes for Sale

Click on links below to take you to homes for sale in New Mexico and Arizona:

New Mexico

Arizona

ADOBE
HOUSE
FOR SALE

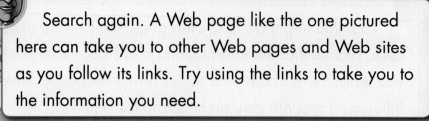

Search again. A Web page like the one pictured here can take you to other Web pages and Web sites as you follow its links. Try using the links to take you to the information you need.

Adobe Architecture

Basic Adobe Structures	Types of Construction	Variations on Adobe Theme
Adobe Homes: Then and Now	Types of Adobe Bricks	Natural Durability and Efficiency

File   Edit   View   Favorites   Tools   Help

http://www.url.n

If you were to click on the link to Adobe Homes: Then and Now, you would find helpful information such as this:

Linking Yesterday and Today

If you were an architect in southwestern Arizona or New Mexico today, you might find yourself designing structures that look like homes of long ago, using materials that have been around for centuries.

Hundreds of years ago, native people of the Southwest constructed their homes of handmade adobe brick. These thick bricks were made of clay and sand mixed with water. Sometimes straw and other natural materials were added for extra strength. The thick mud mixture was either poured into rectangular forms or shaped by hand; then the bricks were set out in the hot sun to dry.

A few of these ancient adobe structures still stand today, such as the thousand-year-old adobe buildings in Taos, New Mexico. Modern people still like the look of these buildings that are descended from the Southwest's Native American heritage.

That's why a growing number of today's homes in the United States Southwest look so much like the homes that people lived in long ago.

Click on another link to find out more. Use the link to Natural Durability and Efficiency to find details about why adobe structures are still popular today.

Adobe Architecture

Basic Adobe Structures	Types of Construction	Variations on Adobe Theme
Adobe Homes: Then and Now	Types of Adobe Bricks	Natural Durability and Efficiency

File   Edit   View   Favorites   Tools   Help

http://www.url.here

Both ancient and modern adobe-style homes have flat roofs that are often held in place by wooden beams called *vigas.* The natural materials of the brick give adobe homes a reddish color that blends with the surrounding landscape of foothills and mountains.

Ever since ancient times, adobe homes have been both durable and energy-efficient. Thick adobe bricks are made to withstand the extreme temperature changes of desert climates. They keep heat in when it is cold outside and keep the inside as

cool as a refreshing cave when the air outside is hot.

Though the cost of adobe homes is high, they are becoming more popular because of their "green" properties and because of their links to the traditional Southwest.

Common Core State Standards

Language 4.d. Verify the preliminary determination of the meaning of a word or phrase (e.g., by checking the inferred meaning in context or in a dictionary). **Also Informational Text 10., Speaking/Listening 1., Language 4.a.**

Let's Learn It!

READING STREET ONLINE
ONLINE STUDENT EDITION
www.ReadingStreet.com

Vocabulary

Unknown Words

Dictionary/Glossary When you are reading and come across a word you do not know, it is important to look it up in a dictionary or a glossary such as the one at the end of this book. In either place you can also find out how to pronounce the word.

Practice It! Find the word *artifacts* on page 243. If you do not know this word, turn to the glossary on page 484. For more information, refer to a dictionary, which may also give other words that are related to *artifact*. Remember that building a better vocabulary means checking the meanings of words you do not know.

Fluency

Appropriate Phrasing

Remember that when you read aloud, you should pay attention to phrasing, or how you group words and when you pause between them. Group words in a way that reflects their meanings and the ideas they express. Use punctuation cues to help with your phrasing.

Practice It! With a partner, read aloud the last page of *Stones, Bones, and Petroglyphs* (page 255). Using punctuation as your guide, practice until you're reading smoothly.

264

Listening and Speaking

Get Ready For High School

When you are part of a group presentation, be sure to take turns and listen to each other.

Panel Discussion

In a panel discussion, a group of experts takes turns sharing ideas and information about one topic.

Practice It! Work with a group to present a panel discussion about the different things that archaeologists do. Each person will research one part of the topic in an encyclopedia or on the Internet. Choose one student to be the moderator. Refer to *Stones, Bones, and Petroglyphs* for information.

Tips

Listening . . .

- Determine each speaker's main and supporting ideas.
- Wait until the end of the discussion to make comments.

Speaking . . .

- Research your topic.
- Make eye contact when you speak and answer questions.

Teamwork . . .

- Identify the different aspects of the topic and divide them up fairly.
- Consider the suggestions and opinions of other group members.

265

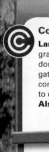
Common Core State Standards

Language 6. Acquire and use accurately grade-appropriate general academic and domain-specific words and phrases; gather vocabulary knowledge when considering a word or phrase important to comprehension or expression.
Also Speaking/Listening 1., 1.c.

Oral Vocabulary

Let's Talk About

Future Homes

- Share opinions about what it might be like to live on another planet.

- Express opinions about the risks someone might take to explore space.

- Describe what a home of the future might look like.

READING STREET ONLINE
CONCEPT TALK VIDEO
www.ReadingStreet.com

You've learned
0 8 0
Amazing Words
so far this year!

Common Core State Standards

Literature 3. Describe how a particular story's or drama's plot unfolds in a series of episodes as well as how the characters respond or change as the plot moves toward a resolution. **Also Literature 1.**

Envision It! | Skill Strategy

Skill

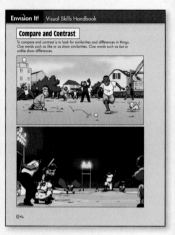

Strategy

Comprehension Skill

🎯 Compare and Contrast

- To compare and contrast means to tell how two or more things are alike and different.

- Clue words such as *like* or *as* show similarities. Words such as *unlike* and *however* show differences.

- Ask questions while you read to compare and contrast, such as "How are these two characters alike and different?" or "What does this situation remind me of?"

- Use a graphic organizer like the one below to compare and contrast Anna and Charlie in "My Siblings."

Character X	Both	Character Y
Trait	Trait	Trait
Trait	Trait	Trait

Comprehension Strategy

🎯 Story Structure

Recognizing story structure will help you understand how the components fit together to form a framework for the story.

My Siblings

My older sibling is Anna, and my younger sibling is Charlie. We all come from the same family, but Anna and Charlie are like night and day.

Skill Based on the phrase "like night and day," do you think that Anna and Charlie are similar? Why or why not?

Anna is 13, and I've never seen a better worker. She is as efficient and orderly as a perfectly programmed robot and can multitask like you wouldn't believe. Anna can clean her room while doing her homework and talking on the phone. Everything she does turns out great. Sometimes I think that Anna is a powerful computer that has somehow acquired a human body.

Strategy The structure of the story uses description to tell about the characters. How else is the story arranged?

Then there's Charlie, a very different species. It's clear to everyone in the family that he's from another planet. Charlie is the most imaginative creature I know. Despite being only 6 years old, he can build fabulous structures out of blocks, invent weird and wonderful games, and make up odd words and names. His mind is like a swarm of bees—constantly moving and swirling. He is a walking tornado, always leaving gigantic, complex messes in his wake. Kind? Yes—but as unique as they come.

Skill Here is one point of contrast: how Anna and Charlie affect the family home. How are they different?

What about me, you ask? Well, I'm nothing like either of them.

Your Turn!

 Need a Review? See the *Envision It! Handbook* for help with comparing and contrasting and story structure.

 Ready to Try It? Use what you've learned about comparing and contrasting as you read *Good-bye to the Moon*.

Envision It! | Words to Know

combustion

dingy

waft

negotiate

traversed

waning

Vocabulary Strategy for
Unfamiliar Words

Context Clues When you come across a word you do not know, use context clues—the words and sentences around the word—to figure out the meaning of the new word.

1. Reread the sentence in which the unfamiliar word appears. Look for a synonym, example, or other clue around the word that gives a clue to the word's meaning.

2. If you need more help, read the sentences around the sentence with the unknown word.

3. Stop and ask yourself, "What is this selection about?" The content itself may help you clarify the word's meaning.

4. Add up the clues you have found and predict the word's meaning. See if your meaning makes sense in the sentence.

Read "Lunar Love Affair." Look for context clues to determine meanings of unfamiliar words.

Words to Write Reread "Lunar Love Affair." Imagine you are traveling to the moon. Write a journal entry about your trip. Use words from the Words to Know list as you write.

Lunar Love Affair

The love affair of humans for all things lunar reaches far back into history. For many thousands of years, humans have watched the moon in the night sky. They saw it gradually waxing, or growing round, and then waning, or growing ever smaller, until only a sliver remained. It excited wonder and curiosity. No matter how dingy or ugly or hard life on Earth might be, the moon always glowed with a soft, pure light in the darkness. The perfume of blossoms might waft in the breeze, gently blowing faces turned up to gaze at the mysterious moon.

Then, not so long ago, people invented internal-combustion engines. By burning fuel in an enclosed space, they harnessed great power to drive vehicles, then airplanes, then jets. Before long, humans looked at the moon with a new question: Why not go there ourselves?

By 1969, astronauts had traversed outer space to go to the moon! Cameras showed us men in spacesuits taking great leaps across the rocky surface of the moon. It seemed the beginning of a new age. However, it seems that people have more plans than money for space travel. NASA, the U.S. agency responsible for space exploration, has to negotiate carefully for funding. Rather than return to the moon, humans have explored farther into space.

Your Turn!

▮▮ Need a Review? For help using context clues to determine the meanings of unfamiliar words, see *Words!*

▷ Ready to Try It? Read *Good-bye to the Moon* on pp. 272–285.

GOOD-BYE
to the
MOON

by Monica Hughes
illustrated by Mick Coulas

Genre

Science fiction is fantasy based on science that takes the reader into an imaginary time and environment, often the future. As you read, look for the clues that indicate this story is science fiction.

Question of the Week

How can a focus on the future help us imagine new possibilities?

I sat in the darkened room of the space station and looked out at Earth. It was strangely familiar to me. The photograph of the blue globe with its whip-cream swirls of cloud hung in the Control Center of Lunar Lab 21. There was a small copy of the same famous picture in our own living unit. To my mother and father, it had meant home.

What was this Earth to me? It was a shining silver disk, waxing from crescent to full, and waning back again to crescent, that traversed the skies of our long lunar nights. It was the song my mother sang to me, the first child born on Moon:

Earth-shine, Earth-bright,
Grant the wish I wish tonight.

But that was long, long ago. Mother had been dead for five years, and I, Kepler Masterman, son of Moon Governor, was

actually going to Earth myself. Already I was over the first hurdle, the wearisome three-day journey on the old beat-up Moon ferry to the space station.

It was great to stretch my legs again and enjoy the low-grav of the station's slow spin after the weight of the moon-rocket's acceleration. I looked down at Earth, so close I felt I could reach out and touch it. What was down there? . . . The Sphinx . . . the Taj Mahal . . . skyscrapers. All the fantastic things I'd read about. I looked at my watch. Fifteen minutes to wait.

Restlessly I left the viewing room and glided down the long passageway to the hub of the space station. In the VIP lounge I could see Father, surrounded by reporters. Time for one last good-bye to Moon.

Down the passage to the right here. The view room was empty, and I slid into a couch in the center front row. The room was dark, and the window was set in an angle that fooled the eye. It was as if nothing separated me from the black infinity of space and from Moon. It was so small now, my Moon, no bigger than the silver identidisk on the chain around my neck.

My eyes picked out the familiar features. The terminator, that razor-edge between night and day, arced down through the Ocean of Storms. The oblique sunlight etched clearly in black shadow the huge circle of Copernicus, and, to its left, right on the edge of the terminator, I could see Kepler, the crater in which Lunar Lab was built. Home! Down there, a new Moon-day was just starting. The viewing ports of the labs and the living units would automatically darken as the brilliant rays of the sun stabbed down white-hard against the rocks of the crater. The heat-exchange units would slowly adjust from two weeks of warming up the buildings to cooling them, as for the next fifteen days the sun would shine down on Lunar Lab 21.

Down there at home the kids would be getting ready for the party. There'd always been a party at sunrise, ever since I could remember, and I was the oldest kid on Moon. The adults used to tease us sometimes . . . "Imagine having a party every *day!*" But it was only twelve or thirteen times a year, and there was something special about the sunlight creeping so slowly across the surface of Moon, striking the peaks of the Apennines, sending shadows chasing across the Sinus

Aestuum, each Earth-day a little closer, until finally the two long weeks of night were over, and we were bathed in sunlight again. The astronomers hated daytime, except for the solar experts. They couldn't see the stars and had to stay in their rooms catching up on their paperwork. But everyone else loved it, especially the kids.

I sighed and thought of Ann. Wonder who'd be taking her to the party? We'd stood at the air lock to say goodbye. Ann had been crying, and her eyes were red. But she was as beautiful as ever. There had been an awful lump in my throat as I blurted out the words.

"I'll be seeing you, Ann."

"Oh, Kepler, take care of yourself."

"Sure. You, too, Ann. I'll write, I promise."

It was a terrible farewell. I'd worked out ahead of time exactly what I was going to say. It was terrific. It'd have bowled her over. But standing there by the air lock, I'd forgotten it all.

I squirmed at the memory and hoped that Ann wouldn't remember and laugh. Well, at least I could write. I knew I couldn't expect letters from Ann. Letter rates to Earth were crippling—so was the cost of everything that had to make the 240,000-mile haul. But I could write to

Ann. That was one advantage of having the Lunar Governor as Father. I could slip my letters into the diplomatic bag, and they would go rocketing to Moon with no questions asked. But six months away from home . . . I was going to miss her. *That* was the disadvantage of having a Governor for Father.

The door swung open behind me, letting in a shaft of light and a babble of excited voices. There was a waft of exotic perfume. Real French perfume! The ferry from Earth must have arrived. These would be passengers on Moon Safari. This was a trip only for the very, very, wealthy. In fact, the tourist complex on the Sea of Serenity helped pay for some of the research expenses that the Moon administration was unable to wring from the reluctant cashbox of Earth.

I slipped out of the suddenly crowded room and down the passage to the central concourse. Father was standing there. There were last minute good-byes.

"Good luck, George."

"We're counting on you, Governor!"

"See you in six months, at the latest."

I walked beside him, trying to copy his casual stroll. I wasn't about to look like some country Rube, even if it was my first Earth trip. But my first sight of the Earth-ferry threw me, and my jaw

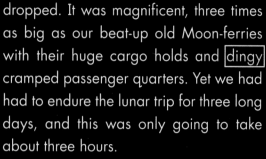

dropped. It was magnificent, three times as big as our beat-up old Moon-ferries with their huge cargo holds and dingy cramped passenger quarters. Yet we had had to endure the lunar trip for three long days, and this was only going to take about three hours.

"Is everything on Earth this fancy?" I whispered to Father, as I snuggled down into the deep plush of my contour seat and buckled my harness around me.

"Pretty much so—in the parts of the world you'll be seeing, anyway. It's a far cry from home, isn't it?"

Was it ever! I tried to imagine our living unit with a deep blue pile carpet and walls of cream

stippled with gold, instead of the standard-issue green vinyl floor and plastic-coated steel walls. When I was a kid, I was always roaming into the wrong unit. They were all identical, and there just wasn't the money to ferry up from Earth the sort of things that would have made them look homey. . . .

. . . The ferry shivered delicately and then moved slowly out of its holding dock. I could feel my body pressing gently against the padded couch as the ferry surrendered itself to Earth-grav. It was amazingly quiet and comfortable. I'd hardly slept on the trip down from Moon, and now, in spite of myself, I found my eyes shutting.

It seemed only a few minutes before Father's voice woke me. "You're a pretty blasé traveler, Kepler! But you mustn't miss this sight. We're just turning into Earth orbit. Look!"

I craned my neck eagerly and looked through the port. I recognized the narrow spindle of Central America, and then the steely shimmer of the Atlantic lay beneath us. It went on and on.

"The planet's all water!" I gasped.

"Seven-tenths of it is," Father agreed.

"But . . . but. Oh, wow!" It was feeble, but what words could I have for it? A world that was seven-tenths *water!* Why, on Moon, water was harder to get than oxygen, much harder. Breathing was free. You could breathe as deeply and as often as you wished. Now that the hydroponic gardens were going, we didn't have to pay for our oxygen any more. But water was something else.

Every ounce of it was worth its weight in Moon minerals. Dirt was removed by electrostatic filters in the labs and living units. Washing was a luxury and drinking a special delight.

There was no free water on the Moon. Every ounce we used was extracted in the refinement of the ores we sent down to Earth. And the mining companies charged us for it—every drop! I had grown up thinking water was the most precious stuff in the Universe. Now, with my own eyes I could see that Earth was covered with the stuff—slopping over with it.

We orbited across North Africa and Arabia. From my port I could see the island-spangled blueness of the Indian Ocean. Then the Pacific. I felt suddenly tired and a little sick. What sort of a place was this Earth, and what were its people like? Half a world made of water, and yet they had charged us for every single cup. I shut my eyes and turned away from the port.

"You feeling groggy?" Father's voice was sympathetic. "They're starting their braking orbit, and I guess you'll really notice the weight difference. Don't worry. It'll get worse before it gets better. But it will get better. Just hang on!"

To the Earth passengers from the space station, I suppose the discomforts were minimal. Their apparent weight increased to double and momentarily three times their normal weight. I had not realized until this moment what my birthright of one-sixth Earth weight was going to mean when I tried to return "home." It was like a barrier separating me from all these other people. Already I weighed six times my normal weight. As the braking continued, it increased to twelve times, to. . . . The weight on my chest . . . I couldn't breathe. I felt as if my brain was going to burst.

When I came back to my senses, the enormous pressure had lifted. I felt heavy and very tired. I lifted my head and looked blurrily around. We had landed! There was a bustle of unstrapping harnesses, collecting belongings. I struggled with my own safety straps, and Father leaned over to help me. The expression on his face told me I didn't look good.

"Lie still, Kepler. You've had a nosebleed. I'll get a stewardess to help."

"I'm okay, Father." My tongue felt thick, and the words were blurry. The stewardess hurried over. She bent down to wash my face.

"I can do it," I muttered thickly, trying to take the cloth away from her.

"You just lie still, sonny. I'm just going to get you an ice pack. You really took the 'Gs' badly. You'll have two beautiful shiners in the morning."

Sonny! How old did she think I was, anyway? Two black eyes . . . oh, brother! That was really starting out on the right foot. Look out, Earth. Here comes Kepler Masterman—on a banana skin!

She glided back with the ice pack. How could she move so lightly on the heavy planet, I wondered. She looked no heavier than a grain of moondust.

She spoke to my father. "Governor, the press and TV are waiting for you. Are you ready to leave the ferry yet?"

"Oh, sure. I'll come right away." He swung himself up from his couch and stretched. He was a big man, my father, and muscular. I wondered if I'd ever catch up. I was at the weedy stage, and in spite of secret body-building in my own room, I wasn't making much headway.

"Strange feeling going up to 170 pounds again. Don't think I like it much. Kepler, lie still and take your time. I'm sure this young lady will look after you."

I watched his broad back down the aisle and through the hatch, and then I took off the ice pack and swung my legs down to the floor. My head throbbed a bit, but it wasn't too bad. Standing was tougher, and walking was a nightmare of

281

wading through glue. I gritted my teeth and practiced, one foot and then the other, up and down the aisle, holding on to the seat backs for support.

Six months on this planet. How was I ever going to make out? I saw the stewardess watching me from the galley door. I wished she'd go away, but when she saw I'd seen her, she came down the aisle toward me.

"I could get you a wheelchair," she volunteered. "This low-grav syndrome can be a problem. It's happened before, you know, though I guess you're the first person who's never experienced Earth-weight in his life."

"I'm going to be fine, thanks. It just takes a little practice, that's all."

"Of course. Perhaps you'd like to clean up before you leave?" I took her hint and plodded back down the aisle to the washroom. Good grief, I was a disaster area! I took off my jacket—how crudely cut it looked in comparison

with the Earth fashions I'd seen on the ferry, and what rough material. Then I washed the rest of the blood off my face and combed my hair, what there was of it. It looked like a convict cut by Earth standards, but it would grow. There were red smudges under my eyes, but the shiners the stewardess had promised hadn't shown up yet.

I put on my jacket and plodded down to the exit hatch. I hesitated, my hand on the ramp rail, looking at the crowd of exotically dressed reporters, cameramen, and casual bystanders milling around my father. It really was a new world down there at the end of the ramp.

"Good luck," the stewardess said softly. She wasn't a bad sort, really, only a bit old to understand. I managed a smile, swallowed, and walked down the ramp to join my father. I was drowned in a storm of voices. How loudly these Earth people talked, as if they were constantly trying to shout each other down.

"Governor, would you say the differences between Earth and Moon people are irreconcilable?"

"I certainly would not. On the contrary, I am convinced that with a clearer understanding of our problems, the differences between us will be settled amicably."

"What do you intend to do if the U.N. vote goes against you?"

"I'm not even considering that possibility at the moment."

"Governor, how long do you intend to spend on Earth this trip?"

"I anticipate that it may take as long as six months to settle our differences, though of course we could strike lucky. . . ."

"One last question, Governor. Now you are back on Earth again, will you tell our listeners—which is really home to you, Earth or Moon?"

"That's a difficult question to answer. All my cultural ties are with Earth. But, like all immigrants who flocked to the New World and shaped it into a nation, I guess I must say that it is in this Newer World, Moon, that my present and future lie. My son was born there. My wife was buried there. My work is there. Yes, gentlemen, it is good to be back on Earth. But Moon is home!"

He saw me standing jammed among the reporters and casually gave me his arm. We walked together across the sun-splashed concrete of the landing pad. The sun was gently warm on my body and our shadows ran out ahead of us, soft, muzzy-edged. I looked up. The sky was a delicate blue with fluffy cumulus clouds, just like the ones in my old video tapes. They sailed gracefully across the sky, unbelievably beautiful. A sudden white shape plunged and screeched. I jumped and clutched Father's arm.

"What was that? . . . a bird?"

"Yes, Kepler. A seagull."

I walked along, breathing real air, not the canned stuff. It was strange being outdoors without a spacesuit, scary but exciting. It looked as if Earth was going to be fun. If only my legs didn't ache so. . . .

"Is it far to the magnetrain, Father?"

"Hang on, son. It's right ahead."

Once aboard with my feet up, I didn't feel so much of a country cousin. The magnetrain had been developed on Moon, where the absence of any atmosphere had precluded the use of conventional jet, hovercraft, or internal-combustion engines. Up there, we had perfected the magnetic lift system of propulsion, and our trains networked the lunar surface with silent pollution-free speeds of 500 miles an hour.

The idea had been enthusiastically adopted by an ecology-conscious Earth, and one of the items on my father's agenda was to negotiate an acknowledgment in terms of royalties of the Lunar discovery.

I lay back and thought of the pyramids and the Taj Mahal, the temples of Angkor Wat, and the mysterious jungle buildings of the Incas. Would six months be time enough to see it all?

Common Core State Standards
Literature 1. Cite textual evidence to support analysis of what the text says explicitly as well as inferences drawn from the text. **Also Literature 2., Writing 9.**

Envision It! Retell

Think Critically

1. Kepler had a new experience when he felt the impact of Earth's gravity on his weight. When have you had a totally new experience that surprised you? **Text to Self**

2. The story is fiction (make-believe) plus science (natural world and technology). Cite examples to show how the author combines the two elements of fiction and science. **Think Like an Author**

3. Kepler mentions many similarities and differences between life on the Moon and life on Earth. Name at least two similarities and two differences he mentions. Then choose which difference you would have the most trouble adjusting to. Explain why.
   Compare and Contrast

4. Briefly summarize the main story problem, key events, climax, and resolution. **Story Structure**

5. **Look Back and Write** What does "the reluctant cashbox of Earth" (p. 276) tell you about the relations between Earth and the Moon in this futuristic story? Write the answer and explain why this phrase is important to the story. Provide evidence to support your answer.
   Key Ideas and Details • Text Evidence

Monica Hughes

Monica Hughes, born in Liverpool, England, lived her first five years in Cairo, Egypt. She was in the Women's Royal Naval Service during World War II and moved to Canada in 1952, when she was 27. Later she moved with her husband and four children to Edmonton, Alberta, where she became an award-winning author of science fiction and fantasy stories for young people. Ms. Hughes believed that ideas are everywhere, and she wrote them down quickly. Because she was interested in "the tension between scientific progress and the health of the environment," she put newspaper clippings about scientific facts and human-interest stories into her files of ideas. Ms. Hughes died in 2003.

Other books by Monica Hughes: *Invitation to the Game* and *A Handful of Seeds*

Use the Reading Log in the *Reader's and Writer's Notebook* to record your independent reading.

Common Core State Standards

Writing 3. Write narratives to develop real or imagined experiences or events using effective technique, relevant descriptive details, and well-structured event sequences. **Also Writing 3.b., Language 1.**

Let's Write It!

Key Features of a Fantasy

- may have made-up events, characters, or settings

- some elements of the story may be realistic

- setting is often in the future or another world

READING STREET ONLINE
GRAMMAR JAMMER
www.ReadingStreet.com

Fantasy

A **fantasy** tells an imaginary story that could not be true because of its characters, plot, or setting. Fantasy stories are often set in environments unlike our own. The student model on the next page is an example of a fantasy.

Writing Prompt Think about a place where people might live in the future. Now write a fantasy about that place and describe life there.

Writer's Checklist

Remember, you should . . .

✓ write about people, places, or events that could not really exist.

✓ maintain some realistic elements, such as typical dialogue.

✓ include vivid descriptions of characters and settings.

A Transport to Earth's Core

"Hurry!" calls my mom. "We'll be late. The last transport to Earth's core is leaving in fifteen minutes. I don't want to miss it!"

I slip into the interior pod of the transport vehicle. The sun rises and sets, rises and sets again, fiery in its orange brilliance. It takes almost twelve minutes before we leave, during which we see three sunrises and sunsets.

Our vehicle roars into the tunnel, and the heat shields clamp down. I look through the viewing window, knowing that if we don't arrive at the shuttle deck on time, we have to turn back. Then we'd have to wait three months for the next trip.

Through the window, I see bubbling pools of liquid fire. I know that this kind of trip hadn't been possible before heat shields and interior pods were invented.

We zap onto the shuttle deck just an instant before it closes for the season. What a trip!

Genre
A **fantasy** includes unreal events that are still reasonable within the framework of the story.

Writing Trait Word Choice
Vivid verbs and adjectives give color to the writer's ideas.

Subject-verb agreement is used correctly.

Conventions

Subject-Verb Agreement

Remember A verb must agree with its subject in number. A singular subject needs a singular verb (the planet rotates), and a plural subject needs a plural verb (the planets rotate). Recall that nouns and pronouns can be plural or singular. Singular pronouns are I, you, she, he, and it. Plural pronouns are you, we, and they.

Common Core State Standards
Literature 10. By the end of the year, read and comprehend literature, including stories, dramas, and poems, in the grades 6–8 text complexity band proficiently, with scaffolding as needed at the high end of the range.

Science in Reading

Genre
Science Fiction

- Science fiction is writing based on science. It often tells about life in the future.

- Science fiction tells stories about events that couldn't happen or that haven't happened—yet.

- Science fiction stories are related to technology rather than to magic.

- Read "Zoo" and look for the events in the story that identify it as science fiction.

Zoo

by Edward D. Hoch

The children were always good during the month of August, especially when it began to get near the twenty-third. It was on this day that the great spaceship carrying Professor Hugo's Interplanetary Zoo settled down for its annual six-hour visit to the Chicago area.

Before daybreak the crowds would form long lines of children and adults both, each one clutching his or her dollar and waiting with wonderment to see what race of strange creatures the Professor had brought this year.

In the past they had sometimes been treated to three-legged creatures from Venus, or tall, thin men from Mars, or even snake-like horrors from somewhere more distant. This year, as the great round ship settled slowly to Earth in the huge tri-city parking area just outside of Chicago, they watched with awe as the sides slowly slid up to reveal the familiar barred cages. In them were some wild breed of nightmare— small, horse-like animals that moved with quick, jerking motions and constantly chattered in a high-pitched tongue. The citizens of Earth clustered around as Professor Hugo's crew quickly collected the waiting dollars, and soon the good Professor himself made an appearance, wearing his many-colored rainbow cape and top hat.

"Peoples of Earth," he called into his microphone. The crowd's noise died down and he continued.

PROFESSOR HUGO

Let's **Think** About...

Which details in the illustration of Professor Hugo are realistic? Which details are fantasy?
Science Fiction

Let's **Think** About...

Do you think "Zoo" will be a story that could never happen, or one that hasn't yet happened?
Science Fiction

291

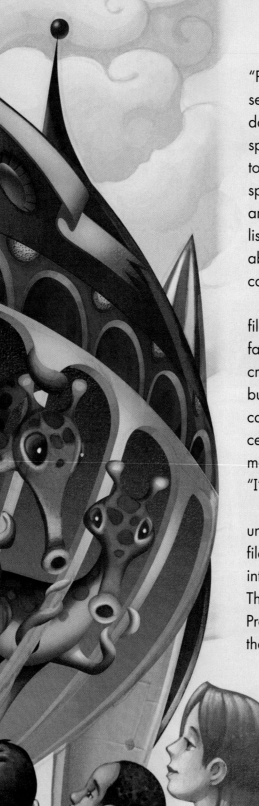

Let's **Think** About...

What details on this page make the story seem more realistic?

Science Fiction

"Peoples of Earth, this year you see a real treat for your single dollar—the little-known horse-spider people of Kaan—brought to you across a million miles of space at great expense. Gather around, see them, study them, listen to them, tell your friends about them. But hurry! My ship can remain here only six hours!"

And the crowds slowly filed by, at once horrified and fascinated by these strange creatures that looked like horses but ran up the walls of their cages like spiders. "This is certainly worth a dollar," one man remarked, hurrying away. "I'm going home to get the wife."

All day long it went like that, until ten thousand people had filed by the barred cages set into the side of the spaceship. Then, as the six-hour limit ran out, Professor Hugo once more took the microphone in hand.

"We must go now, but we will return next year on this date. And if you enjoyed our zoo this year, telephone your friends in other cities about it. We will land in New York tomorrow, and next week on to London, Paris, Rome, Hong Kong, and Tokyo. Then on to other worlds!"

He waved farewell to them, and as the ship rose from the ground, the Earth peoples agreed that this had been the very best Zoo yet. . . .

Some two months and three planets later, the ship of Professor Hugo settled at last onto the familiar jagged rocks of Kaan, and the odd horse-spider creatures filed quickly out of their cages. Professor Hugo was there to say a few parting words, and then they scurried away in a hundred different directions, seeking their homes among the rocks.

In one house, the she-creature was happy to see the return of her mate and offspring. She babbled a greeting in the strange tongue and hurried to embrace them. "It was a long time you were gone. Was it good?"

And the he-creature nodded. "The little one enjoyed it especially. We visited eight worlds and saw many things."

The little one ran up the wall of the cave. "On the place called Earth it was the best. The creatures there wear garments over their skins, and they walk on two legs."

"But isn't it dangerous?" asked the she-creature.

"No," her mate answered. "There are bars to protect us from them. We remain right in the ship. Next time you must come with us. It is well worth the nineteen commocs it costs."

And the little one nodded. "It was the very best Zoo ever. . . ."

Let's Think About...

Reading Across Texts

In both *Good-bye to the Moon* and "Zoo," a father travels with his child. Tell how each trip was different for the characters in the stories.

Writing Across Texts Which parent and child do you think enjoyed themselves more? Write a paragraph telling why.

Common Core State Standards
Language 4.a. Use context (e.g., the overall meaning of a sentence or paragraph; a word's position or function in a sentence) as a clue to the meaning of a word or phrase. **Also Literature 10., Speaking/Listening 6.**

Let's Learn It!

Vocabulary

Unfamiliar Words

Context Clues Remember that surrounding words and phrases can help you identify the meaning of a word. If these context clues do not define the word, predict a meaning for it. Then try out the meaning in the sentence.

Practice It! From the classroom or media center, select a magazine article you have not read. Find two or three words that are not familiar to you. Use context clues as you work to figure out the meaning of each word.

Fluency

Expression

When you read aloud, think about the way people usually speak words and phrases in conversation. Use different tones of voice to show emotion such as suspense, reflection, or excitement in a story. If you are reading dialogue, use a different tone of voice for each character.

Practice It! With a partner, practice reading aloud the beginning of *Good-bye to the Moon*, from page 274 to the first four lines of page 275. Read with emphasis and rhythmic feeling, and offer each other feedback.

Listening and Speaking

Get Ready For High School

When you are part of a dramatization, listen for your cues and speak clearly and loudly enough.

Dramatization

A dramatization is a version of a story that is written to be performed for an audience. Dramatizations use dialogue between characters to show what happens in the story. A dramatization should be based on a good story with interesting characters.

Practice It! Work with a group to reenact a scene from *Good-bye to the Moon*. Assign roles and rehearse your dramatization before you present it to the class.

Tips

Listening . . .

- Listen attentively to each speaker.
- Pay attention to facial expressions to help understand the speaker.

Speaking . . .

- Make eye contact with the audience.
- Speak loudly and enunciate clearly.

Teamwork . . .

- Participate in discussions about the dramatization by asking for and considering suggestions from others in your group.
- Listen attentively so that you speak at the right time.

Common Core State Standards

Language 6. Acquire and use accurately grade-appropriate general academic and domain-specific words and phrases; gather vocabulary knowledge when considering a word or phrase important to comprehension or expression.
Also Speaking/Listening 1., 1.c.

Oral Vocabulary

Let's Talk About

Ancient Egypt

- Share what you know about Egypt.

- Ask questions about ancient Egypt.

- Express opinions about why ancient Egypt is important to us.

READING STREET ONLINE
CONCEPT TALK VIDEO
www.ReadingStreet.com

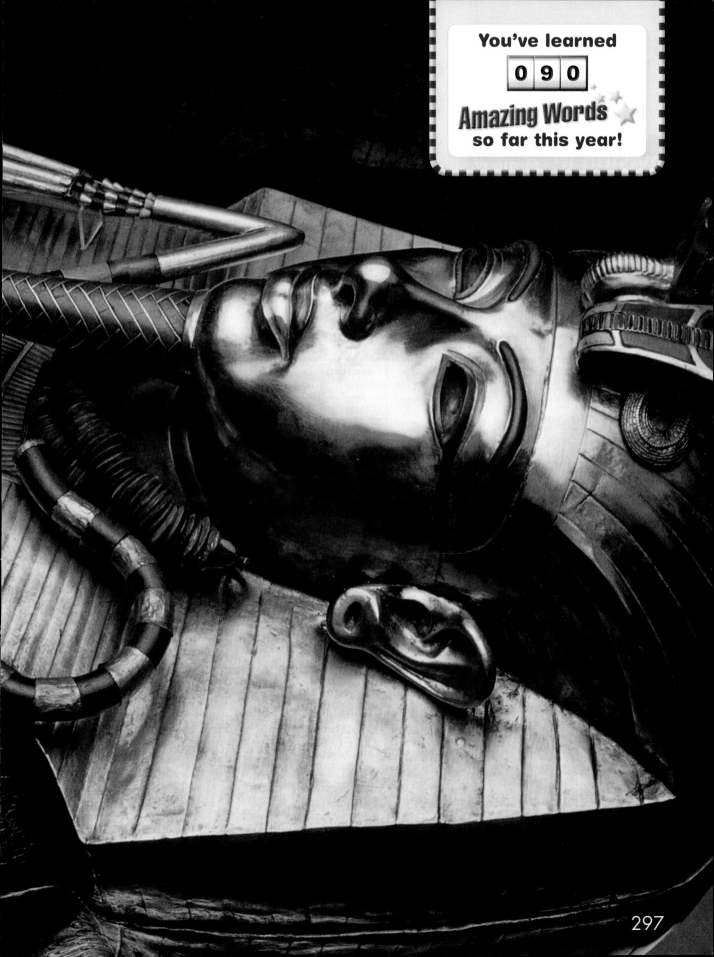

Common Core State Standards
Informational Text 1. Cite textual evidence to support analysis of what the text says explicitly as well as inferences drawn from the text. **Also Informational Text 2.**

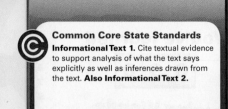

Envision It! | Skill Strategy

Skill

Strategy

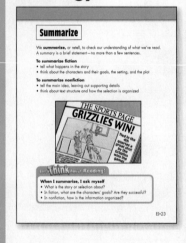

Comprehension Skill

🎯 Graphic Sources

- Graphic sources such as maps, charts, diagrams, pictures, and schedules give information visually.

- Graphic sources are often used to summarize complex information.

- Use a graphic source like the two-column chart below with the map on page 299 to make better sense of the information you will read in "The Land of Egypt."

Rainfall in Egypt

Location	Rainfall as Inches per Year
Alexandria	7
Northern Sinai	5
Cairo	1
Aswan	1/10

Comprehension Strategy

🎯 Summarize

Summarizing helps you determine which information in an article is the most important. Summaries state only the important ideas and do not include minor details. A summary also can be in the form of a chart, graph, time line, or some other graphic aid, because the key information is put into the graphic with as few words as possible.

The Land of Egypt

The Nile The Nile River is the most important body of water in Egypt. Aside from being the main source of fresh water, this mighty river divides Egypt into two sections, the Western and Eastern Deserts. A third area, the Sinai, is also a desert.

Mountains Egypt is not a completely flat country. There are mountains along the coast of the Red Sea. The highest of these rises 7,175 feet. The Sinai holds Egypt's highest mountain, Mount Catherine, which has an elevation of 8,668 feet.

Climate Egypt is a very sunny place. It averages 12 hours of sunshine per day in the summer and about 10 hours in the winter. Winters are usually cool, with temperatures around 65°F. In summer, the highs range from 91°F in Cairo to 106°F in Aswan. Long winter cold spells and summer heat waves are not uncommon.

Precipitation On average, Egypt receives very little rain. Most of the rain comes during the winter months. However, the amount varies from place to place. The farther south you go in Egypt, the less it rains.

Strategy What is the most important information you read in this paragraph? Summarize this first paragraph in one sentence.

Skill How does the map below help you better understand the information in this paragraph?

Skill How does the "Rainfall in Egypt" graphic on page 298 help you better understand the information presented in this article?

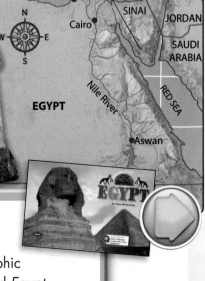

MEDITERRANEAN SEA
ISRAEL
Mount Catherine
Alexandria
N
W — E
S
SINAI
JORDAN
Cairo
SAUDI ARABIA
EGYPT
Nile River
RED SEA
Aswan

Your Turn!

❚❚ Need a Review? See the *Envision It! Handbook* for help with graphic sources and summarizing.

▶ Ready to Try It? Use what you've learned about graphic sources as you read *Egypt*.

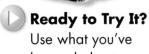

Envision It! | Words to Know

artifacts

decrees

receded

abundant

eternity

immortal

reigned

READING STREET ONLINE
VOCABULARY ACTIVITIES
www.ReadingStreet.com

Vocabulary Strategy for
Greek and Latin Roots

Word Structure Many words in English are derived from Greek and Latin roots. If you recognize and know the meaning of a root in a word, you can probably figure out the word's meaning. For example, *-mort-* is a Latin root meaning "death" (A *mortal* wound is a deadly one.), and *-reg-* or *-rex-* means "king." (*Tyrannosaurus rex* was king of the dinosaurs.)

Choose one of the Words to Know that is unfamiliar to you and follow these steps.

1. Look at the unfamiliar word. Examine the word to see if you recognize a Latin or Greek root in it.

2. Ask yourself how the meaning of the Latin or Greek root influences the meaning of the word.

3. Review the context in which the word is used. Does this meaning make sense?

4. If not, read on for other clues.

As you read "The Pharaohs of Egypt," look for Greek or Latin roots to help you determine the meanings of words. If you still can't find the meaning, use the glossary or a dictionary.

Words to Write Reread "The Pharaohs of Egypt." Study the pictures on these two pages and choose one to write about. Use as many words from the Words to Know list as you can to describe the meaning of your picture.

The Pharaohs of Egypt

It has been more than 2,300 years since the last of the pharaohs reigned in Egypt, but we are still fascinated by these powerful rulers. They were believed to be gods. A pharaoh's power was absolute. The decrees of the ruler had to be obeyed. His every wish would be carried out.

Artifacts from the tombs of the pharaohs tell us that they had fabulous wealth. Pharaohs were buried along with objects of solid gold inlaid with beautiful jewels. A royal tomb had many rooms in which abundant containers, furniture, and personal belongings were placed. Egyptians believed that the person who died would keep his earthly body in the next life, so he would need these belongings. In other words, Egyptians believed that a person could be immortal. He or she could enjoy food and clothing for all eternity.

We can only imagine what life was like for Egyptians so long ago. We know that a few were rich and many were poor. However, those favored few lived in regal splendor.

That ancient age of Egypt has receded like the waters of the Nile River. Each year, the Nile's waters would rise and flood its banks. When the floods ended and the water went down, rich soil was left behind. Like the Nile's waters, the kings of Egypt have left a rich history.

Your Turn!

Need a Review? For help with word structure and Latin and Greek roots, see *Words!*

Ready to Try It? Read *Egypt* on pp. 302–315.

EGYPT

by Ann Heinrichs

Question of the Week

Why is it important to understand ancient civilizations?

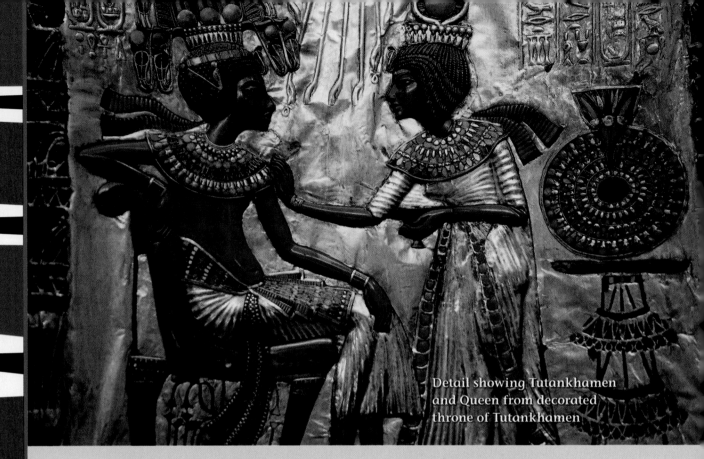

Detail showing Tutankhamen
and Queen from decorated
throne of Tutankhamen

Land of the Pharaohs

People were farming along the Nile as early as 7000 B.C. Eventually, they settled into two kingdoms—Upper Egypt in the south, and Lower Egypt in the northern Delta. In about 3100 B.C., Menes, a king of Upper Egypt, united the two kingdoms. Menes was honored as Egypt's first pharaoh, or king. (The word *pharaoh* comes from the words *per 'aa*, meaning "big house.")

Pharaohs liked to keep their power in the family. Ancient Egypt was governed by one dynasty, or ruling family, after another. Thirty-one dynasties of pharaohs reigned in Egypt between 3100 B.C. and 332 B.C.

Levels of Society

The pharaoh and his family were at the top rung of Egyptian society. They lived in great luxury. Alabaster lamps, golden beds and chairs, and exotic woods inlaid with ivory decorated their homes. Servants took care of their every need. Musicians and dancers amused guests at their lavish banquets. Other members of the upper class were priests, nobles, doctors, and high-ranking army officers.

Ancient Egyptian society greatly valued scribes. This painted limestone sculpture is on display at the Louvre Museum in Paris, France.

Artisans, merchants, and engineers made up the middle class. Scribes, or professional writers, held a special place of honor. Every family hoped to have a son who would become a scribe. The scribes wrote letters and government documents and recorded the pharaoh's decrees.

The common people were farmers, laborers, and soldiers. Farming took only part of the year, so many farmers spent several months working on the pharaoh's construction projects.

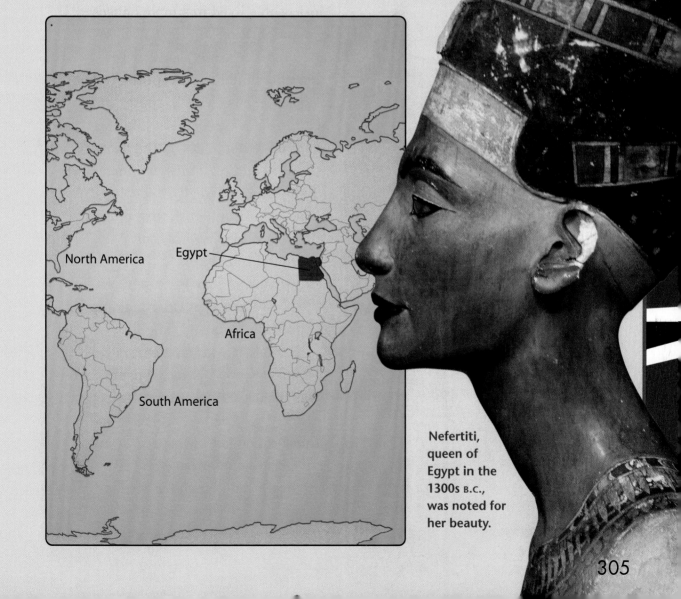

North America

Egypt

Africa

South America

Nefertiti, queen of Egypt in the 1300s B.C., was noted for her beauty.

Love and Marriage

In ancient Egypt, love was an important part of marriage. Egyptians wrote beautiful love poems and songs. Druggists mixed love potions to help people charm their beloved. Pharaohs could keep several wives, but one wife was customary for everyone else.

Women in ancient Egypt had more rights than women in many cultures have today. They could own property, buy and sell goods, and inherit wealth. Wives could even sue for divorce if they had a good reason.

Statuette of Akhenaten and Nefertiti

Homes, Adornments, and Games

Most people lived in simple houses made of mud bricks. Very few of these houses remain today. Centuries of rain and wind have swept the soft materials away. In these simple homes, people sat and slept on woven mats on the floor. Candles and oil lamps provided light at night. Wealthy people had beautiful homes with dozens of rooms. Some were built around courtyards with gardens and pools.

Women kept their makeup in tiny bowls and jars. Cosmetics were made from minerals and plants. Gypsum was mixed with soot to make a sparkly eye shadow. A black substance called kohl was used as an eyeliner. Other substances made red coloring for lips and blush for cheeks.

Women also painted their fingernails and wore hair ornaments. Upper-class women wore earrings, bracelets, armbands, and necklaces of gold and precious stones.

Both men and women wore lightweight linen skirts or robes. Lower-class people went barefoot, while the upper classes wore leather sandals. Shoulder-length head coverings protected workers from the heat of the sun. Upper-class men and women wore wigs. On festive evenings, women sometimes wore a cone of perfumed animal fat on their heads. As the night wore on, the fat melted, drenching them with sweet-smelling oil.

Ancient paintings and artifacts show how much the Egyptians loved games. Children played leapfrog and tug-of-war. Girls played catch with a ball, sometimes while riding piggyback. Wooden toys included monkeys on horseback and animals on wheels. Grown-ups played a game called *senet* by moving pieces on a checkered board. They played "snake" on a round board shaped like a coiled snake.

Ancient Cuisine

Egyptians ate using the first three fingers of the right hand. A typical meal might include vegetables such as broad beans, lentils, peas, cucumbers, or cabbage. People also enjoyed onions, garlic, turnips, and lettuce. Their fruit trees yielded figs, dates, and pomegranates. Other favorite fruits were melons and grapes.

Hunters went into the desert for wild game such as antelope and gazelle. In marshy areas, they shot ducks and geese with bows and arrows. Quail, pigeon, and beef were grilled or roasted. Fish from the Nile were salted or hung out to dry. Food was sweetened with honey collected from beehives.

Bread was a basic, everyday food. Pharaohs and nobles had their own bakeries. In most homes, women ground wheat and barley into flour and baked the loaves in clay pots or beehive-shaped clay ovens.

A wall relief that depicts men bearing poultry and joints of meats

The Cycle of Floods

Ancient Egyptians divided the year into three seasons of four months each. The new year began with the flooding of the Nile in July. This was the season of *akhet*. In November, as the waters receded, *peret*—the plowing and planting season—began. The dry season, *shemu*, lasted from March to July. Then crops were harvested and stored before the rains came again.

The floodwaters left a deposit of silt that fertilized the fields and produced abundant crops. Mud along the riverbank was made into pots, jars, tiles, and other ceramics. People measured the rise and fall of the Nile's water level with a *nilometer*—a series of marks on riverside rocks or cliffs.

Farmers produced more than enough food for Egypt's people. The pharaohs' storehouses brimmed over with food they collected as taxes. Ancient Egypt has been called the "granary [grainhouse] to the world." Grain and other crops were traded with neighboring peoples in Africa and Asia.

Nebamun hunting in marshes.

Animal Life

Ancient Egypt swarmed with animals that no longer live there. Hippopotamuses bobbed in the Nile and lounged along the shore. Lions wandered in from the desert for water. Baboons and wildcats screeched in the thickets, and herds of gazelles trotted by. Golden jackals scoured the valleys for animal and human remains. Great flocks of rose-colored flamingos swooped in to nest along the Nile, and red-breasted geese flew in to winter in the marshes.

As the climate grew hotter and dryer, human settlements spread, and these animals went away. We know they once lived there because Egyptians left paintings of them. Ancient animals that still live in Egypt

Ancient Egyptian lion fresco

include cobras, crocodiles, vultures, falcons, quails, and cows. Many animals were drawn in hieroglyphic symbols, and some were honored as gods.

Hieroglyphs

Egyptians were writing with picture symbols called hieroglyphs as early as 3000 B.C. Some hieroglyphs represented an object. For example, wavy lines stood for water, and a bird was—a bird. But a picture could also stand for an idea. Walking feet meant movement or the passage of time.

Some hieroglyphic symbols were homophones— words that sound alike but have different meanings. For example, the pharaoh Narmer's name was written as *n'r* (fish) plus *mr* (chisel). (Vowel sounds were often left out.) Some symbols stood for sounds. Others showed whether a word was singular or plural or a noun or a verb. By 300 B.C., the Egyptian alphabet consisted of more than seven hundred hieroglyphic symbols.

A loop with a royal name inside it was called a cartouche. You can make your cartouche using the symbols shown in the hieroglyphic chart.

Chart of hieroglyphic symbols

Life Everlasting

The age of 110 was believed to be the perfect life span, but it was more an ideal than a reality. Most people in those days did not live past their thirties.

Hieroglyphs cover this obelisk at Luxor Temple.

But every Egyptian, from pharaoh to laborer, believed in life after death. Given the proper burial rites, they could be immortal.

The Egyptians believed that the jackal-headed god, Anubis, escorted each soul into the afterlife. Osiris, god of the underworld, made a final judgment by the "weighing of the heart." A feather was put on one side of a scale, and the person's heart on the other side. If the heart was as light as the feather, the soul could enter eternity.

Egyptians also believed that the dead would enjoy all their earthly comforts in the afterlife. Burial chambers were filled with favorite possessions, clothes, furniture, games, and food. Even pet cats were preserved and buried with their masters.

Mummies

After death, the body was made into a mummy to keep it from decaying. This ensured a successful journey into the afterlife. Mummification could take as long as seventy days. First, the body was packed in a salt called natron, which dried the tissues and kept them from breaking down. Then the internal organs were removed. Some were preserved in jars and buried with the body. Other organs were treated with herbs and replaced in the body. The brain, believed to be worthless, was thrown away. Embalming fluids and pastes were then applied to preserve the skin and the body's interior.

Finally, the body was wrapped round and round with white linen strips. Mummies of some pharaohs were encased in jewel-encrusted gold and placed in a sarcophagus, or stone coffin,

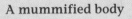

A mummified body

311

in the burial chamber. Scrolls of the *Book of the Dead* were buried with the body. They contained special prayers and instructions for getting through the mysterious world of the dead.

Pyramids

To make sure they would have eternal life, pharaohs built fabulous tombs for themselves. The earliest pharaohs built tombs called *mastabas*—low, flat-topped, mud-brick structures with slanting sides.

Djoser, a pharaoh of the Third Dynasty, wanted a more glorious tomb, so his architect, Imhotep, built the first pyramid. It is called a step pyramid because its sides are like stair steps. Djoser's step pyramid still stands at Saqqara, near Memphis.

Fourth Dynasty pharaohs built the most famous pyramids—the three pyramids of Giza, just west of Cairo. Khufu built the largest one, called the Great Pyramid, around 2600 B.C.

> **GREAT PYRAMID FACTS**
>
> **Height:** 481 feet (147m)—taller than a forty-story building
>
> **Length of One Side:** 755 feet (230 m), or one-seventh of a mile
>
> **Area Covered:** 13 acres (5 ha), or about seven city blocks
>
> **Number of Limestone Blocks:** About 2.5 million
>
> **Average Weight of a Block:** 2.5 tons
>
> **Weight of Heaviest Blocks:** 15 tons
>
> **Contents:** Stolen by grave robbers, probably in ancient times

These are two of the three pyramids of Giza. The capped pyramid of Khafre stands behind the Great Pyramid, also known as the Pyramid of Khufu.

This is a side view of the Great Sphinx in Giza, Egypt. The pyramid of Khufu looms in the background.

Khufu's pyramid was made of limestone blocks covered with sheer granite slabs that glistened in the sun. People could slide right down the sides. In later centuries, the granite was removed to make buildings in Cairo.

Khufu's son Khafre and the pharaoh Menkaure built the two other Giza pyramids. Nearby stands the Great Sphinx, a massive stone lion with the head of a man.

How Did They Build the Pyramids?

The ancient Egyptians left only a few clues about how they built the pyramids. From rock quarries at Aswan, stone blocks were floated down the Nile on rafts for 500 miles (800 km). Then the blocks were probably put on runners, like sleds, and hauled up wooden or stone ramps.

The Greek historian Herodotus says that 100,000 men worked on the Great Pyramid in three-month shifts. Then another 100,000 went to work. This went on for more than twenty years. How were the blocks lifted into place? According to Herodotus, they were lifted with a kind of crane that rested on lower-level stones.

313

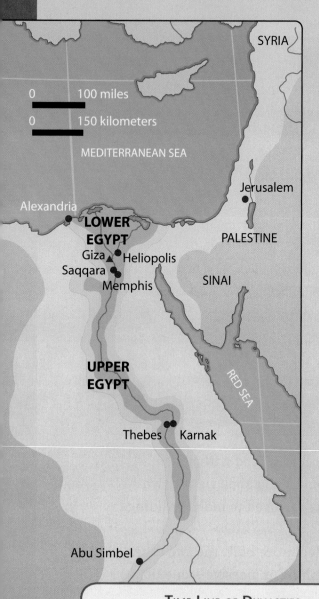

SYRIA

MEDITERRANEAN SEA

Jerusalem

Alexandria

LOWER EGYPT

PALESTINE

Giza Heliopolis
Saqqara
Memphis

SINAI

UPPER EGYPT

RED SEA

Thebes Karnak

Abu Simbel

TIME LINE OF DYNASTIES

3110 B.C.	Founding of united Egypt by King Menes
C. 2686 B.C.–2160 B.C.	Old Kingdom
C. 2040 B.C.–1786 B.C.	Middle Kingdom
1570 B.C.–330 B.C.	New Kingdom

Ancient Egypt

- Old Kingdom
- Middle Kingdom
- New Kingdom

Kingdoms Unite and Divide

The history of ancient Egypt may be divided into three major periods—the Old Kingdom, the Middle Kingdom, and the New Kingdom. Memphis was Egypt's capital during the Old Kingdom period, beginning around 2686 B.C. Memphis lies about 15 miles (24 km) south of what is now Cairo. Even in this early period, Egyptians were making paper from papyrus fibers and writing in hieroglyphs.

In time, the pharaohs' power weakened, and Egypt once again broke into separate districts. Mentuhotep II pulled the kingdom together again around 2040 B.C. He built his capital at Thebes, on the Nile's east bank in Upper Egypt. His reign marks the beginning of the Middle Kingdom period. During this time, construction began on the temple of Amon at Karnak.

Asian people called the Hyksos rose to power in the 1600s B.C. They began ruling from their capital at Avaris in the Delta and later spread to Thebes. Egyptians learned much about the art of war from these foreign rulers. The Hyksos introduced horse-drawn chariots, bronze and iron swords, and other military gear.

The New Kingdom: Conquests and Construction

Ahmose, a Theban prince, drove the Hyksos out in the 1500s B.C. This began the New Kingdom period, with Thebes as the capital. With their new military skills, Egyptians now became a major world power. Under Thutmose III, they took over Nubia, Palestine, Syria, and northern Iraq. New lands meant new sources of wealth. Slaves, exotic woods, ivory, and precious metals and stones poured into the pharaohs' warehouses.

To show off their power, New Kingdom pharaohs built huge temples, monuments, and statues of themselves. Ramses II ("Ramses the Great") was the greatest builder of all. He built the temples of Abu Simbel and enlarged the temple at Karnak. Scholars also believe he was the pharaoh mentioned in the Bible's Book of Exodus story, in which Moses led the Hebrews out of slavery in Egypt.

For their tombs, New Kingdom rulers built huge necropolises, or cities of the dead. These tomb sites were on the west bank of the Nile, across from Thebes. Today they are named the Valley of the Kings, the Valley of the Queens, and the Tombs of the Nobles.

In 1995, archaeologist Kent Weeks discovered what may be the largest tomb in the Valley of the Kings. It holds most of Ramses II's fifty-two sons. So far, about sixty tombs have been found in the Valley of the Kings—only a fraction of those waiting to be discovered.

THE BOY KING

We know about Tutankhamen, or "King Tut," from his lavish tomb in the Valley of the Kings. Tutankhamen, the "boy king," reigned in the 1300s B.C. He died when he was about eighteen years old. More than five thousand objects were found in his tomb, including furniture, games, weapons, and a golden chariot.

Common Core State Standards

Informational Text 1. Cite textual evidence to support analysis of what the text says explicitly as well as inferences drawn from the text. **Also Informational Text 2., Writing 9.**

Envision It! | Retell

Think Critically

1. Some Egyptian hieroglyphs represented ideas and actions. What modern picture-symbols do people today understand no matter what language they speak? Describe a few examples. **Text to World**

2. Nonfiction can be concise; that is, it can give much information in not very much space. Explain, through examples, how Ann Heinrichs has made this article concise. **Think Like an Author**

3. How do the graphic sources, such as the photos of Egyptian artifacts and the chart of hieroglyphic symbols, help you to better understand the text? Explain your answer. **Graphic Sources**

4. In a few sentences, summarize the most influential parts of ancient Egypt's culture and explain how Egyptian culture has affected our own. **Summarize**

5. **Look Back and Write** How long did Egypt exist under the thirty-one dynasties? Why is the length of time important? Look on page 304 for help, and review the sections that describe different dynasties. As you write your answer, provide evidence from the selection.

   Key Ideas and Details • Text Evidence

Meet the Author

Ann Heinrichs

While growing up in Arkansas, Ann Heinrichs read Doctor Doolittle books and became fascinated by faraway places. She has since traveled throughout the United States, Europe, Asia, and Africa. Her experiences in Egypt provided the background for this selection. She visited pyramids and tombs, and she rode a camel in the desert. She says, "Trips are fun, but the real work—tracking down all the factual information for a book—begins at the library. I head straight for the reference department. My favorite resources include United Nations publications, world almanacs, and the library's computer databases." An author of more than one hundred books about countries throughout the world, Ms. Heinrichs has two college degrees in piano performance and is an award-winning martial artist who practices t'ai chi, nan chuan, and kung fu sword.

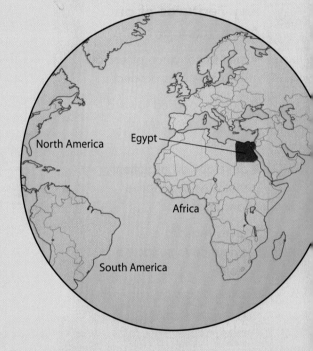

North America

Egypt

Africa

South America

Other books by Ann Heinrichs: *Pakistan* and *Afghanistan*

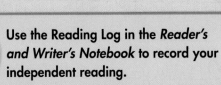

Use the Reading Log in the *Reader's and Writer's Notebook* to record your independent reading.

Argument/Persuasive

Let's Write It!

Key Features of an Advertisement

- tries to convince others of the value of a product

- may be geared toward specific purposes or groups

- develops an argument that uses descriptive language

- gives reasons and evidence to support a claim

READING STREET ONLINE
GRAMMAR JAMMER
www.ReadingStreet.com

Advertisement

An **advertisement** tries to persuade someone to purchase a product by developing a convincing argument. The student model on the next page is an example of an advertisement.

Writing Prompt *Egypt* describes ancient Egyptian culture. Write an advertisement for a product you might have found in ancient Egypt. Be sure to develop an argument that supports your claim with reasons and relevant evidence.

Writer's Checklist

Remember, you should . . .

✓ give reasons and evidence that will persuade someone to buy your product.

✓ keep your audience's interests, wants, and needs in mind.

✓ clearly state what you are selling.

✓ use strong, persuasive language to support your argument.

✓ know your purpose for writing.

OWN A GAME TREASURED BY KINGS!

For a limited time! When our great leader Pharaoh Tutankhamen **is sealed** in his tomb in the Valley of the Kings, **he will count** a Tep Brothers' senet board among his treasured artifacts. And now you, too, **can own** an exact replica of Pharaoh Tutankhamen's board!

You know the game, now get the board!

Our Limited Edition Pharaoh Tutankhamen Senet Board **is the highest-quality** senet board available. Master craftsmen **hand-carved** the playing pieces out of the finest ivory. The board is made of ebony, ivory, lapis, and gold.

Buy a Tep Brothers' Limited Edition Pharaoh Tutankhamen Senet Board today, before the tomb is sealed!

About Us

Tep Brothers brand board games **have been** entertaining royalty and commoners alike since the late Hyksos dynasty. Our bestselling senet boards **can be found** throughout the kingdom.

Genre An **advertisement** tries to sell a product.

Past, present, and **future verb tenses** are used correctly.

Writing Trait Organization The writer uses topic headings to separate ideas.

Conventions

Past, Present, and Future Tenses

Remember The tense of a verb shows when something happens. **Present tense** verbs show action that happens now (and often end in -s). **Past tense** verbs show action that has already happened (and often end in -ed). **Future tense** verbs show action that will happen.

Common Core State Standards
Informational Text 9. Compare and contrast one author's presentation of events with that of another (e.g., a memoir written by and a biography on the same person). **Also Informational Text 1., 10.**

Social Studies in Reading

Genre
Expository Text

- Expository text gives facts that explain a person, thing, or event.

- Expository text may use a question-and-answer text structure to deliver information more quickly.

- Some expository texts include graphics, such as charts and photos, to give readers even more information.

- Read "The Rosetta Stone" and look for information about ancient Egyptian culture. Look, too, for how the mystery of the Rosetta Stone was finally solved.

The Rosetta Stone

FROM THE BRITISH MUSEUM'S WEB SITE

What is the Rosetta Stone?
The Rosetta Stone is a stone with writing on it in two languages (Egyptian and Greek), using three scripts (hieroglyphic, demotic, and Greek).

Why is it in three different scripts?
The Rosetta Stone is written in three scripts because when it was written, there were three scripts being used in Egypt.

- The first was hieroglyphic, which was the script used for important or religious documents.

- The second was demotic, which was the common script of Egypt.

- The third was Greek, which was the language of the rulers of Egypt at that time.

The Rosetta Stone was written in all three scripts so that the priests, government officials, and rulers of Egypt could read what it said.

When was the Rosetta Stone made?
The Rosetta Stone was carved in 196 B.C.

When was the Rosetta Stone found?
The Rosetta Stone was found in 1799.

Who found the Rosetta Stone?

The Rosetta Stone was found by French soldiers who were rebuilding a fort in Egypt.

Where was the Rosetta Stone found?

The Rosetta Stone was found in a small village called Rosetta (Rashid) in the delta of the Nile River.

Why is it called the Rosetta Stone?

It is called the Rosetta Stone because it was discovered in a town called Rosetta (Rashid).

What does the Rosetta Stone say?

The Rosetta Stone is a text written by a group of priests in Egypt to honor the Egyptian pharaoh. It lists all of the things that the pharaoh had done that were good for the priests and the people of Egypt.

Detail of hieroglyphic and demotic script on the Rosetta Stone

Who deciphered hieroglyphs?

Many people worked on deciphering hieroglyphs over several hundred years. However, the structure of the script was very difficult to work out.

After many years of studying the Rosetta Stone and other examples of ancient Egyptian writing, Jean-François Champollion deciphered hieroglyphs in 1822.

How did Champollion decipher hieroglyphs?

Champollion could read both Greek and Coptic (the extinct language of Egypt that developed from ancient Egyptian).

He was able to figure out what the seven demotic signs in Coptic were. By looking at how these signs were used in Coptic he was able to work out what they stood for. Then he began tracing these demotic signs back to hieroglyphic signs.

By working out what some hieroglyphs stood for, he could make educated guesses about what the other hieroglyphs stood for.

Let's Think About...

How can the text structure help you summarize the main facts presented on these two pages?
Expository Text

Let's Think About...

Reading Across Texts The Rosetta Stone honors an Egyptian pharaoh. What other ways of honoring pharaohs were stated in *Egypt*?

Writing Across Texts Make a list of ways in which pharaohs were honored in ancient Egyptian society.

Common Core State Standards
Language 4.b. Use common, grade-appropriate Greek or Latin affixes and roots as clues to the meaning of a word (e.g., *audience, auditory, audible*).
Also Speaking/Listening 1.b., 6.

Let's
Learn
It!

READING STREET ONLINE
ONLINE STUDENT EDITION
www.ReadingStreet.com

Vocabulary

Latin and Greek Roots

Word Structure Remember that knowing the meanings of Latin and Greek roots will help you figure out the meanings of unfamiliar English words. When you read an unfamiliar word, analyze its parts. If you recognize the root, then you are close to understanding the word's meaning. You may use a dictionary for help.

Practice It! Look back at *Egypt* and "The Rosetta Stone" and choose several words that have Latin or Greek roots. Create a chart with two columns. In the first column, list the chosen words and their meanings. You may use a dictionary. In the second column, write each word's root and another word that has the same root.

Fluency

Expression

Remember when you read aloud to use your voice to change the emphasis on what you are reading. It is important to keep things interesting to your listeners, so vary your tone of voice to suit what's going on or who is taking part in the action.

Practice It! With a partner, read two different kinds of writing to see how you naturally vary your expression. First read the top of page 308 from *Egypt,* with its familiar words and ideas. Then read page 321, column 2, from "The Rosetta Stone." What differences do you hear?

Listening and Speaking

Making facts easy to understand is very important when you present a newscast.

Newscast

In a newscast, TV or radio reporters read news stories. The purpose of a newscast is to inform people about important events in a way that is easy to understand.

Practice It! Imagine that three of you are reporters traveling through ancient Egypt. Prepare a special report for a three-part newscast back home. Keep your reports to two minutes, using only the most important details. Then discuss how news reports are different from talk shows and advertisements.

Tips

Listening . . .

- Look directly at each reporter.

- Consider the reporter's credibility.

- Draw conclusions about what the reporter says or doesn't say.

Speaking . . .

- Present your most important idea first and follow it with facts.

- Follow the conventions of language.

- Face your audience and maintain eye contact.

Teamwork . . .

- Divide the topics for your reports fairly and take turns.

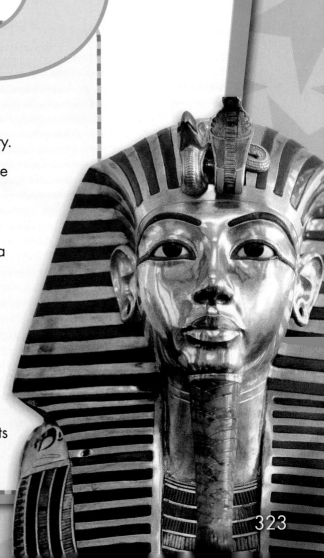

Common Core State Standards
Literature 5. Analyze how a particular sentence, chapter, scene, or stanza fits into the overall structure of a text and contributes to the development of the theme, setting, or plot. **Also Literature 4., 10.**

Poetry

- Poems give pleasure to the reader by evoking emotions and imagination.

- **Lyrical poems** are both personal and descriptive. They use rhymes and a regular meter, or rhythm, much like song lyrics, to help create images.

- **Free verse poems** don't have regular rhymes or meter. They may not even use capital letters or punctuation.

- Read these five poems about space and time. Compare the lyrical poem "Tradition" to the free verse of "Fossils" and to the two limericks on page 326.

Tradition

by Eloise Greenfield

Pineapples! pumpkins! chickens! we
carry them on our heads you see
we can glide along forever
and not drop a thing, no never
never even use our hands
never put a finger to it
you know how we learned to do it?
knowledge came from other lands
Africans of long ago
passed it down to us and so
now we pass it on to you
for what is old is also new
pineapples, pumpkins, chickens, we
carry more than the things you see
we also carry history

Fossils

by Lilian Moore

Older than
books,
than scrolls,

older
than the first
tales told

or the
first words
spoken

are the stories

in the forests that
turned to
stone

in ice walls
that trapped the
mammoth

in the long
bones of
dinosaurs—

the fossil
stories that begin
Once upon a time

Let's **Think** About...

What three things make "Tradition" a lyrical poem?

Let's **Think** About...

"Tradition" rhymes; "Fossils" doesn't. Their meters and stanzas differ. Why are both of them considered poems?

Arrival

**by Florence Parry Heide
and Judith Heide Gilliland**

A very fast runner named Fay
ran faster and faster each day.
She was very athletic
and so energetic
she arrived at tomorrow today.

The Time Machine

**by Florence Parry Heide and
Judith Heide Gilliland**

There was an inventor named Breen
who invented a Time Machine.
By mistake one time
he pressed rewind
and woke in his crib with a scream.

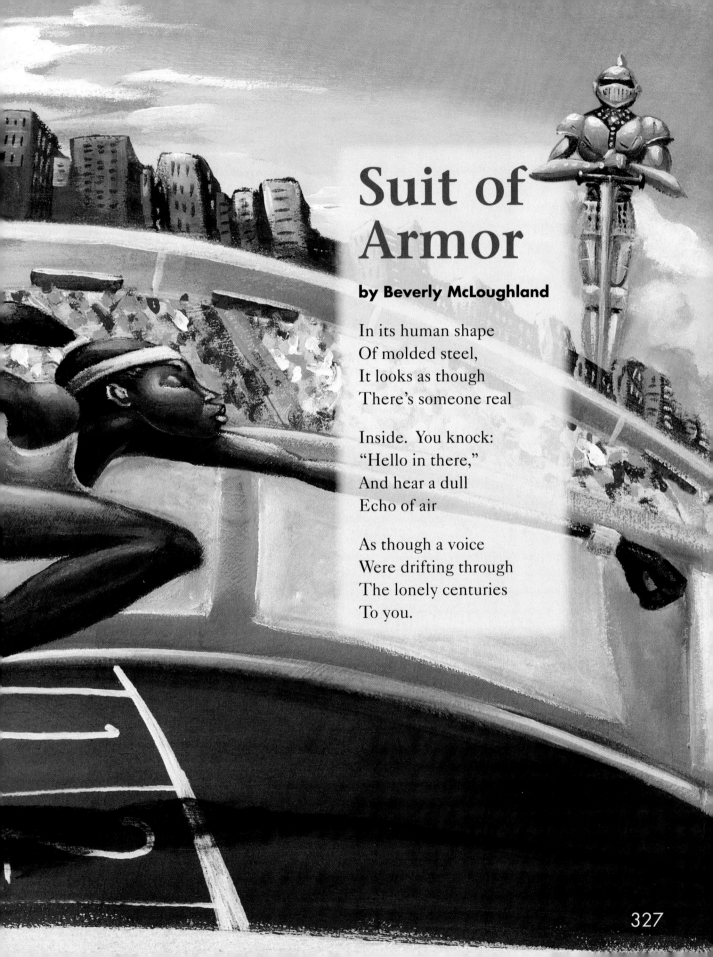

Suit of Armor

by Beverly McLoughland

In its human shape
Of molded steel,
It looks as though
There's someone real

Inside. You knock:
"Hello in there,"
And hear a dull
Echo of air

As though a voice
Were drifting through
The lonely centuries
To you.

Challenges and Obstacles

How are the results
of our efforts sometimes
greater than we expect?

Let's **Think** About Reading!

Common Core State Standards
Language 6. Acquire and use accurately
grade-appropriate general academic and
domain-specific words and phrases;
gather vocabulary knowledge when
considering a word or phrase important
to comprehension or expression.
Also Speaking/Listening 1.c.

Oral Vocabulary

Let's Talk About

Survival in Nature

- Describe how nature can challenge us.

- Suggest what might be needed to survive in the wilderness.

- Share ideas about how to prepare for being out in nature.

READING STREET ONLINE
CONCEPT TALK VIDEO
www.ReadingStreet.com

331

Common Core State Standards

Literature 3. Describe how a particular story's or drama's plot unfolds in a series of episodes as well as how the characters respond or change as the plot moves toward a resolution. **Also Literature 1.**

Envision It! | Skill Strategy

Skill

Strategy

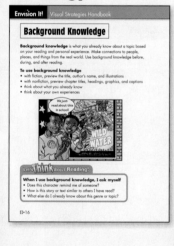

READING STREET ONLINE
ENVISION IT! ANIMATIONS
www.ReadingStreet.com

Comprehension Skill

Sequence

- Sequence is the order of events in a story. Clue words such as *first, next, then,* and *finally* often indicate sequence.

- If events happen at the same time, look for clue words such as *while* and *during*.

- Use a graphic organizer like the one below to keep track of the sequence of events in "Incident at the Street Fair."

End

fourth event

third event

second event

first event

Beginning

Comprehension Strategy

Background Knowledge

Background knowledge is what you already know about a topic from your reading or from your real-life experience. Use background knowledge before, during, and after reading to monitor your comprehension.

Incident at the Street Fair

One Saturday Caleb, his sister Mandy, and their father rode the train downtown to the Garfield Street Festival. The street fair was packed with people!

First they treated themselves to some barbecued chicken and corn at a food booth and listened to a live salsa band entertaining the crowd from the main stage. While his father surveyed his festival map, Caleb gazed up at the glistening skyline, tilting his head w-a-a-a-y back.

"Dad, look at that awesome skyscraper," Caleb said, but there was no reply. Caleb anxiously glanced all around, but he didn't see a single familiar face.

Wide-eyed, Caleb wandered around, looking for his family in all directions. At one point he was sure he saw his father—the shirt was the same. But when Caleb tapped on the shirt and the person wearing it turned around, all Caleb saw was an old man eating a sloppy sandwich with barbecue sauce all over his face. Caleb was getting nervous.

The crowd swelled larger, and people bumped and jostled him. A rock band was now playing ear-blasting music. Then suddenly he saw Mandy and, a moment later, his father's face. It held a strange mixture of anger and relief.

Skill Which of the following events took place at the same time Caleb was looking at the skyline?
a) He began to walk around.
b) His father looked at a map.
c) He ate chicken and corn.

Strategy Have you ever been separated from your family in a crowd? How would that experience help you understand how Caleb is feeling at this point?

Skill What is the last event in the story?

Your Turn!

⏸ **Need a Review?** See the *Envision It! Handbook* for help with sequencing and background knowledge.

Let's Think About...

▶ **Ready to Try It?** Use what you've learned about sequencing as you read *Hatchet*.

Common Core State Standards
Language 4.a. Use context (e.g., the overall meaning of a sentence or paragraph; a word's position or function in a sentence) as a clue to the meaning of a word or phrase.

hatchet

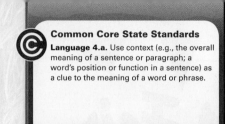

quill

smoldered

ignite

painstaking

registered

stiffened

Vocabulary Strategy for
🎯 Word Endings -ed, -ing

Word Structure An ending is a letter or letters added to the end of a base word. For example, the endings -ed and -ing can be added to verbs to change their tense. You may be able to use endings to help you figure out the meanings of words.

1. Cover the ending and read the base word.

2. Think about the meaning of the base word. If you do not know its meaning, reread the sentence for clues that can help you.

3. See how the ending affects the meaning of the verb: -ed makes a verb show past action; -ing makes a verb show ongoing or current action. Sometimes the -ed or -ing form of a verb is used as an adjective, to describe.

4. Choose a meaning that seems correct and see if it makes sense in the sentence.

Read "Wilderness Camp." Use word endings -ed and -ing to help you figure out the meanings of words you do not know.

Words to Write Reread "Wilderness Camp." Write a paragraph describing how you would start a fire without matches or how you would survive in the woods. Use as many words from the Words to Know list as you can.

Wilderness Camp

I woke early to unfamiliar sounds. Slowly it registered in my mind that I was not at home but in a tent in the north woods of Michigan. My whole body had stiffened from sleeping with only a sleeping bag between me and the remarkably hard ground. Why had I signed on for Wilderness Camp? I wasn't sure I could take a month of roughing it.

Soon everyone was up and concentrating on breakfast. First we would have to build a fire. We had sat up late last night until the campfire was only ash and embers that smoldered. Our counselor, Daniel, had doused it well with water from the river. An unattended campfire could start a forest fire, and we didn't want that.

I took a hatchet and began to cut a dead branch into firewood. Daniel built the fire, using painstaking care. He started with wadded-up newspaper and small dead twigs. We would lean the larger pieces of wood around this and then ignite the paper. As we worked, I showed Daniel the curious hollow stick I had found yesterday. He told me it was a quill from a porcupine.

Your Turn!

⏸ Need a Review?
For help with word endings, see *Words!*

Let's Think About...

▶ Ready to Try It?
Read *Hatchet* on pp. 336–349.

335

Hatchet

by Gary Paulsen

Question of the Week
How does facing challenges help us learn about ourselves?

Let's **Think** About **Reading!**

Brian is on his way to visit his father in northern Canada, when the pilot of the small, single-engine plane in which he is flying suffers a fatal heart attack. Forced to crash-land the plane, Brian suddenly finds himself alone in the Canadian wilderness, with only a hatchet to help him survive.

AT FIRST HE THOUGHT IT WAS A GROWL. In the still darkness of the shelter in the middle of the night his eyes came open and he was awake and he thought there was a growl. But it was the wind, a medium wind in the pines had made some sound that brought him up, brought him awake. He sat up and was hit with the smell.

It terrified him. The smell was one of rot, some musty rot that made him think only of graves with cobwebs and dust and old death. His nostrils widened and he opened his eyes wider, but he could see nothing. It was too dark, too hard dark with clouds covering even the small light from the stars, and he could not see. But the smell was alive, alive and full and in the shelter. He thought of the bear, thought of Bigfoot and every monster he had ever seen in every fright movie he had ever watched, and his heart hammered in his throat. Then he heard the slithering. A brushing sound, a slithering brushing sound near his feet——and he kicked out as hard as he could, kicked out and threw the hatchet at the sound, a noise coming from his throat. But the hatchet missed, sailed into the wall where it hit the rocks with a shower of sparks, and his leg was instantly torn with pain, as if a hundred needles had been driven into it. "Unnnngh!"

Let's Think About...

How do the author's vivid descriptions help to convey Brian's terror in the night?
Story Structure

338

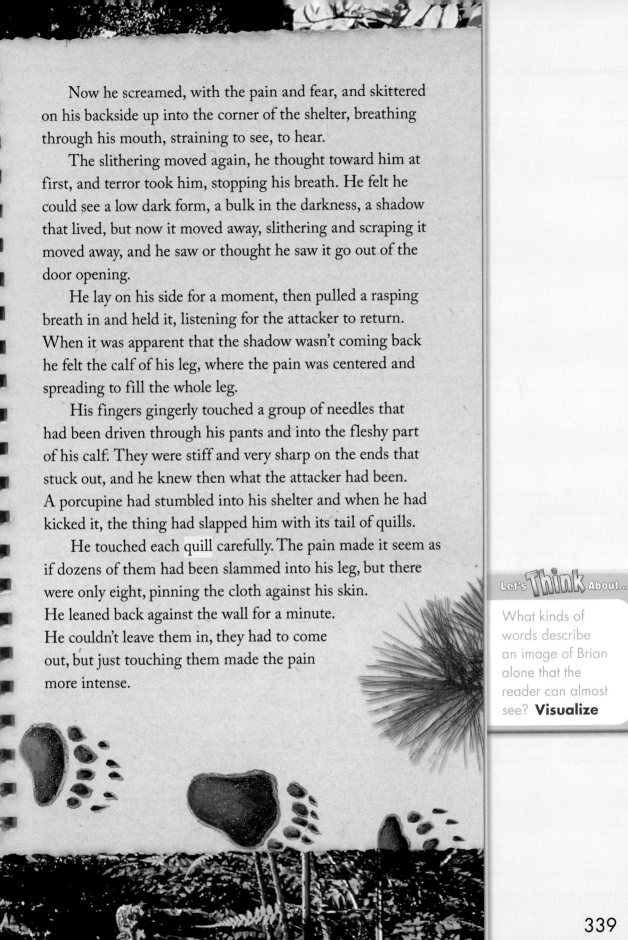

Now he screamed, with the pain and fear, and skittered on his backside up into the corner of the shelter, breathing through his mouth, straining to see, to hear.

The slithering moved again, he thought toward him at first, and terror took him, stopping his breath. He felt he could see a low dark form, a bulk in the darkness, a shadow that lived, but now it moved away, slithering and scraping it moved away, and he saw or thought he saw it go out of the door opening.

He lay on his side for a moment, then pulled a rasping breath in and held it, listening for the attacker to return. When it was apparent that the shadow wasn't coming back he felt the calf of his leg, where the pain was centered and spreading to fill the whole leg.

His fingers gingerly touched a group of needles that had been driven through his pants and into the fleshy part of his calf. They were stiff and very sharp on the ends that stuck out, and he knew then what the attacker had been. A porcupine had stumbled into his shelter and when he had kicked it, the thing had slapped him with its tail of quills.

He touched each quill carefully. The pain made it seem as if dozens of them had been slammed into his leg, but there were only eight, pinning the cloth against his skin. He leaned back against the wall for a minute. He couldn't leave them in, they had to come out, but just touching them made the pain more intense.

Let's Think About...

What kinds of words describe an image of Brian alone that the reader can almost see? **Visualize**

So fast, he thought.
So fast things change.

When he'd gone to sleep he had satisfaction and in just a moment it was all different. He grasped one of the quills, held his breath, and jerked. It sent pain signals to his brain in tight waves, but he grabbed another, pulled it, then another quill. When he had pulled four of them he stopped for a moment. The pain had gone from being a pointed injury pain to spreading in a hot smear up his leg, and it made him catch his breath.

Some of the quills were driven in deeper than others, and they tore when they came out. He breathed deeply twice, let half of the breath out, and went back to work. Jerk, pause, jerk——and three more times before he lay back in the darkness, done. The pain filled his leg now, and with it came new waves of self-pity. Sitting alone in the dark, his leg aching, some mosquitos finding him again, he started crying. It was all too much, just too much, and he couldn't take it. Not the way it was.

I can't take it this way, alone with no fire and in the dark, and next time it might be something worse, maybe a bear, and it wouldn't be just quills in the leg, it would be worse. *I can't do this*, he thought, again and again. *I can't.* Brian pulled himself up until he was sitting upright back in the corner of the cave. He put his head down on his arms across his knees, with stiffness taking his left leg, and cried until he was cried out.

He did not know how long it took, but later he looked back on this time of crying in the corner of the dark cave and thought of it as when he learned the most important rule of survival, which was that feeling sorry for yourself didn't work. It wasn't just that it was wrong to do, or that it was considered

Let's **Think** About...

Think about a time when you felt sorry for yourself. Does that help you identify with Brian?

Background Knowledge

340

incorrect. It was more than that——it didn't work. When he sat alone in the darkness and cried and was done, was all done with it, nothing had changed. His leg still hurt, it was still dark, he was still alone, and the self-pity had accomplished nothing.

Let's **Think** About...

What can you do to find exactly when Brian decided not to give in to feelings of self-pity?
Monitor and Clarify

At last he slept again, but already his patterns were changing and the sleep was light, a resting doze more than a deep sleep, with small sounds awakening him twice in the rest of the night. In the last doze period before daylight, before he awakened finally with the morning light and the clouds of new mosquitos, he dreamed. This time it was not of his mother, but of his father at first and then of his friend Terry.

In the initial segment of the dream his father was standing at the side of a living room looking at him, and it was clear from his expression that he was trying to tell Brian something. His lips moved but there was no sound, not a whisper. He waved his hands at Brian, made gestures in front of his face as if he were scratching something, and he worked to make a word with his mouth but at first Brian could not see it.

Then the lips made an *mmmmm* shape but no sound came. *Mmmmm-maaaa.* Brian could not hear it, could not understand it and he wanted to so badly; it was so important to understand his father, to know what he was saying. He was trying to help, trying so hard, and when Brian couldn't understand he looked cross, the way he did when Brian asked questions more than once, and he faded. Brian's father faded into a fog place Brian could not see, and the dream was almost over, or seemed to be, when Terry came.

He was not gesturing to Brian but was sitting in the park at a bench looking at a barbecue pit and for a time nothing happened. Then he got up and poured some charcoal from a bag into the cooker, then some starter fluid, and he took a flick type of lighter and lit the fluid. When it was burning and the charcoal was at last getting hot he turned, noticing Brian for the first time in the dream. He turned and smiled and pointed to the fire as if to say, *see, a fire.*

But it meant nothing to Brian, except that he wished he had a fire. He saw a grocery sack on the table next to Terry. Brian thought it must contain hot dogs and chips and mustard, and he could think only of the food. But Terry shook his head and pointed again to the fire, and twice more he pointed to the fire, made Brian see the flames, and Brian felt his frustration and anger rise and he thought *all right, all right, I see the fire but so what? I don't have a fire.*

I know about fire;
I know I need a fire.
I know that.

Let's **Think** About...

How does the dream about his father lead Brian to think about the importance of fire?
Story Structure

His eyes opened and there was light in the cave, a gray dim light of morning. He wiped his mouth and tried to move his leg, which had stiffened like wood. There was thirst, and hunger, and he ate some raspberries from the jacket. They had spoiled a bit, seemed softer and mushier, but still had a rich sweetness. He crushed the berries against the roof of his mouth with his tongue and drank the sweet juice as it ran down his throat. A flash of metal caught his eye, and he saw his hatchet in the sand where he had thrown it at the porcupine in the dark.

He scooted up, wincing a bit when he bent his stiff leg, and crawled to where the hatchet lay. He picked it up and examined it and saw a chip in the top of the head.

The nick wasn't large, but the hatchet was important to him, was his only tool, and he should not have thrown it. He should keep it in his hand and make a tool of some kind to help push an animal away. *Make a staff,* he thought, *or a lance, and save the hatchet.* Something came then, a thought as he held the hatchet, something about the dream and his father and Terry, but he couldn't pin it down.

"Ahhh . . ." He scrambled out and stood in the morning sun and stretched his back muscles and his sore leg. The hatchet was still in his hand, and as he stretched and raised it over his head it caught the first rays of the morning sun. The first faint light hit the silver of the hatchet and flashed a brilliant gold in the light. Like fire. *That is it,* he thought. *What they were trying to tell me.*

Let's **Think** About...

What other stories have you read or heard about on how to survive in the wilderness?

Background Knowledge

Fire. The hatchet was the key to it all. When he threw the hatchet at the porcupine in the cave and missed and hit the stone wall, it had showered sparks, a golden shower of sparks in the dark, as golden with fire as the sun was now.

sandstone

The hatchet was the answer. That's what his father and Terry had been trying to tell him. Somehow he could get fire from the hatchet. The sparks would make fire.

Brian went back into the shelter and studied the wall. It was some form of chalky granite, or a sandstone, but imbedded in it were large pieces of a darker stone, a harder and darker stone. It only took him a moment to find where the hatchet had struck. The steel had nicked into the edge of one of the darker stone pieces. Brian turned the head backward so he would strike with the flat rear of the hatchet and hit the black rock gently. Too gently, and nothing happened. He struck harder, a glancing blow, and two or three weak sparks skipped off the rock and died immediately.

He swung harder, held the hatchet so it would hit a longer, sliding blow, and the black rock exploded in fire. Sparks flew so heavily that several of them skittered and jumped on the sand beneath the rock, and he smiled and struck again and again.

There could be fire here, he thought.

Let's Think About...

What did you know about starting a fire that helps you understand what Brian is going through?

⊙ Background Knowledge

I will have a fire here, he
thought, and struck again.
I will have fire from
the hatchet.

Brian found it was
a long way from sparks to fire.

Clearly there had to be something for the sparks to ignite,
some kind of tinder or kindling——but what? He brought some
dried grass in, tapped sparks into it and watched them die.
He tried small twigs, breaking them into little pieces, but that
was worse than the grass. Then he tried a combination of the
two, grass and twigs.

Nothing. He had no trouble getting sparks, but the tiny
bits of hot stone or metal——he couldn't tell which they
were——just sputtered and died.

He settled back on his haunches in exasperation, looking
at the pitiful clump of grass and twigs.

He needed something finer, something soft and fine and
fluffy to catch the bits of fire.

Shredded paper would be nice, but he had no paper.

"So close," he said aloud, "so close. . . ."

He put the hatchet back in his belt and went out of the
shelter, limping on his sore leg. There had to be something,
had to be. Man had made fire. There had been fire for thousands,
millions of years. There had to be a way. He dug in his pockets
and found the twenty-dollar bill in his wallet. Paper. Worthless
paper out here. But if he could get a fire going. . . .

Let's Think About...

What do you think
Brian will do with
his twenty-dollar
bill? **Predict**

He ripped the twenty into tiny pieces, made a pile of pieces, and hit sparks into them. Nothing happened. They just wouldn't take the sparks. But there had to be a way—some way to do it.

Not twenty feet to his right, leaning out over the water were birches, and he stood looking at them for a full half-minute before they registered on his mind. They were a beautiful white with bark like clean, slightly speckled paper.

Paper.

He moved to the trees. Where the bark was peeling from the trunks it lifted in tiny tendrils, almost fluffs. Brian plucked some of them loose, rolled them in his fingers. They seemed flammable, dry, and nearly powdery. He pulled and twisted bits off the trees, packing them in one hand while he picked them with the other, picking and gathering until he had a wad close to the size of a baseball.

Then he went back into the shelter and arranged the ball of birchbark peelings at the base of the black rock. As an afterthought he threw in the remains of the twenty-dollar bill. He struck and a stream of sparks fell into the bark and quickly died. But this time one spark fell on one small hair of dry bark— almost a thread of bark—and seemed to glow a bit brighter before it died.

The material had to be finer. There had to be a soft and incredibly fine nest for the sparks.

I must make a home for the sparks, he thought. A perfect home or they won't stay or they won't make a fire.

Let's Think About...

What kinds of details show how hard Brian is trying to find materials that will ignite?
Visualize

He started ripping the bark, using his fingernails at first, and when that didn't work he used the sharp edge of the hatchet, cutting the bark in thin slivers, hairs so fine they were almost not there. It was painstaking work,

slow work, and he stayed with it for over two hours. Twice he stopped for a handful of berries and once to go to the lake for a drink. Then back to work, the sun on his back, until at last he had a ball of fluff as big as a grapefruit——dry birchbark fluff.

He positioned his spark nest——as he thought of it——at the base of the rock, used his thumb to make a small depression in the middle, and slammed the back of the hatchet down across the black rock. A cloud of sparks rained down, most of them missing the nest, but some, perhaps thirty or so, hit in the depression and, of those, six or seven found fuel and grew, smoldered and caused the bark to take on the red glow.

Then they went out.

Close——he was close. He repositioned the nest, made a new and smaller dent with his thumb, and struck again.

More sparks, a slight glow, then nothing.

Let's Think About...

Why does the author seem to be telling what happens so slowly, almost minute by minute?
Story Structure

It's me, he thought. *I'm doing something wrong. I do not know this——a cave dweller would have had a fire by now, a Cro-Magnon man would have a fire by now——but I don't know this. I don't know how to make a fire.*

Maybe not enough sparks. He settled the nest in place once more and hit the rock with a series of blows, as fast as he could. The sparks poured like a golden waterfall. At first they seemed to take, there were several, many sparks that found life and took briefly, but they all died.

Starved.

He leaned back. They are like me. They are starving. It wasn't quantity, there were plenty of sparks, but they needed more.

I would kill, he thought suddenly, *for a book of matches. Just one book. Just one match. I would kill.*

What makes fire? He thought back to school. To all those science classes. Had he ever learned what made a fire? Did a teacher ever stand up there and say, "This is what makes a fire . . ."

He shook his head, tried to focus his thoughts. What did it take? *You have to have fuel*, he thought——and he had that. The bark was fuel. Oxygen——there had to be air.

He needed to add air. He had to fan on it, blow on it.

He made the nest ready again, held the hatchet backward, tensed, and struck four quick blows. Sparks came down and he leaned forward as fast as he could and blew.

Too hard. There was a bright, almost intense glow, then it was gone. He had blown it out.

Another set of strikes, more sparks. He leaned and blew, but gently this time, holding back and aiming the stream of air from his mouth to hit the brightest spot. Five or six sparks had fallen in a tight mass of bark hair, and Brian centered his efforts there.

"Fire!" He yelled. "I've got fire! I've got it, I've got it. I've got it. . . ."

Let's Think About...

What can you do to better understand Brian's attempts to start a fire?

Monitor and Clarify

The sparks grew with his gentle breath. The red glow moved from the sparks themselves into the bark, moved and grew and became worms, glowing red worms that crawled up the bark hairs and caught other threads of bark and grew until there was a pocket of red as big as a quarter, a glowing red coal of heat.

And when he ran out of breath and paused to inhale, the red ball suddenly burst into flame.

But the flames were thick and oily and burning fast, consuming the ball of bark as fast as if it were gasoline. He had to feed the flames, keep them going. Working as fast as he could he carefully placed the dried grass and wood pieces he had tried at first on top of the bark and was gratified to see them take.

But they would go fast. He needed more, and more. He could not let the flames go out.

He ran from the shelter to the pines and started breaking off the low, dead, small limbs. These he threw in the shelter, went back for more, threw those in, and squatted to break and feed the hungry flames. When the small wood was going well he went out and found larger wood and did not relax until that was going. Then he leaned back against the wood brace of his door opening and smiled.

I have a friend, he thought——*I have a friend now. A hungry friend, but a good one. I have a friend named fire.*

"Hello, fire. . . ."

The curve of the rock back made an almost perfect drawing flue that carried the smoke up through the cracks of the roof but held the heat. If he kept the fire small it would be perfect and would keep anything like the porcupine from coming through the door again.

A friend and a guard, he thought.

So much from a little spark. A friend and a guard from a tiny spark.

Let's Think About...

Why does the author call Brian's fire "a friend and a guard"?
Monitor and Clarify

Envision It! | Retell

READING STREET ONLINE
STORY SORT
www.ReadingStreet.com

Think Critically

1. Think about the many challenges and struggles that faced people in the years before today's technologies were developed. List five things you can do today without much time and effort but that took a lot of time, effort, and perseverance many years ago. **Text to World**

2. Read parts of pages 339 and 340 aloud, slowly and deliberately. Notice how the pace of your reading matches the pace of Brian's movements. How does writing that is deliberately slow in pace help *Hatchet* come alive? **Think Like an Author**

3. Describe the sequence of events that occurred between the time Brian made sparks by throwing his hatchet against a rock and when he actually made a fire. **Sequence**

4. Have you ever seen someone lay and light a fire? How would this experience help a reader understand what is happening as Brian tries to start his fire and keep it going? **Background Knowledge**

5. **Look Back and Write** Look back at page 340. Brian believes he has learned the most important rule of survival. Write that rule and why it is important. Provide evidence from the remainder of the selection to support your answer. **Key Ideas and Details • Text Evidence**

Meet the Author

Gary Paulsen

Gary Paulsen is one of America's most important writers of books for young people. *Hatchet,* a modern-day classic, is a Newbery Honor Book, as are his novels *Dogsong* and *The Winter Room*. Mr. Paulsen's life changed the wintry day he went into a Minnesota library to warm up. He says, "The librarian asked me if I would like a library card. I was a real cocky kid and said, 'Sure, why not?' So she gave me a card, and the most astonishing thing happened. This silly little card with my name on it gave me an identity I had not had. I felt I had become somebody"— and he read up to a book a day. When he was young, Mr. Paulsen tried a number of jobs to support himself, from migrant worker to ranch hand to truck driver. Many of his books about the outdoors are based on his early life as a hunter and trapper and his later years running the Iditarod dog sled race and sailing the Pacific. He now lives with his wife in New Mexico.

Here are other books about survival:
Brian's Winter and *My Side of the Mountain*

Reading Log

Use the Reading Log in the *Reader's and Writer's Notebook* to record your independent reading.

351

Common Core State Standards

Writing 4. Produce clear and coherent writing in which the development, organization, and style are appropriate to task, purpose, and audience. **Also Writing 2.b., Language 1.**

Expository

Speech

A **speech** is a public address given for a specific purpose. It is typically written in advance, and includes details, explanations, reasons, or examples that support a main idea or thesis statement. The student model on the next page is an example of a speech.

Writing Prompt Think about a natural resource or wilderness area that is important to you. Now write a speech about what makes this resource or area special.

Let's Write It!

Key Features of a Speech

- meant to be formally presented to an audience

- delivers a message, argument, or story

- has a main idea or thesis statement

Writer's Checklist

Remember, you should . . .

✓ begin with an interest grabber.

✓ support the thesis statement with details, explanations, reasons, or examples.

✓ consider how your speech will be spoken as you write it.

✓ remember your purpose and audience as you write.

My Favorite Wilderness

Yosemite Valley is the most scenic place on Earth. It is my favorite wilderness area: a beautiful, broad, flat valley, with towering walls, carved into amazing shapes by nature. There is no more beautiful place in the United States.

Waterfalls crash down into the valley from surrounding cliffs. They flow into a river that winds through the valley. At the bottom of one waterfall is the gorgeous Mirror Lake.

The valley floor is covered with meadows that flower in the spring. Sequoia trees, or redwoods, also grow there. These trees are the largest living things on Earth. They can grow to be 100 feet high, and 25 feet in diameter.

Since I love Yosemite so much, I wanted to learn about it. The area has been a national park since 1890, one of the first national parks in the country. I am happy to know that the place I love will always stay as beautiful as it is now, because it is protected as a national park.

Due to its remarkable beauty and wonder, Yosemite Valley will always be my favorite place.

Writing Trait Focus/Ideas This speech has a clear thesis statement.

Genre A **speech** is an oral address shared with an audience.

Principal parts of regular verbs are used correctly.

Conventions

Principal Parts of Regular Verbs

Remember A verb's tenses are made from four basic forms. These are called the **principal parts,** and include present, past, present participle, and past participle. A **regular verb** forms its past and past participle by adding -d or -ed to the present form.

353

Common Core State Standards
Informational Text 1. Cite textual evidence to support analysis of what the text says explicitly as well as inferences drawn from the text. **Also Informational Text 2.**

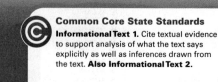

Genre
Expository Text

- Expository text provides information about people, places, events, and activities.

- Photos can help the reader better understand the information presented.

- Expository text may include quotes from sources or people.

- Read "Call of the Deep Wilds" and see if the text makes you want to experience the adventures that are described.

Call of the Deep Wilds

by Helen Strahinich

A summer camp teaches life skills to young people.

Jeannie McGartland used to be afraid of lots of things. She was frightened of the dark. She would get spooked by bees, hornets, and spiders, and she was so afraid of fire that she wouldn't even light a match.

Then one day, when Jeannie was ten years old, she enrolled in Deep Wilds, an unusual school in Brattleboro, Vermont. At overnight camps and day programs operated by Deep Wilds, kids learn how to survive, and even thrive, in the wilderness with little more than the clothes on their backs.

354

At Deep Wilds, Jeannie learned many useful skills, including how to make a fire using only two sticks. If Jeannie were to get lost in the woods now, she would know just how to use branches and leaves to make a shelter sturdy enough to withstand a fierce storm. And if she were to run out of food, no problem: Jeannie has learned to tell the difference between the plants that will nourish her and those that are poisonous. She can even distinguish beavers, bobcats, and coyotes from the appearance of their tracks.

Thanks to Deep Wilds, Jeannie, who lives in southern New Hampshire, has learned other valuable lessons as well: "I really learned about myself. I learned how to be aware of myself in my surroundings and of other people around me. I'm not as self-absorbed as I used to be."

Jeannie's words are music to the ears of her teachers, Mark Morey and Steve Young. When Morey and Young founded Deep Wilds in 1994, their goal was to help kids understand the natural world and find their place in it. The two met during a wilderness survival course in upstate New York. Until then, Steve had been confused about what he wanted to do with his life. But he and Mark discovered they shared the same passions for nature and for teaching.

"Mark wanted to make a difference in the world, and so did I," Steve recalls.

Let's **Think** About...

Do you understand how and why Jeannie changed?
Expository Text

Since then, Deep Wilds has blossomed into a full array of overnight and day camps. For kids ages seven to eleven, Deep Wilds offers the River Otter Day Camp. For girls ages nine to twelve and boys ten to twelve, there's overnight Raccoon Camp. And for teenagers ages thirteen to seventeen, Deep Wilds hosts its Coyote Camp.

Whatever their ages, Deep Wilds campers acquire all the skills necessary to survive in the wilderness. They learn how to forage for Indian cucumbers, wild groundnuts, onions, and nutritious greens, as well as blueberries, raspberries, and blackberries. They also learn to bake berry pies in "wilderness ovens," as Mark calls them, which campers make from mud, clay, stones, and straw. As well, they fashion their own spoons and bowls using hot charcoals and knives. Deep Wilds staffers also teach campers how to make "wilderness sleeping bags" from branches and leaves.

Let's Think About...

List the types of skills that campers of all ages learn at Deep Wilds.
Expository Text

"This is real-time living off the land," says Mark. "We don't mess around. We don't need backpacks, sleeping bags, or tents. This is what our ancestors did to stay alive. *All* our ancestors."

But Deep Wilds is also about having fun. Campers learn to make slings with rope harvested from milkweed fibers. They make the bows and arrows they use from hickory branches and animal feathers. And at the end of the day, they get to break into smaller groups and play all-night tag games, using their wilderness tracking and stalking skills.

Primitive cooking—using a stick to start a fire

When Deep Wilds campers are ready, they get to do a "solo," which entails spending a whole night alone in the woods (under staff supervision, of course). Thirteen-year-old Liam Purvis, who lives in upstate New York, did his first solo last summer. He says it taught him how to be "a more self-reliant individual."

A camper writing a letter in the wild

"When you're out there in the middle of everything, you find out who you are inside the baggy pants and the tee shirt."

As for Jeannie McGartland, she says, "I used to be a fearful person. Now I'm learning how to help others conquer their fears."

Here is a recipe for a snack that nut-allergy-free campers often pack for nourishment on the go—Trail Mix, or GORP (good old raisins and peanuts):

Ingredients:

2 parts sunflower or roasted pumpkin seeds or peanuts

2 parts raisins

2 parts granola

2 parts dried fruit of your choice (e.g., apricots, cranberries, dates)

1 part chocolate chips (optional)

Combine all ingredients in an airtight container. Dried fruits will get sticky after a few days in warm weather, but Trail Mix will keep at room temperature for quite a long time.

Let's Think About...

How do the photographs help you understand and imagine the Deep Wilds experience?
Expository Text

Let's Think About...

Reading Across Texts How would Brian from *Hatchet* have been better off if he'd gone to Deep Wilds?

Writing Across Texts Write about how Brian could have benefited from Deep Wilds.

Common Core State Standards
Language 4.a. Use context (e.g., the overall meaning of a sentence or paragraph; a word's position or function in a sentence) as a clue to the meaning of a word or phrase. **Also Speaking/Listening 1.a., 4.**

READING STREET ONLINE
ONLINE STUDENT EDITION
www.ReadingStreet.com

Vocabulary

Word Endings *-ed, -ing*

Word Structure A word ending is a letter or letters added to the end of a base word. The endings *-ed* and *-ing* can be added to verbs to change their tense. Sometimes they change the part of speech of a word. If you know the meaning of the base word, you can use it with the meaning of the ending to figure out the form or meaning of any new word. Use a dictionary to check the form of the new word.

Practice It! Find the word *slithering* in this sentence at the bottom of p. 338: "Then he heard the *slithering*." Cover the *-ing* ending and read the base word. Think about the meaning of the verb *slither*. See how the *-ing* ending has turned the verb into a noun. And, in the next sentence, the same ending turns *slithering* into an adjective in "a *slithering* brushing sound."

Fluency

Appropriate Phrasing

When you read aloud, pay attention to phrasing, or how you group words and when you pause between them. Group words in a way that reflects their meaning. Use punctuation as the guide to when you should pause between words: a short pause for a comma; a longer pause for a semicolon, colon, or dash; and a full stop for a period.

Practice It! With a partner, take turns reading from *Hatchet*, the two full paragraphs on page 341. Practice appropriate phrasing, using punctuation cues as your guide. Give each other feedback.

Listening and Speaking

When giving a speech, do your research and speak clearly and concisely.

Informational Speech

In a speech, a speaker gives a formal talk to an audience for a specific purpose. An informational speech provides listeners with facts and details about a specific topic.

Practice It! Prepare a three-minute informational speech about one aspect of *Hatchet*. Research the topic you choose in an encyclopedia or on the Internet. Look for key facts and interesting details. Take notes and then make note cards to use during your speech. Using your own words, direct your speech to your classmates. Stick to your time limit and practice first with a partner.

Tips

Listening ...

- Listen attentively.
- Determine the speaker's main ideas.

Speaking ...

- Speak clearly and concisely.
- Time your speech carefully.
- Look up from your note cards to make eye contact.

Teamwork ...

- Ask questions thoughtfully.
- If you can't hear, raise your hand to let the speaker know.

Common Core State Standards

Language 6. Acquire and use accurately grade-appropriate general academic and domain-specific words and phrases; gather vocabulary knowledge when considering a word or phrase important to comprehension or expression. **Also Speaking/Listening 1.c.**

Oral Vocabulary

Let's Talk About

Determination

- Share opinions about what it takes to have determination.

- Discuss what it takes to reach a goal.

- Describe the ways that people show their determination.

READING STREET ONLINE
CONCEPT TALK VIDEO
www.ReadingStreet.com

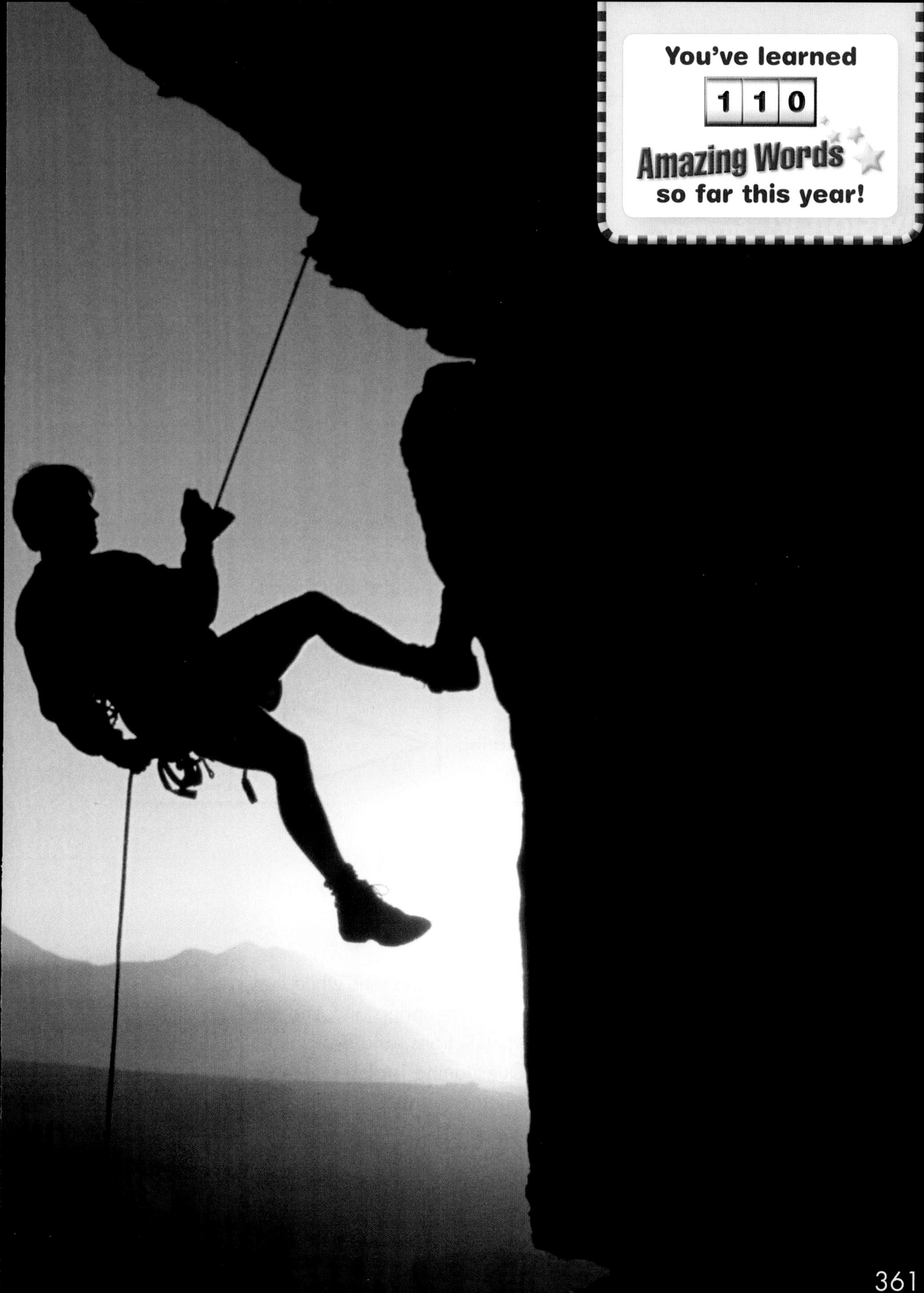

You've learned

110

Amazing Words

so far this year!

Common Core State Standards
Literature 1. Cite textual evidence to support analysis of what the text says explicitly as well as inferences drawn from the text. **Also Literature 2., 6.**

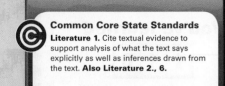

Envision It! | Skill Strategy

Skill

Strategy

Comprehension Skill

🎯 Generalize

- Sometimes authors write broad statements that apply to many examples. These statements are called generalizations. Often, clue words such as *most, all, sometimes, always,* and *never* identify generalizations.

- Generalizations supported by facts and logic are called valid generalizations. Faulty generalizations are not supported by facts and logic.

- Generalizations should always be supported with facts from the text or from your knowledge of the world.

- Use a graphic organizer like the one below to help you generalize as you read "Ashley Helps Out."

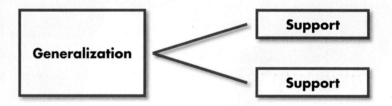

Comprehension Strategy

🎯 Questioning

Active readers ask questions while they read. This can help them understand and evaluate the text, make predictions, and determine the author's purpose. Questioning is also useful when deciding whether or not an author's generalizations are valid or faulty. To evaluate generalizations, ask "Is this statement accurate?" or "Do facts support this statement?"

Ashley Helps Out

Strategy Asking questions before you read can help you predict what a story might be about. What questions come to mind from the title alone? Are they answered as you read?

"I'll get it, Mom," said Ashley. She walked quickly to the buzzer and pressed it so her friend Karina could enter. Ashley loved living in the apartment with her mother, but who wouldn't? Apartments are always better to live in than houses because you don't have to trim the hedges, and they are always luxurious inside.

"Mom, Karina and I are going to the shelter now, okay?"

Skill How can you determine if the author's generalization about apartments is valid or faulty?

"Okay, baby," said a groggy voice from the back bedroom. Ashley's mother usually worked nights and had to sleep during the day.

At the homeless shelter, the girls volunteered to help serve dinner. Although the food wasn't very tasty (it never is at homeless shelters), Ashley dispensed the food with a smile and an encouraging word. Several hours later, the girls finished up and returned to the apartment.

"Mom, we're home," Ashley called as they entered. She and Karina fixed tuna sandwiches and a Greek salad to surprise Ashley's mom.

"Aw, sweetie, you're too much!" she said when she walked into the kitchen.

Skill Is the generalization about food at homeless shelters valid or faulty? Why do you think so?

Your Turn!

▐▐ Need a Review?
See the *Envision It! Handbook* for help with generalizing and questioning.

▶ Ready to Try It?
Use what you've learned about generalizing as you read *When Marian Sang*.

Common Core State Standards

Language 4.a. Use context (e.g., the overall meaning of a sentence or paragraph; a word's position or function in a sentence) as a clue to the meaning of a word or phrase.

Envision It! Words to Know

application

enraged

recital

dramatic	formal
momentous	opera
prejudice	
privileged	

READING STREET ONLINE
VOCABULARY ACTIVITIES
www.ReadingStreet.com

Vocabulary Strategy for

🎯 Suffixes -ic, -ous, -ation

Word Structure A suffix is a word part added to the end of a base word that changes its meaning, the way it is used in a sentence, and sometimes how it is spelled. The suffix -ic adds the meaning "pertaining to or associated with," as in *romantic*. The suffix -ous adds the meaning "full of," as in *joyous*. The suffix -ation makes a noun out of a verb, usually adding the meaning "the state of being," as in *starvation*. Knowing the meaning of a suffix may help you figure out the meaning of a word.

1. Look at the word. See if you recognize a base word in it.

2. Check to see if the suffix -ic, -ous, or -ation has been added to the base word.

3. Ask yourself how the added suffix changes the meaning of the base word.

4. See if your meaning makes sense in the sentence.

As you read "From a Different Planet?" use what you know about the suffixes -ic, -ous, and -ation to figure out the meanings of words.

Words to Write Reread "From a Different Planet?" Select one of the examples given of dramatic moments and write about it. Use as many words from the Words to Know list as you can.

From a Different Planet?

The world of opera is much like another planet to some people. Not only do they have a difficult time trying to understand it, but they also try to avoid it. Admittedly, this mixture of drama and music is much too formal for the taste of many Americans. Opera is quite different from other forms of recital and concert that some people are more familiar with. However, the roots of prejudice against this art form are fed by other oddities.

To begin with, opera is usually sung in a language other than English. That means we are privileged to get to see opera because it opens our eyes to another culture and language. Attending an opera is meant to be enjoyable, not like filling out a job application!

Another fault we find with opera is actually one of its great strengths. It forces us to look at momentous occasions in someone's life. It takes a dramatic moment and multiplies its feelings times ten. Love brings the greatest joy. Loss brings awful sadness and even death. Jealousy drives an enraged lover to murder. The pageant of life is acted out before us with great feeling and color. If we can learn to live in this intense world for a few hours, we come away richer in spirit.

 **Your Turn!**

 Need a Review?
For help using suffixes, see *Words!*

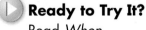 **Ready to Try It?**
Read *When Marian Sang* on pp. 366–379.

When Marian Sang

by Pam Muñoz Ryan
illustrations by Brian Selznick

Genre A **biography** is the story of a real person's
life, written by another person. As you read,
note dates and other clues that indicate
this story is about a real person.

Question of the Week
How can our determination affect our ability to succeed?

367

No one was surprised

that Marian loved to sing. After all, she listened to Father singing in the morning as he dressed. Mother often hummed while she worked in the kitchen. Sometimes Marian and her little sisters, Ethel May and Alyse, sang songs all afternoon.

> *Let us break bread together*
> *   on our knees*
> *Let us break bread together*
> *   on our knees*
> *When I fall on my knees*
> *   with my face to the rising sun*
> *O Lord, have mercy on me.*

However, *her* voice was distinct—strong and velvety and able to climb more than twenty-four notes.

Everyone wanted to hear Marian sing.

Alexander Robinson, the choir director at the Union Baptist Church in South Philadelphia, wanted to hear Marian sing even though she was not quite eight years old and sometimes sang *too* loud. He asked her to perform a duet with her friend Viola Johnson. As Viola sang the high part and Marian sang the low, their harmony blended like a silk braid.

> *Dear to the heart of the Shepherd*
> *Dear are the sheep of His fold*
> *Dear is the love that He gives them*
> *Dearer than silver or gold.*

Church folks started whispering and followed with out-and-out talking about Marian's remarkable gift.

Neighboring churches heard the news and invited Marian to perform. One advertisement said: "COME AND HEAR THE BABY CONTRALTO, TEN YEARS OLD." And people came.

When Marian sang, it was often with her eyes closed, as if finding the music within. Audiences heard not only words, but feelings too: spirited worship, tender affection, and nothing short of joy.

She was chosen for the celebrated People's Chorus, a hundred voices from all the black church choirs in Philadelphia. She was one of the youngest members and had to stand on a chair so those in the back could see the pride of South Philadelphia.

Her father was proud too, but protective. He didn't want anyone taking advantage of his child. Father's love made Marian feel important. When he died after an injury at the Reading Terminal where he sold ice, tragedy filled Marian's heart and sometimes her songs.

> *Were you there when they laid Him*
> *in the tomb?*
> *Were you there when they laid Him*
> *in the tomb?*
> *Oh . . . oh . . . sometimes it causes me*
> *to tremble, tremble, tremble*
> *Were you there when they laid Him*
> *in the tomb?*

Mother was happy for Marian's success but reminded her that no matter what she studied, she should take a little extra time and do it well.

Marian didn't need extra encouragement when it came to singing. She practiced her part of each song and often learned all the other parts too. For her, music was serious business, and more than anything, she hoped to someday go to music school. Church members promised tuition for "our Marian" if she was accepted.

Since Father's death, Marian worked at odd jobs and sang in concert programs in order to help support her family. It wasn't until 1915, when Marian was eighteen, that she finally went to a music school and patiently waited in

line for an application. But the girl behind the counter helped everyone except Marian. Was she invisible?

Finally, the girl said, "We don't take colored!" Her voice sounded like a steel door clanking shut.

Marian knew about prejudice. She had seen the trolley drive past her family as they stood at the corner. She knew that her people were always the last to be helped in a store. But she could not understand how anyone who was surrounded by the spirit and beauty of music could be so narrow-minded.

She felt sick in her stomach and in her heart. Didn't they know that her skin was different but her feelings were the same? Couldn't she be a professional singer if she was Negro?

With unwavering faith, Mother told her that there would be another way to accomplish what would have been done at that school. Marian believed her mother. She took voice lessons in her own neighborhood, continued with the choirs, and sometimes performed at Negro churches and colleges.

When Marian saw a Metropolitan Opera performance of the tragic opera *Madame Butterfly,* thoughts of a formal music education again came to mind. How wonderful it would be to sing on a grand stage, act out a dramatic role, and wear beautiful costumes. The passionate music inspired her and she was determined to study. But opera was simply the sun and the moon—a dream that seemed too far away to reach.

> He's got the wind and the rain
> in His hands
> He's got the sun and the moon
> right in His hands
> He's got the wind and the rain
> in His hands
> He's got the whole world in His hands.

As a young woman in her twenties, Marian was invited to many states to sing. Sometimes she traveled with her accompanist by train where they were seated in the dirty and crowded Jim Crow car reserved for Negroes. When she arrived at her destination, she often sang the same program twice, to separate audiences—one white and one black—or to segregated groups, whites in the best seats and blacks in the balcony. Many times, she was welcomed enthusiastically by her audiences, and then could not get a hotel room because she was Negro.

No matter what humiliations she endured, Marian sang her heart with dignity. Her voice left audiences weeping or in hushed awe as they strained to hold on to the memory of every opulent note.

When Israel was in Egypt's Land
Let my people go
Oppressed so hard they could not stand
Let my people go
Go down Moses
Way down in Egypt's Land
Tell ol' Pharaoh
To let my people go.

Marian still wanted to advance her singing with master teachers. With the help of friends, she was granted an audition with the fierce yet famous Giuseppe Boghetti.

When she arrived at his studio, Mr. Boghetti announced that he didn't have time or room for new students. Too afraid even to look at him, Marian took a deep breath. Slowly, with great emotion, she sang,

"Deep river, my home is over Jordan
Deep river, Lord, I want to cross over
*   into campground*
Don't you want to go to that gospel feast
That promised land where all is peace?
O, deep river, Lord, I want to cross over
*   into campground."*

Marian finally lifted her eyes.

"I will make room for you right away," Mr. Boghetti said firmly, "and I will need only two years with you. After that, you will be able to go anywhere and sing for anybody."

Again, Marian's devoted church community raised the money for her lessons.

Marian worked hard with Mr. Boghetti, and sometimes, for practice, she sang scenes from Italian operas with him. Her recitals now included German songs too, but other languages troubled her. She didn't want simply to sing beautiful words like *Dunkel, wie dunkel in Wald und in Feld!* She wanted to know that the words meant *Dark, how dark in the woods and the fields!*

Other Negro singers had gone overseas to develop their voices and learn foreign languages. Why not her? After all, Europe was different. There, she would be able to sing to mixed audiences and travel without the restrictions put on her people in America.

Marian needed to grow and Mother agreed.

A bundle of trepidation and excitement, Marian boarded the *Ile de France* in October 1927. She had never been so far from her family. She knew her sisters would take good care of Mother, but still she already felt twinges of homesickness.

Sometimes I feel like a motherless child
Sometimes I feel like a motherless child
Sometimes I feel like a motherless child
A long ways from home. A long ways from home.

Sometimes I feel like I'm almost gone
Sometimes I feel like I'm almost gone
Sometimes I feel like I'm almost gone
A long ways from home. A long ways from home.

Marian studied and was eventually invited to perform in concert halls in Norway, Sweden, Finland, and Denmark. The enthusiasm for her singing was so overwhelming that one newspaper in Sweden called it "Marian Fever."

Audiences applauded in London, cheered in Paris, and pounded on the stage for encores in Russia. In Austria, the world-

375

famous conductor, Arturo Toscanini, announced that what he had heard, one was privileged to hear only once in a hundred years.

Marian felt as if she had finally achieved some success. She even asked Mother if there was anything she wanted that would make her happy because now Marian could afford to buy it for her. Mother said that all she wanted was for God to hold Marian in the highest of His hands.

It seemed like she was already there.

Mr. Boghetti had been right. She *could* go anywhere and sing for anyone . . .

. . . until she came home to the United States.

In 1939, Howard University in Washington, D.C., booked a concert with Marian Anderson and began looking for an auditorium big enough to hold the audience she attracted. They decided that the 4,000-seat Constitution Hall would be perfect. But the manager of the hall said it wasn't available *and* no other dates were offered because of their *white performers only* policy.

Marian's agent, Sol Hurok, wrote to the hall manager, pointing out that Marian Anderson was one of the greatest living singers of our time. But it did no good.

Enraged fans wrote letters to the newspaper. In protest, Eleanor Roosevelt, the First Lady of the United States, resigned from the organization that sponsored Constitution Hall.

Howard University then tried to reserve a large high school auditorium from an all-white school. Again, they were denied.

Now teachers were angry and marched in support of Marian
in front of the Board of Education. Washington, D.C., was a boiling
pot about to spill over.

Wasn't there someplace in her own country's capital where
Marian Anderson's voice could be heard?

Committees formed and held meetings. Finally, with President
Roosevelt's approval, the Department of the Interior of the United
States government invited Marian to sing on the steps of the
Lincoln Memorial on Easter Sunday. Her country was offering
her a momentous invitation, but she had concerns. Would people
protest? Was it dangerous? Would anyone come?

Examining her heart, Marian realized that although she was
a singer first and foremost, she also had become a symbol to her
people and she wanted to make it easier for those who would
follow her.

She said yes.

Standing in the shadow of the statue of Lincoln, waiting to be
called out, she read the engraved words:

. . . THIS NATION UNDER GOD SHALL HAVE A NEW BIRTH OF
FREEDOM. . . .

Marian looked out on a river of 75,000 people. Her heart beat
wildly. Would she be able to utter one note?

She took a deep breath and felt the power of her audience's
goodwill surge toward her. Marian's sisters were there, and

Mother too. Marian stood straight and tall. Then she closed her eyes and sang,

> *"My country 'tis of thee*
> *Sweet land of liberty . . .*
> *Let freedom ring!"*

A roaring cheer followed every song. At the end of the program, the people pleaded for more.

When she began her thought-provoking encore,

> *"Oh, nobody knows the trouble I see*
> *Nobody knows my sorrow. . . ."*

. . . silence settled on the multitudes.

For almost sixteen years after the Lincoln Memorial performance, Marian sang for kings and queens, presidents and prime ministers, famous composers and conductors. She received medals, awards, and honorary degrees for her magnificent voice. But there was still one place Marian had not sung. When she was finally invited, a dream came true.

Marian wondered how people would react. No Negro singer had ever done such a thing. She would be the first. But she didn't need to worry. After she signed the contract, someone said, "Welcome home."

On opening night excitement charged the air. As Marian waited in the wings, the orchestra began. Her stomach fluttered. She walked onto the grand stage. Trembling, she straightened her costume and waited for the pounding music she knew to be her cue.

Tonight was her debut with the Metropolitan Opera. At long last, she had reached the sun and the moon.

The curtain parted . . .

. . . and Marian sang.

In order to address the era in which this story took place, the author has, with the greatest respect, stayed true to the references to African Americans as colored or Negro. Marian Anderson referred to herself and others of her race in this manner in the entirety of her autobiography.

Common Core State Standards

Informational Text 1. Cite textual evidence to support analysis of what the text says explicitly as well as inferences drawn from the text. **Also Informational Text 2., Writing 9.**

Envision It! Retell

Think Critically

1. Marian finally reached a goal she had dreamed of for many years. What is a goal you would like to accomplish? How do you plan to accomplish this goal? **Text to Self**

2. The tone of a story shows how the author feels about his or her subject. Read and show parts of *When Marian Sang* that best convey the tone of this biography. **Think Like an Author**

3. Why did so many people show up to see and hear Marian Anderson at the Lincoln Memorial in 1939? **Generalize**

4. What do you think is the most important message the author wants readers to remember about Marian Anderson? **Questioning**

5. **Look Back and Write** Look back at pages 376–378. Summarize the concert Marian gave at the Lincoln Memorial on Easter Sunday in 1939. Explain how this event came about and why it was historically important. Use evidence from the text in your summary.

   Key Ideas and Details • Text Evidence

Meet the Author

Pam Muñoz Ryan

Pam Muñoz Ryan has written more than twenty-five books for young people, often about the Latino experience in the United States. She was born in California's San Joaquin Valley, where summers are sweltering, and when she was a girl, she spent days reading inside the air-conditioned library. She became a lifelong lover of books. While working on *When Marian Sang*, Ms. Ryan grew increasingly interested in her subject. "Like many people, I knew a little about Marian Anderson—specifically her Lincoln Memorial concert. . . . I began researching and became fascinated by the depth of her talent. Marian Anderson was someone of whom all Americans could be proud. I wanted more people to know about her inspiring story." Ms. Ryan and her husband live in Southern California.

Other books about musicians:
Duke Ellington and
Ella Fitzgerald

Use the Reading Log in the *Reader's and Writer's Notebook* to record your independent reading.

Common Core State Standards
Writing 4. Produce clear and coherent writing in which the development, organization, and style are appropriate to task, purpose, and audience.
Also Writing 2.b., Language 1.

Let's Write It!

Key Features of a Biography

- tells the story of someone else's life

- may include the subject's entire life or only a part of the subject's life

- written in third person

READING STREET ONLINE
GRAMMAR JAMMER
www.ReadingStreet.com

Expository

Biography

A **biography** is the story of a person's life, written by someone other than that person. The student model on the next page is an example of a biography.

Writing Prompt *When Marian Sang* is a biography of singer Marian Anderson. Think of an important person you know about. Write a biography of that person.

Writer's Checklist

Remember, you should . . .

✓ write about someone else's life.

✓ only include information from reliable sources.

✓ tell interesting information about the person's life.

✓ never include untrue information or details you have made up about the person's life.

382

Maya Angelou

The talented woman we **know** as Maya Angelou had a different name when she was born in 1928: Marguerite Johnson. She changed her first name to match the way her brother pronounced it when he was a child: "Maya."

Angelou was born in Missouri, but she moved to Arkansas when she was very young. African Americans were not treated well there at that time. They were not allowed to have the same jobs as others and couldn't even eat in the same restaurants where white people **ate**. Angelou had difficulties in her life, but worked hard to help others.

Angelou was interested in dancing, acting, singing, and writing. She moved to New York City in the late 1950s. There, she **found** people who encouraged her to write. She lived in the Harlem section of New York City, where many talented African American writers and artists lived.

Angelou **wrote** many famous books, poems, songs, and speeches. While she **won** awards for her work, she was also working to improve conditions for other people in the world.

Genre
A **biography** tells about true events in someone else's life.

Principal parts of irregular verbs are used correctly.

Writing Trait Conventions
The writer shows control and accuracy in spelling and grammar.

Conventions

Principal Parts of Irregular Verbs

Remember Usually you add -ed to show past tense. **Irregular verbs** do not follow this rule. Instead of having -ed forms to show past tense, irregular verbs usually change to other words: *sing, sang, sung.*

Social Studies in Reading

Genre
Expository Text

- Expository text offers factual information about the natural or social world.

- Though expository text presents facts, it can do so with vivid description.

- Expository texts are usually written in the third person and often follow a logical order.

- Some expository texts may contain portions of speeches or other literary works.

- Read "The Lincoln Memorial" and the excerpt from Dr. Martin Luther King Jr.'s I Have a Dream speech and look for realistic language.

The *Lincoln* Memorial
by Sheri Buckner

Located in Washington, D.C., the Lincoln Memorial commemorates the sixteenth President of the United States, Abraham Lincoln. Sitting on top of a three-tiered stack of steps, the Memorial covers about the same area as a football field. It was designed by Henry Bacon in 1912 to resemble a classic Greek temple. Construction on the Memorial began in 1914 and took eight years, lasting through World War I.

The outside of the building features thirty-six columns, one for each state in the Union at the time of Lincoln's death in 1865. There are three rooms inside. The central room features a statue by Daniel Chester French of the seated Lincoln.

At nineteen feet high, this sculpture is almost as imposing as the Memorial itself. If the statue could stand, it would reach a towering height of twenty-eight feet. The sculptor had a little help with the statue too. Casts, or molds, of Lincoln's hands and face were taken five years before his death. Daniel Chester French used these casts to help him recreate Lincoln's features.

In the south room of the Memorial, Lincoln's Gettysburg Address is etched, or cut, into a stone tablet. Lincoln's second inaugural address is etched on a tablet in the north room. Above the Gettysburg Address is a mural showing the freeing of a slave; above the inaugural address is a mural on the theme of unity between the North and South.

Let's **Think** About...

What are some of the facts that help you recognize this article as expository text?
Expository Text

Let's **Think** About...

How do the descriptions and photos of the Memorial help you understand more about this historic site?
Expository Text

385

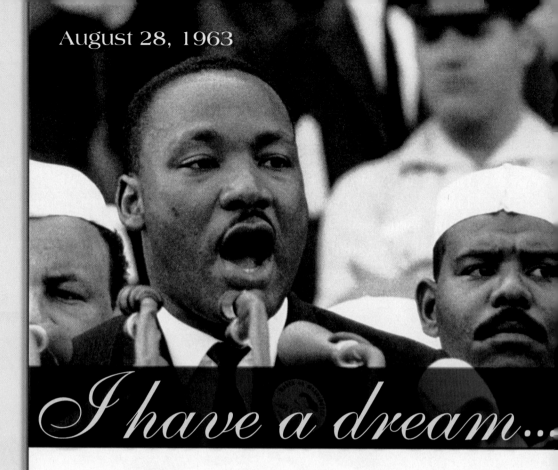

August 28, 1963

I have a dream...

Let's **Think** About...

What vivid details do you find in the article and in Dr. King's famous speech?
Expository Text

. . .*I have a dream that one day this nation will rise up and live out the true meaning of its creed: "We hold these truths to be self-evident, that all men are created equal."*

I have a dream that one day on the red hills of Georgia, the sons of former slaves and the sons of former slave owners will be able to sit down together at the table of brotherhood. . . .

I have a dream that my four little children will one day live in a nation where they will not be judged by the color of their skin but by the content of their character. . . .

Marian Anderson's 1939 Concert at the Memorial

From all walks of life, people have come to be inspired by Abraham Lincoln's determination to save the Union and end the Civil War, as well as his great concern for those people who had been denied their freedom through slavery. The Memorial honors these accomplishments. But it has also become a place where people have come together to draw attention to similar causes and issues.

Since its dedication on May 30, 1922, the Memorial has played host to a number of important historical events. In 1939, singer Marian Anderson gave a concert on the Memorial steps. She was not allowed to sing in any concert halls in Washington, D.C., because of the color of her skin. The free concert, on Easter Sunday, drew more than 70,000 people. It was the largest concert crowd in the history of the city. It was also the first major gathering for the cause of civil rights at the feet of Lincoln. But it would not be the last.

Twenty-four years later, on August 28, 1963, Dr. Martin Luther King Jr. delivered an address to more than 200,000 civil rights supporters at the Memorial. His I Have a Dream speech expressed the hopes of the civil rights movement and moved a nation of citizens. But the Lincoln Memorial is not just a symbol of civil rights. Antiwar protesters came to the Memorial in the late 1960s and early 1970s to raise their voices against the war in Vietnam. In the years since, others have used the Memorial as a backdrop for rallies and protests.

The Lincoln Memorial, besides being a beautiful monument to an important President, has also come to symbolize the ideals of American civil rights.

Let's **Think** About...

What facts about the concert and the speech let you know that they are important historical events?
Expository Text

Let's **Think** About...

Reading Across Texts Make a Venn diagram to compare and contrast how *When Marian Sang* and "The Lincoln Memorial" describe Marian's landmark concert.

Writing Across Texts Using your diagram and vivid details, write your own account of the concert.

Common Core State Standards
Language 4.a. Use context (e.g., the overall meaning of a sentence or paragraph; a word's position or function in a sentence) as a clue to the meaning of a word or phrase. **Also Informational Text 7., 10.**

Let's Learn It!

READING STREET ONLINE
ONLINE STUDENT EDITION
www.ReadingStreet.com

Vocabulary

Suffixes *-ic, -ous, -ation*

Word Structure A suffix is a word part added to the end of a base word to change its meaning. The suffix *-ic* adds the meaning "pertaining to" or "associated with." The suffix *-ous* adds the meaning "full of." The suffix *-ation* adds the meaning "the state of being."

Practice It! Read the words below. Write the base word for each. Then explain how the suffix changes the meaning of the base word, and how understanding the meaning of the suffix helps you understand the meaning of the word.

metallic   nervous   desperation

Fluency

Expression

Remember to show appropriate emotion when you read aloud. Express anger, surprise, sadness, fear, or joy in ways that make sense for what you are reading. If you are reading dialogue, be sure to read it as a character would speak. Pause at commas and ellipses, and stop at end punctuation.

Practice It! With a partner, practice reading aloud page 378 of *When Marian Sang*, from the words "*My country 'tis of thee . . .*" to "*. . . and Marian sang.*" Show appropriate expression as you read, and give each other feedback.

388

Listening and Speaking

When you participate in a presentation to the class, take turns.

Analyze a Photograph

When you analyze a photo, first study what the subject looks like and then observe what background details tell you about the subject.

Practice It! In a small group, look up and print photos of Marian Anderson from the Internet. Based on these photos, what kind of person do you think Marian Anderson was? Do you recognize any other famous people or places in the photos? When you have explanations for your photos, present them to the class.

Tips

Listening . . .

- Pay attention.

- Listen to learn and to enjoy.

- Ask relevant questions.

Speaking . . .

- Give information about the photos you have found, such as dates they were taken.

- Speak clearly and distinctly.

- Take time to answer questions.

Teamwork . . .

- If someone else has found the same photo you did, try to find different information about it to relate to the class.

Common Core State Standards

Language 6. Acquire and use accurately grade-appropriate general academic and domain-specific words and phrases; gather vocabulary knowledge when considering a word or phrase important to comprehension or expression. **Also Speaking/Listening 1.c.**

Oral Vocabulary

Let's Talk About

Meeting Emergencies

- Describe examples of emergencies.

- Share ideas about how people can stay calm in emergencies.

- Ask questions about how a person can prepare for emergencies.

READING STREET ONLINE
CONCEPT TALK VIDEO
www.ReadingStreet.com

390

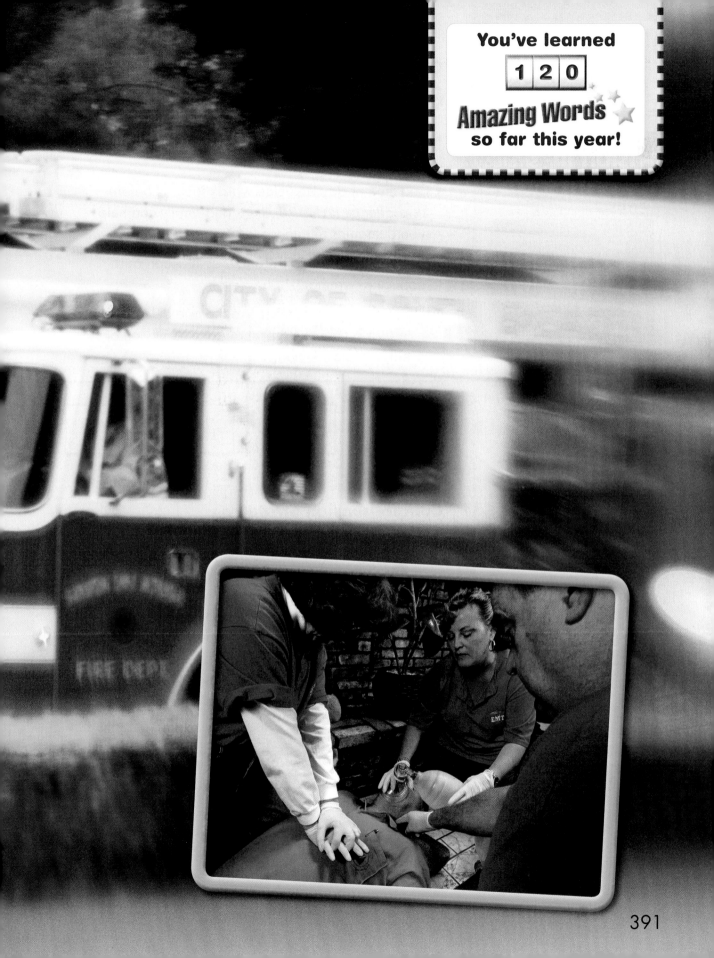

You've learned
1 2 0
Amazing Words
so far this year!

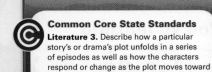

Common Core State Standards

Literature 3. Describe how a particular story's or drama's plot unfolds in a series of episodes as well as how the characters respond or change as the plot moves toward a resolution. **Also Literature 5.**

Envision It! | **Skill Strategy**

Skill

Strategy

READING STREET ONLINE
ENVISION IT! ANIMATIONS
www.ReadingStreet.com

Comprehension Skill

🎯 Sequence

- Sequence is the order in which events take place, from first to last.

- The time of day and clue words such as *before* and *after* or *first, next, then,* and *finally* can help you determine sequence.

- Sequence is used to organize both fiction and nonfiction writing.

- Use a graphic organizer like the one below to establish a time line that shows the sequence of events in "Slow Down!"

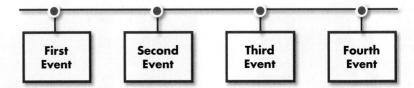

| First Event | Second Event | Third Event | Fourth Event |

Comprehension Strategy

🎯 Predict and Set Purpose

Before reading, good readers predict what will happen or what they will learn and then establish a purpose for reading. Setting a purpose can help you understand a text. When you've finished reading, look back to see if your predictions were accurate.

Slow Down!

Thunder boomed. Glen and Felix huddled under an overhanging rock, but Dave, standing, said, "Let's keep going."

"No way," Felix said, as it thundered and lightning flashed. Glen nodded. Dave scowled.

Once the storm passed, the three young men resumed their hike. They walked through a small woods, then out across a meadow where a herd of elk was grazing. An hour later the three approached a river. It was wide and fast. Glen and Felix walked along the bank to find a safer place to cross, where the water was shallower and the current not so strong. Dave stopped.

"C'mon already!" Dave yelled. Felix and Glen didn't reply; it was crazy to even consider crossing there. A minute later Felix glanced back and saw Dave striding into the deep, churning water. Felix rushed down the bank, but the current was already hurtling Dave downstream.

"The rope!" Felix yelled to Glen, who quickly pulled it out of his pack. Glen threw one end of the rope to Dave and dragged him to shore.

"I could've made it," Dave said, standing on shore. Felix and Glen just rolled their eyes.

Skill What phrase at the beginning of this paragraph is a clue to sequence? What other clue words and phrases are in this paragraph?

Strategy Think of how Dave acted during the storm. What do you predict he will do next?

Skill What do you think the last important event should be on your time line of this story?

Your Turn!

⏸ **Need a Review?** See the *Envision It! Handbook* for help with sequencing and with predicting and setting a purpose for reading.

▶ **Ready to Try It?** Use what you've learned about sequencing as you read *Learning to Swim*.

393

Common Core State Standards
Language 5.c. Distinguish among the connotations (associations) of words with similar denotations (definitions) (e.g., *stingy, scrimping, economical, unwasteful, thrifty*). **Also Language 4.a.**

Envision It! | Words to Know

frantic

stunned

treaded

customary

emphasized

Vocabulary Strategy for

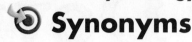

Synonyms

Context Clues When you find a word you do not know, look at words near it. Often the author will provide clues to help you figure out the meaning of the word. One kind of clue is a synonym, a word or phrase that means the same or almost the same thing.

1. Reread the sentence in which the unknown word appears.

2. Look for another word or words that give a clue to the word's meaning.

3. Are two things being compared? Look for nearby words that point to similarity such as *like, also,* or *similarly.*

4. Identify the synonym and think about its meaning.

5. See if this meaning can be substituted for the unknown word. Does the sentence make sense?

Read "Water Safety at the Beach." Look for synonyms to help you figure out the meanings of words.

Words to Write Reread "Water Safety at the Beach." Write what you know about keeping safe in another dangerous situation. Use words from the Words to Know list in your writing.

Water Safety at the Beach

A day at the beach sounds relaxing and fun. Who doesn't enjoy building sand castles, napping, and splashing in the blue-green water? However, if you choose to swim in the ocean, find out about what may be waiting in the waters.

It is customary for a beach to post a sign with any important information about swimming there. On the usual list, safety rules are emphasized. The sign may also focus on when and where the water becomes deep and whether there are riptides, which are dangerous currents that flow swiftly outward from the shore.

People are often stunned to learn that a riptide can pull a good swimmer far out to sea in minutes. Many fight the current, trying to swim against it back to the beach. They become frantic as they see they are losing ground. Despite their frenzied work, they move farther out to sea. Too late, a swimmer may realize that he or she should have treaded water to save strength. The best strategy is to swim at an angle to the current. Passing beyond it, the swimmer can then safely swim back toward shore.

Your Turn!

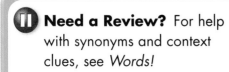 **Need a Review?** For help with synonyms and context clues, see *Words!*

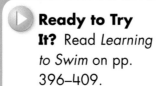 **Ready to Try It?** Read *Learning to Swim* on pp. 396–409.

Learning to Swim

by Kyoko Mori

illustrated by Kazuhiko Sano

I was determined to swim at least twenty-five meters in the front crawl. As we did every summer, my mother, younger brother, and I were going to stay with my grandparents, who lived in a small farming village near Himeji, in Japan. From their house it was a short walk through some rice paddies to the river where my mother had taught me how to swim when I was six. First, she showed me how to float with my face in the water, stretching my arms out in front of me and lying very still so my whole body was like a long plastic raft full of air. If you thought about it that way, my mother said, floating was as easy as just standing around or lying down to sleep. Once I got comfortable with floating, she taught me to kick my legs and paddle my arms so I could move forward, dog-paddling with my face out of the water.

Now I was too old to dog-paddle like a little kid. My mother had tried to teach me the front crawl the previous summer. I knew what I was supposed to do——flutter kick and push the water from front to back with my arms, while keeping my face in the water and turning sideways to breathe——but somehow there seemed to be too much I had to remember all at once. I forgot to turn my head and found myself dog-paddling again after only a few strokes. This summer, I thought, I would work harder and learn to swim as smoothly and gracefully as my mother. Then I would go back to school in September and surprise my classmates and my teachers. At our monthly swimming test, I would swim the whole length of our pool and prove myself one of the better swimmers in our class.

At our school, where we had monthly tests to determine how far each of us could swim without stopping, everyone could tell who the best and the worst swimmers were by looking at our white cloth swimming caps. For every five or ten meters we could swim, our mothers sewed a red or black line on the front of the cap. At the last test we had, in late May, I had made it all the way across the width of the pool in an awkward combination of dog paddle and front crawl, earning the three red lines on my cap for fifteen meters. That meant I was an average swimmer, not bad, not great. At the next test, in September, I would have to try the length of the pool, heading toward the deep end. If I made it all the way across, I would earn five red lines for twenty-five meters. There were several kids in our class who had done that, but only one of them had turned around after touching the wall and swum farther, heading back toward the shallow end. He stopped halfway across, where the water was up to our chests. If he had gone all the way back, he would have earned five black lines, meaning "fifty meters and more." That was the highest mark.

All the kids who could swim the length of the pool were boys. They were the same boys I competed with every winter during our weekly race from the cemetery on the hill to our schoolyard. They were always in the first pack of runners to come back——as I was. I could beat most of them in the last dash across the schoolyard because I was a good sprinter, but in the pool they easily swam past me and went farther. I was determined to change that. There was no reason that I should spend my summers dog-paddling in the shallow end of the pool while these boys glided toward the deep end, their legs cutting through the water like scissors.

My brother and I got out of school during the first week of July and were at my grandparents' house by July 7——the festival of the stars. On that night if the sky was clear, the Weaver Lady and the Cowherd Boy would be allowed to cross the river of Heaven—— the Milky Way——for their once-a-year meeting. The Weaver Lady and the Cowherd Boy were two stars who had been ordered to live on opposite shores of the river of Heaven as punishment for neglecting their work when they were together.

On the night of the seventh, it was customary to write wishes on pieces of colored paper and tie them to pieces of bamboo. On the night of their happy meeting, the Weaver Lady and the Cowherd Boy would be in a generous mood and grant the wishes. I wished, among other things, that I would be able to swim the length of the pool in September. Of course I knew, as my mother reminded me, that no wish would come true unless I worked hard.

Every afternoon my mother and I walked down to the river in our matching navy blue swimsuits. We swam near the bend of the river where the current slowed. The water came up to my chest, and I could see schools of minnows swimming past my knees and darting in and out among the rocks on the bottom. First I practiced the front crawl, and then a new stroke my mother was teaching me: the breaststroke.

"A good thing about this stroke," she said, "is that you come up for air looking straight ahead, so you can see where you are going."

We both laughed. Practicing the front crawl in the river——where there were no black lines at the bottom——I had been weaving wildly from right and left, adding extra distance.

As we sat together on the riverbank, my mother drew diagrams in the sand, showing me what my arms and legs should be doing. Then we lay down on the warm sand so I could practice the motions.

"Pretend that you are a frog," she said. "Bend your knees and then kick back. Flick your ankles. Good."

We got into the water, where I tried to make the motions I had practiced on the sand, and my mother swam underwater next to me to see what I was doing. It was always harder to coordinate my legs and arms in the water, but slowly, all the details that seemed so confusing at first came together, so I didn't have to think about them separately. My mother was a good teacher. Patient and humorous, she talked me out of my frustrations even when

401

I felt sure I would never get better. By mid-August, in both the front crawl and the breaststroke, I could swim easily downstream——all the way to the rock that marked the end of the swimming area. My mother thought that the distance had to be at least fifty meters. When I reached the rock, I would turn around and swim against the current. It was harder going that way. I had to stop several times and rest, panting a little. But swimming in a pool where the water was still, I was sure I could easily go on for twenty-five meters.

That summer, during the third week of August, two of my uncles, their wives, and my mother decided to take a trip to the Sea of Japan for the weekend, bringing my brother, our cousins, and me. All of us kids were excited about going to the seacoast. It was on the less populated side of our country, which faced China, Korea, Russia, and other faraway northern places.

I had never been to that sea, though the river we swam in ended there. When my mother warned me not to swim past the rock that marked off the swimming area——because the current got strong——she said, "We don't want you carried past Ikaba, all the way to the Sea of Japan." Ikaba, a village to the north, got its name, which meant "fifty waves," because the river was so turbulent and wavy there. I imagined the water tumbling down rocky mountains from Ikaba to the faraway sea.

The next morning after breakfast, we dressed in our swimsuits and walked to the beach, which was just down the road from the inn. On a narrow strip of white sand, a few families were clustered around bright red, blue, and pink beach towels. Some people were already in the water. Even a long way out, the water came only to their waists or chests. Big waves were hitting the rocks on a piece of land that jutted out to the sea to our left.

While my uncles and aunts and their kids spread out their beach towels on the sand, my mother and I walked to the water's edge, leaving my brother behind with my cousins. I had never swum in the sea before, but I had seen pictures in my geography book of people floating on the Dead Sea. The writing underneath said that the salt in the water made it easier for people to float.

The sea was cold as my mother and I walked in——much colder than the pool or the river——but it was a hot sunny morning. I knew I would get used to it soon. We went in and splashed around for a while; then I started practicing my front crawl.

I couldn't tell if it really was easier to float. A big wave came and hit my face sideways just as I was turning my head to breathe. I stood up coughing. The water didn't taste like the salt water that I gargled with when I had a cold. Instead, it had a strong bitter taste that stung my nostrils and my throat. My eyes burned.

"Try floating on your back," my mother suggested, flopping back and closing her eyes. "It's easy."

She was right. In the pool I could float on my stomach, but never on my back. But in the sea, my legs and head didn't start sinking while my chest and stomach stayed afloat. All of me was floating; I could almost take a nap.

Once we got tired of floating, my mother and I started jumping the waves. Side by side holding hands, we treaded water, each paddling with one arm instead of two, waiting for the next big wave to come surging our way. If we stopped moving at just the right time, we could crest over the top and glide down to the other side, falling slowly down the gentle slope till another wave came and lifted us up. All around us, other grownups and kids were doing the same thing. There were so many waves coming and going. Sometimes we couldn't see people who were only a few feet away until a wave lifted us up and dropped us almost on top of them. Laughing, we would apologize before another wave swept us away.

I don't know how long we were riding the waves before I noticed that my mother and I hadn't seen anyone for a long time. I thought of another thing too. When we first started, my feet had brushed against the sand bottom almost every time we came down. In the lull between the waves, I'd be standing in the water only up to my chest. That hadn't happened for a while. My feet hadn't touched bottom for at least twenty waves now. I stretched my body as straight as I could, trying to touch bottom with my toes. Nothing. Just as I opened my mouth to point that out to my mother, a big wave came, my head went under, and my hand was swept loose from hers. When I came up again, I was turned around, facing the shore for the first time. I couldn't believe what I saw. The people on the beach looked so small that I couldn't tell our family from anyone else's.

Before I really understood what this meant, another wave rose, my head went under again, and I came up coughing and spitting. My mother, to my relief, was right beside me, treading water.

"Mom," I tried to warn her, but the look on her face told me that she already knew. Her eyes were wide open and there was a big frown between her eyebrows.

"Turn around and swim," she said. "It's not as far as you think."

"I can't," I gasped before a wave pounded me, filling my mouth with a burning, bitter taste.

My mother was beside me again, treading water. She couldn't reach out and hold my hand now, I realized suddenly, because even she needed both of her arms to stay afloat. The water was moving underneath, pulling us sideways. The beach looked farther and farther away. It was all I could do to keep my head from going under.

My mother started flinging her hand upward, trying to wave it from side to side. She was calling for help. That meant we were drowning.

Before the next wave hit us, I kicked my legs as hard as I could and lunged toward my mother, making up the short distance between us. The wave hit. We came up, both of us coughing and spitting, my arms clutched tightly around her neck.

"Listen," my mother said, in a choked-up voice. "You have to let go."

"But I'll drown," I wailed.

She stopped moving her arms for just a moment—long enough to put them around me and draw me closer. I could feel my shoulders, wet and slippery, pressed against her collarbone. "Let go," she said in a voice that sounded surprisingly calm. "Now, or we'll both drown."

By the time the next wave went over my head I was swimming alone, flailing my arms and legs to come up for air, and my mother was beside me. If it weren't for me, I thought, she could easily swim back to the shore. She was a strong swimmer. We were drowning because of me.

"Stay calm," she said, "and float."

We treaded water for a while, and between the waves my mother looked around, no doubt trying to measure the distance we had to swim.

"Look over there," she said, turning away from the shore and pointing toward the piece of land jutting into the sea. "We can't swim back to the beach, but we can make it to those rocks."

The waves had been pushing us sideways, toward the rocks, as well as farther from the shore. From where we were now, the tip of that land was about as far away as I could swim in the river without stopping if the current was with me. That piece of land was our last chance. If I couldn't make it there, I would surely drown. Heading toward the rocks meant turning away from the beach completely, swimming farther out to sea. If I drifted too far to the side and missed the tip of the land, there wouldn't be anywhere else. Every time I came up for air, I'd better be looking at those rocks, making sure they were still in my sight. The only stroke that would allow me to do that was the breaststroke.

I took a big breath and started kicking my legs with my knees bent, flicking my ankles the way my mother had taught me in the river. The arms, I told myself, should draw nice big arcs, not a bunch of little frantic circles that would make me tired. My mother swam right beside me in her easy graceful breaststroke——she was

between me and the rest of the sea, guiding me toward the rocks, showing me how I should swim.

The waves we had been fighting were suddenly helping us. In just a few minutes, my mother and I stood on the rocky ground of that slip of land, looking back toward the shore. My legs felt wobbly, and I was breathing hard. The two of us looked at each other, too stunned to say anything. For a while we just stood trying to catch our breath, listening to the waves as they continued to crash at our feet. Then we started walking. The rocks formed a steep cliff above us, but at the bottom, there was enough room for us to walk side by side. Cautiously we picked our way back to the beach, trying not to cut our feet or slip back into the sea. On the way we noticed a group of people gathered on the sand, watching us. When we got there, they came rushing toward us. They were my uncles and several other men we had never seen.

"I waved for help," my mother said to them.

"We thought you were just waving for fun," one of my uncles said. "We didn't know anything was wrong until we saw you walking on those rocks."

One of the strangers, an old man in a shirt and trousers, shook his head. "You got caught in a riptide," he said. "A fisherman drowned there a few years ago."

Several people were talking all at once, saying how lucky we were, but I wasn't listening very carefully. My brother was running toward us. Behind him, the beach was more crowded than when we had first started swimming. For the first time, I noticed an ice cream stand not too far away.

"Mom," I said. "My throat hurts from the seawater. I would love some ice cream."

When my mother told people the story of our near drowning, that was the detail she always emphasized——how I had calmly asked for ice cream as soon as we were back on the beach. Every time we remembered this incident, she said to me, "You are a brave girl. You let go of me when you had to."

The way she talked about it, our experience in the Sea of Japan was a great adventure that proved my courage: If I could swim well enough not to drown in a place where a fisherman had died in a riptide, then I never again had to worry about drowning. I did not question her logic——though years later I realized that my mother had said just the right things to prevent me from becoming afraid.

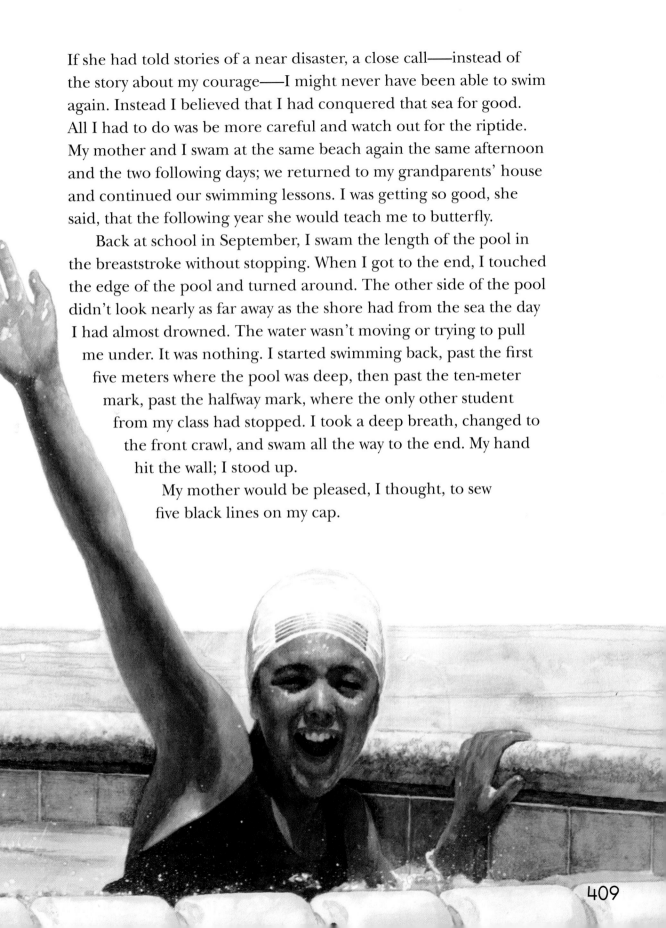

If she had told stories of a near disaster, a close call——instead of the story about my courage——I might never have been able to swim again. Instead I believed that I had conquered that sea for good. All I had to do was be more careful and watch out for the riptide. My mother and I swam at the same beach again the same afternoon and the two following days; we returned to my grandparents' house and continued our swimming lessons. I was getting so good, she said, that the following year she would teach me to butterfly.

Back at school in September, I swam the length of the pool in the breaststroke without stopping. When I got to the end, I touched the edge of the pool and turned around. The other side of the pool didn't look nearly as far away as the shore had from the sea the day I had almost drowned. The water wasn't moving or trying to pull me under. It was nothing. I started swimming back, past the first five meters where the pool was deep, then past the ten-meter mark, past the halfway mark, where the only other student from my class had stopped. I took a deep breath, changed to the front crawl, and swam all the way to the end. My hand hit the wall; I stood up.

My mother would be pleased, I thought, to sew five black lines on my cap.

Envision It! Retell

READING STREET ONLINE
STORY SORT
www.ReadingStreet.com

Think Critically

1. How would you apply the lessons of this story to a challenge in your life, such as taking a test? **Text to Self**

2. No screaming, no choking, no thrashing about: Kyoko Mori's autobiographical account is told so calmly that you may have to think twice before you realize what's happening. Find a sample section to read aloud to demonstrate this calm style. **Think Like an Author**

3. At the beginning of her story, on page 398, Kyoko Mori tells about how she first learned to swim. What swimming basics did she learn first, second, and last in that passage? **Sequence**

4. What do you predict about Kyoko Mori's future as a swimmer? What did you read in the story that helps you make that prediction? **Predict and Set Purpose**

5. **Look Back and Write** Look at pages 407–409 to recall how Kyoko's mother helped her not to be afraid after the near-drowning. In your own words, write what strategy the mother used. Provide evidence to support your answer. **Key Ideas and Details • Text Evidence**

Meet the Author

Kyoko Mori

Kyoko Mori was born in Kobe, Japan, where she learned many ways to be creative from her mother and her mother's family. Later, after her mother's death and a difficult adolescence, Ms. Mori moved to the United States to attend college. After graduate school, where she studied creative writing, she became an award-winning novelist and poet and also a teacher of creative writing. Ms. Mori says, "Much of what I write is based on the things I know. For instance I write about growing up in Japan, being a runner or a gardener, certain feelings I had as a teenager about wanting to be honest and wanting to be liked." Her stories come from what might have happened in her life but not what actually did happen. She says, "I think that the best thing about being a writer is that we get to make up things and tell the truth at the same time."

Other autobiographies:
The Invisible Thread and
Surprising Myself

Use the Reading Log in the *Reader's and Writer's Notebook* to record your independent reading.

411

Common Core State Standards
Writing 3.a. Engage and orient the reader by establishing a context and introducing a narrator and/or characters; organize an event sequence that unfolds naturally and logically. **Also Language 1., 3.a.**

Narrative

Autobiographical Sketch

An **autobiographical sketch** tells about the life or an incident in the life of the writer. The student model on the next page is an example of an autobiographical sketch.

Writing Prompt *Learning to Swim* is an autobiographical sketch from author Kyoko Mori. Now, write your own autobiographical sketch.

Let's Write It!

Key Features of an Autobiographical Sketch

- describes a true event or events in a writer's life
- includes the writer's thoughts and feelings
- may be part of a longer autobiography
- uses first-person point of view

READING STREET ONLINE
GRAMMAR JAMMER
www.ReadingStreet.com

Writer's Checklist

Remember, you should ...

✓ write about a real event from your life.

✓ include specific details as you describe the event or experience.

✓ write with first-person point of view.

✓ vary sentence beginnings to create a natural flow or rhythm.

My tenth birthday was one of the best birthdays that I ever had. My birthday is October 10, the tenth day of the tenth month of the year — so I felt extra special turning ten years old on this day.

On my birthday, my older sister picked me up from school. I didn't know where we were going, but I was just happy not to be on the bus. She drove the car toward the city. Finally, we pulled up in front of a building that had pink flowers planted in front of it. I had no idea where she was taking me. When we walked inside, the first thing I noticed was a sweet smell. We sat down at a small table. I remember there being a lot of pastel colors inside the place.

A waiter brought us menus, but my sister immediately asked him for two slices of red velvet cake. I became excited — I had only seen pictures of this kind of cake! I took a bite and was surprised that it didn't taste like a cherry, since it was so red. Instead, it tasted like my favorite flavor, chocolate. That delicious taste was only the start of the great birthday I shared with my family.

Writing Trait Sentences
The author avoids beginning sentences with the same word or phrase.

Genre
An **autobiographical sketch** tells a real story about the writer's life.

Verbs, objects, and subject complements are used correctly.

Conventions

Verbs, Objects, and Subject Complements

Remember A **direct object** follows an action **verb** and tells who or what receives the action (*Chris told a secret*). An **indirect object** tells to whom or what the action is done (*Chris told **Bill** a secret*). A **subject complement** tells who or what the subject is or is like.

413

21st Century Skills
INTERNET GUY

Use quotes in a **search engine. "Capital of Minnesota"** finds only pages with all the words together. **Capital of Minnesota** finds every page with at least one word. Which is better?

- Use a tool called a search engine to find Web sites on the Internet.

- Brainstorm a list of important words, called keywords, that you want to search for.

- Type your keyword(s) into the search engine window. Then click on the Search button.

- Each item on the list is a link to a Web site that contains your keyword(s). Click on links that look good.

- Read "Staying Safe in the Water" and notice how one link can lead to another.

414

Staying Safe in the Water

Just about everyone likes to be near or in water, whether at a pool, river, lake, or ocean. Water can pose a challenge though. If you wanted to know more about safety in the water, you could type the keywords *water safety* into a search engine and click SEARCH.

The search engine you choose might come up with a long list of Web sites about water safety. You might find results such as those below. You must decide which link will give you the information you want. You decide to click on the second link, *Water Safety.*

http://www.url.here

Search Engine water safety [Search]

Beach Safety. Play It Safe at the Beach tips, safety advice, printable worksheets, and more about **beach safety.**

Water Safety. Playing at the beach, at a water park, by a lake, or in a pool can be a real treat on a hot day. But water can also mean danger.

Keeping Kids Safe at the Beach. Articles. From sun to swimming, we've got the goods on **beach safety.**

A computer screen such as this one appears. Look at the links. You then click on *Beaches* to learn more about ocean safety.

Water Safety

Check out more stuff below!

- Swimming Pools
- Lakes and Ponds
- **Beaches**
- Water Parks

Drowning is the second most common cause of death from injuries among kids under the age of fourteen. Drowning can happen so suddenly—sometimes in less than two minutes after your head goes under the water—that often there's precious little time for someone to rescue you. Many drownings and near-drownings of youths occur when they accidentally fall into a swimming pool, but accidents can occur anywhere—at someone's home or even at your own house. That's why you need to know how to be safe around water.

How do you know which of the three results was clicked on to bring up this Web page?

You find lots of useful information from the *Beaches* link.

View   Favorites   Tools   Help

http://www.url.here

Beaches

Check out more stuff below!

- Swimming Pools
- Lakes and Ponds
- **Beaches**
- Water Parks

"Never underestimate the power of the ocean. It isn't like a swimming pool. The ocean is so large that it's harder to spot you if you get in trouble," Dr. Kate Cronan says. In some places swimmers may encounter strong undertows or ocean currents.

Rip currents are so strong that they can carry swimmers away from shore before they know what's going on. If you are caught in a rip current, swim parallel to the shore until the water stops pulling you, and then swim back to shore.

You probably won't see any sharks, but jellyfish and Portuguese men-of-war are another story. These umbrella-shaped, nearly transparent animals can grow to be as large as several feet in diameter! They are often found floating near the shore. Getting stung is no fun—it can hurt and blister your skin. If you get stung, tell an adult immediately.

More Advice on Beach Safety

You decide to click on the link for more advice on beach safety.

jellyfish

What information would I likely find if I clicked on *Swimming Pools*?

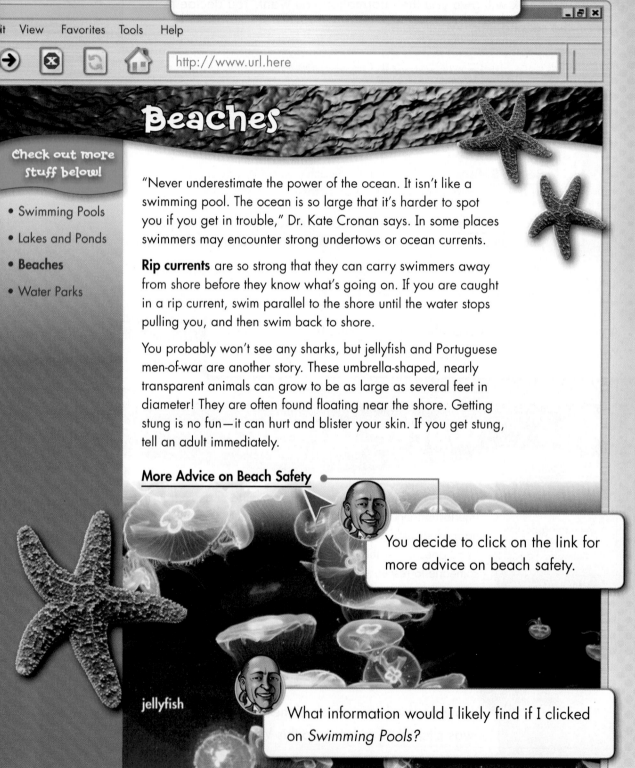

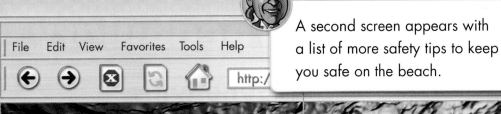

A second screen appears with a list of more safety tips to keep you safe on the beach.

File   Edit   View   Favorites   Tools   Help

http:/

Beaches

Check out more stuff below!

- Swimming Pools
- Lakes and Ponds
- **Beaches**
- Water Parks

Here's some other good advice for the beach:

- Never swim alone, and always swim where a lifeguard can see you.

- Wear protective footwear, especially on rocky beaches.

- Don't swim out too far.

- Never fake trouble or calls for help.

- Don't turn your back to the ocean—you may be swept into the water by waves that come without warning.

417

Common Core State Standards
Language 5.c. Distinguish among the connotations (associations) of words with similar denotations (definitions) (e.g., *stingy, scrimping, economical, unwasteful, thrifty*). **Also Informational Text 10., Speaking/Listening 4., Language 4.a.**

Let's Learn It!

Vocabulary

Synonyms

Context Clues Remember that synonyms are words that have the same or similar meanings. They can help you determine the meaning of a word by serving as context clues for that word in a sentence.

Practice It! Locate each of the Words to Know in *Learning to Swim* to see how it is used in the text. Determine if a sentence contains a synonym that provides a clue to the word's meaning. Create a list of the Words to Know and their synonyms that you find in the text. Then use a thesaurus to find more synonyms for the words. When you are finished, exchange your list with a partner.

Fluency

Rate

Adjusting your reading rate, or speed, allows you to better understand a story or article. Slow your reading when you read sentences with important information or many facts. Speed up a little when you are reading more descriptive passages.

Practice It! With a partner, read aloud from *Learning to Swim*. Start on page 404, at "I don't know how long. . . ." and continue to the middle of page 405. Notice how you naturally vary the rate of your reading to emphasize the key points and words that the characters say. Give each other feedback.

Listening and Speaking

Acknowledge the contributions of others in all classroom projects.

How-to Demonstration

A how-to demonstration describes how to do something. Its purpose is to teach others how to do an activity or make something. The process is told in steps.

Practice It! With a partner, using information from *Learning to Swim* and the Internet, demonstrate how to do two different swimming strokes. Make a drawing and write steps for each stroke. Order the steps. Then present your demonstration to the class.

Tips

Listening . . .

- Follow oral instructions that involve a series of related steps.

- Take notes on multi-step directions.

Speaking . . .

- Use conventions to communicate each step as effectively as you can.

- Use gestures to communicate the action to be taken at each step.

Teamwork . . .

- Work with your partner to develop both visual aids and instructions.

- Identify strengths and weaknesses in your demonstration and redo it as necessary.

Let's Talk About

Trust

- Express opinions about why trust is important.

- Ask questions about what trustworthiness is.

- Share ideas about how trust is earned.

READING STREET ONLINE
CONCEPT TALK VIDEO
www.ReadingStreet.com

Common Core State Standards

Literature 2. Determine a theme or central idea of a text and how it is conveyed through particular details; provide a summary of the text distinct from personal opinions or judgments. **Also Literature 6.**

Envision It! | Skill Strategy

Skill

Strategy

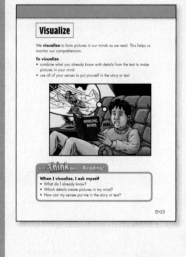

Comprehension Skill

🎯 Generalize

- A generalization is a broad statement or rule that applies to many examples.

- Sometimes when you read, you can generalize. When you are given ideas about several things or people and you can make a statement that applies to all of them, you are generalizing.

- Valid generalizations are supported by examples, facts, or good logic. Invalid generalizations are not supported.

- Use a graphic organizer like the one below to make a generalization about "Tall-Tale Town."

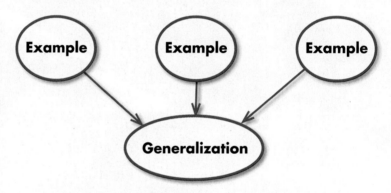

Comprehension Strategy

🎯 Visualize

Good readers visualize, or create mental images, to make sense of what they read. They picture themselves seeing, hearing, feeling, tasting, and smelling things or events in a text. Visualizing is a good way to understand the characters, setting, and events of a story.

Tall-Tale Town

Rahim was the new kid in town. One day he ventured out, looking to shoot some hoops and make some friends in the process.

"Hi," he said, as he approached a boy mowing the lawn. "Like to play basketball?"

"Sure, just yesterday I was shooting some hoops at the playground and made 551 free throws in a row," the boy said.

"That's astounding!" exclaimed Rahim.

"Yeah, but I can't play now. I have to finish mowing the lawn. Maybe later."

Rahim continued on until he came to a boy washing the family car. "Like to play basketball?" he asked.

"Love to. I scored 242 points in a game once. Would have scored more, but my coach took me out for the second half. My knee is bothering me now. Maybe some other time."

Rahim was speechless. "Like to play basketball?" he asked a third boy, a little hesitantly.

"Nope. Soccer's my game. Last week I blocked 863 shots on goal. We won the game, 1–0."

Rahim slowly wandered home.

"How'd it go, honey?" his mother inquired as he entered the back door. "Do you think you'll like it here?"

Rahim paused. "Yeah. Who wouldn't? We just moved to the greatest, smartest, most talented town in the world!"

Strategy Visualize the boy mowing the lawn. What do you see, hear, and smell?

Skill What can you generalize from how the second boy responds? Explain.

Skill What generalization might be suggested about the people in the town?

Your Turn!

Need a Review?
See the *Envision It! Handbook* for help with generalizing and visualizing.

Ready to Try It?
Use what you've learned about generalizing as you read *Juan Verdades: The Man Who Couldn't Tell a Lie.*

Envision It! | Words to Know

confidently

dismounted

flourish

distressed

fulfill

permission

repay

vigorously

Vocabulary Strategy for
🔄 Prefixes *re-* and *dis-*

Word Structure When you come across a word you do not know, see if the word begins with a prefix that might help you to figure out the meaning of the word. For example, the prefix *re-* usually adds the meaning "again" to a word, as in *reschedule*, or "back," as in *rewind*. Usually, the prefix *dis-* adds the meaning "to remove" or "the opposite of," as in *disrespect*. Follow these steps when you come across a word that has a prefix.

1. Cover the prefix.
2. Look at the base word. See if you know what it means.
3. Uncover the prefix. Think about its meaning.
4. Combine the meaning of the prefix with the meaning of the base word.
5. Check the context. Does this meaning make sense in this sentence?

Read "Kindness for Kindness." Use prefixes to help you figure out the meanings of the words.

Words to Write Reread "Kindness for Kindness." What could you do to help someone you love? Write about your plan. Use as many words from the Words to Know list as you can.

Kindness for Kindness

As she rode along the lane, Terry tried to think of a way to repay Miss Posy. The elderly woman had been the one to fulfill Terry's dream of owning her own horse. Miss Posy had offered Terry a job cleaning stalls and grooming horses on her dude ranch. After a year, Terry had enough money to buy Biscuit from Miss Posy. He was old but gentle and easy to ride, and Terry loved the horse to an unreasonable degree.

Arriving at the ranch after a ride, Terry dismounted and put Biscuit in a pasture to graze. Then she got to work. Terry moved confidently among the horses in the barn. As she vigorously forked clean straw into stalls, she thought of something she could do for her employer.

Last winter, Miss Posy had suffered a stroke and now spent much of her time sitting on the porch. This distressed Terry, who knew how much Miss Posy loved walking outdoors. Smiling, Terry marched to the porch and got permission for her project. Soon a beautiful big garden of flowers began to flourish next to Miss Posy's porch.

Your Turn!

⏸ **Need a Review?** For additional help using prefixes, see *Words!*

▶ **Ready to Try It?** Read *Juan Verdades: The Man Who Couldn't Tell a Lie* on pp. 426–439.

425

Juan Verdades

The Man Who Couldn't Tell a Lie

 retold by Joe Hayes
illustrated by Joseph Daniel Fiedler

Question of the Week
How do we demonstrate trustworthiness?

427

One late summer day a group of wealthy rancheros was gathered on the village plaza, joking and laughing and discussing events on their ranches.

One of the men, whose name was don Ignacio, had a fine apple tree on his land. The rancher called the apple tree *el manzano real*—the royal apple tree—and was extremely proud of it. It had been planted by his great-grandfather, and there was something about the soil it grew in and the way the afternoon sun struck it that made the apple tree flourish. It gave sweeter and more flavorful fruit than any other tree in the country round about.

Every rancher for miles around knew about *el manzano real*, and each year they all hoped don Ignacio would give them a small basket of its sweet fruit. And so each of the ranchers asked don Ignacio how the fruit of the apple tree was doing. To each one don Ignacio replied, "It's doing beautifully, amigo, beautifully. My foreman takes perfect care of the tree, and every evening he reports how the fruit is ripening."

When don Ignacio said this to his friend don Arturo, the other man replied, "Do you mean to say, don Ignacio, that you don't tend your magnificent tree yourself? How can you have such faith in your employee? Maybe he's not doing all he says he is. Maybe he's not telling you the truth."

Don Ignacio wagged a finger at his friend. "*Mi capataz* has never failed me in any way," he insisted. "He has never told me a lie."

"Are you sure, *compadre?*" said don Arturo. "Are you sure that he has never lied to you?"

"Absolutely certain, *compadre,* absolutely certain. The young man doesn't know how to tell a lie. His name is Juan Valdez, but everyone calls him Juan Verdades because he is so truthful."

"I don't believe it. There never was an employee who didn't lie to his boss. I'm sure I can make him tell you a lie."

"Never," replied the proud employer.

The two friends went on arguing good-naturedly, but little by little they began to raise their voices and attract the attention of the other men on the plaza.

Finally don Arturo declared loudly, "I'll bet you whatever you want that within two weeks at the most I'll make this Juan Verdades tell you a lie."

"All right," replied don Ignacio. "It's a deal. I'll bet my ranch against yours that you can't make my foreman lie to me."

The other ranchers laughed when they heard that. "Ho-ho, don Arturo," they said, "now we'll see just how sure you are that you're right."

"As sure as I am of my own name," said don Arturo. "I accept the bet, don Ignacio. But you must allow me the freedom to try anything I wish." The two friends shook hands, and the other men in the group agreed to serve as witnesses to the bet.

The gathering broke up, and don Arturo and don Ignacio rode confidently away toward their ranches. But as don Arturo rode along thinking of what he had just done, he no longer felt so sure of himself. When he arrived home and told his wife and daughter about the bet, his wife began to cry. "What will we do when we lose our ranch?" she sobbed. And don Arturo began to think he had made a terrible mistake.

But his daughter, whose name was Araceli and who was a very bright and lively young woman, just laughed and said, "Don't worry, *Mamá*. We're not going to lose our ranch."

Araceli suggested to her father that he make up some excuse for them all to spend the next two weeks at don Ignacio's house. "If we're staying on don Ignacio's ranch," she said, "we'll surely discover a way to come out the winners."

The next day don Arturo rode to don Ignacio's ranch and told his friend, "My men are mending the walls of my house and giving them a fresh coat of whitewash. It would be more convenient for my family to be away. Could my wife and daughter and I stay at your house for a while?"

"Of course, my friend," don Ignacio answered. "Feel perfectly free."

That afternoon don Arturo and his family moved into don Ignacio's house, and the next morning Araceli rose at dawn, as she always did at home, and went to the ranch kitchen to prepare coffee. The foreman, Juan Verdades, was already there, drinking a cup of coffee he had made for himself and eating a breakfast of leftover tortillas. She smiled at him, and he greeted her politely: *"Buenos días, señorita."* And then he finished his simple breakfast and went off to begin his day's work.

That night don Arturo and his daughter made up a plan. Araceli rose before dawn the next day and went to the kitchen to prepare coffee and fresh tortillas for the foreman. She smiled sweetly as she offered them to Juan. He returned her smile and thanked her very kindly. Each morning she did the same thing, and Juan Verdades began to fall in love with Araceli, which was just what the girl and her father expected.

What Araceli hadn't expected was that she began to fall in love with Juan Verdades too and looked forward to getting up early every morning just to be alone with him. She even began to wish she might end up marrying the handsome young foreman. Araceli continued to work on the plan she and her father had made—but she now had a plan of her own as well.

Of course, Juan knew that he was just a worker and Araceli was the daughter of a wealthy ranchero, so he didn't even dream of asking her to marry him. Still, he couldn't help trying to please her in every way. So one morning when they were talking, Juan said to Araceli, "You're very kind to have fresh coffee and warm food ready for me every morning and to honor me with the pleasure of your company. Ask me for whatever you want from this ranch. I'll speak to don Ignacio and see that it's given to you."

This is exactly what the girl and her father thought would happen. And she replied just as they had planned. It was the last thing Juan expected to hear.

"There's only one thing on this ranch I want," she said. "I'd like to have all the apples from *el manzano real*."

The young man was very surprised, and very distressed as well, because he knew he couldn't fulfill her wish.

"I could never give you that," Juan said. "You know how don Ignacio treasures the fruit of that tree. He might agree to give you a basket of apples, but no more. I would have to take the fruit without permission, and then what would I say to don Ignacio? I can give you anything else from the ranch, but not what you're asking for."

With that the conversation ended, and they separated for the day. In the evening Juan reported to don Ignacio, and they exchanged the exact words they said every evening:

"Good evening, *mi capataz*," the rancher said.

"Good evening, *mi patrón*," replied the foreman.

"How goes it with my cattle and land?"

"Your cattle are healthy, your pastures are green."

"And the fruit of *el manzano real*?"

"The fruit is fat and ripening well."

The next morning Juan and Araceli met again. As they sipped their coffee together, Juan said, "I truly would like to repay you for the kindness you've shown me. There must be something on this ranch you would like. Tell me what it is. I'll see that it's given to you."

But again Araceli replied, "There's only one thing on this ranch I want: the apples from *el manzano real*."

Each day they repeated the conversation. Araceli asked for the same thing, and Juan said he couldn't give it to her. But each day Juan was falling more hopelessly in love with Araceli. Finally, just the day before the two weeks of the bet would have ended, the foreman gave in. He said he would go pick the apples right then and bring them to the girl.

Juan hitched up a wagon and drove to the apple tree. He picked every single apple and delivered the wagonload of fruit to Araceli. She thanked him very warmly, and his spirits rose for a moment. But as he mounted his horse to leave, they sank once again. Juan rode away alone, lost in his thoughts, and Araceli hurried off to tell her father

the news and then to wait for a chance to talk to don Ignacio too.

Juan rode until he came to a place where there were several dead trees. He dismounted and walked up to one of them. Then he took off his hat and jacket and put them on the dead tree and pretended it was don Ignacio. He started talking to it to see if he could tell it a lie.

"Good evening, *mi capataz*," he pretended he heard the tree say.

"Good evening, *mi patrón*."

"How goes it with my cattle and land?"

"Your cattle are healthy, your pastures are green."

"And the fruit of *el manzano real*?"

"The . . . the crows have carried the fruit away. . . ."

But the words were hardly out of his mouth when he heard himself say, "No, that's not true, *mi patrón*. I picked the fruit. . . ." And then he stopped himself.

He took a deep breath and started over again with, "Good evening, *mi capataz*."

And when he reached the end, he sputtered, "The . . . the wind shook the apples to the ground, and the cows came and ate them. . . . No, they didn't, *mi patrón*. I . . . ."

He tried over and over, until he realized there was no way he could tell a lie. But he knew he could never come right out and say what he had done either. He had to think

of another way to tell don Ignacio. He took his hat and coat from the stump and sadly set out for the ranch.

All day long Juan worried about what he would say to don Ignacio. And all day long don Ignacio wondered what he would hear from his foreman, because as soon as Araceli had shown the apples to her father, he had run gleefully to tell don Ignacio what had happened.

"Now you'll see, *compadre*," don Arturo gloated. "You're about to hear a lie from Juan Verdades."

Don Ignacio was heartsick to think that all his apples had been picked, but he had agreed that don Arturo could try whatever he wanted. He sighed and said, "Very well, *compadre*, we'll see what happens this evening."

Don Arturo rode off to gather the other ranchers who were witnesses to the bet, leaving don Ignacio to pace nervously up and down in his house. And then, after don Ignacio received a visit from Araceli and she made a request that he couldn't deny, he paced even more nervously.

All the while, Juan went about his work, thinking of what he would say to don Ignacio. That evening the foreman went as usual to make his report to his employer, but he walked slowly and his head hung down. The other ranchers were behind the bushes listening, and Araceli and her mother were watching anxiously from a window of the house.

The conversation began as it always did:

"Good evening, *mi capataz*."

"Good evening, *mi patrón*."

"How goes it with my cattle and land?"

"Your cattle are healthy, your pastures are green."

"And the fruit of *el manzano real*?"

Juan took a deep breath and replied:

"Oh, *patrón*, something terrible happened today.

Some fool picked your apples and gave them away."

Don Ignacio pretended to be shocked and confused. "Some fool picked them?" he said. "Who would do such a thing?"

Juan turned his face aside. He couldn't look at don Ignacio. The rancher asked again, "Who would do such a thing? Do I know this person?"

Finally the foreman answered:

"The father of the fool is my father's father's son.

The fool has no sister and no brother.

His child would call my father 'grandfather.'

He's ashamed that he did what was done."

Don Ignacio paused for a moment to think about Juan's answer. And then, to Juan's surprise, don Ignacio grabbed his hand and started shaking it excitedly.

The other ranchers ran laughing from their hiding places. "Don Arturo," they all said, "you lose the bet. You must sign your ranch over to don Ignacio."

"No," said don Ignacio, still vigorously shaking Juan's hand. He glanced toward the window where Araceli was watching and went on: "Sign it over to don Juan Verdades. He has proved that he truly deserves that name, and he deserves to be the owner of his own ranch as well."

Everyone cheered and began to congratulate Juan. Don Arturo's face turned white, but he gritted his teeth and forced a smile. He shook Juan's hand and then turned to walk away from the group, his shoulders drooping and his head bowed down.

But Araceli came running from the house and put her arm through her father's. "*Papá,*" she said, "what if Juan Verdades were to marry a relative of yours? Then the ranch would stay in the family, wouldn't it?"

Everyone heard her and turned to look at the girl and her father. And then Juan spoke up confidently. "*Señorita* Araceli, I am the owner of a ranch and many cattle. Will you marry me?"

Of course she said she would, and don Arturo heaved a great sigh. "Don Juan Verdades," he said, "I'll be proud to have such an honest man for a son-in-law." He beckoned his wife to come from the house, and they both hugged Juan and Araceli.

The other ranchers hurried off to fetch their families, and a big celebration began. It lasted all through the night, with music and dancing and many toasts to Juan and Araceli. And in the morning everyone went home with a big basket of delicious apples from *el manzano real*.

Common Core State Standards
Literature 1. Cite textual evidence to support analysis of what the text says explicitly as well as inferences drawn from the text. **Also Literature 2., Writing 9.**

Envision It! | Retell

Think Critically

1. Think about times when it is difficult to tell the truth. Give three examples of situations in which some people find it hard not to tell a lie. **Text to Self**

2. Joe Hayes is a storyteller, so it's no wonder that a riddle appears in this story, for riddles find their way into stories everywhere. Why does the storyteller tell a riddle instead of having Juan say, "I am ashamed to admit it, but I picked those apples"? **Think Like an Author**

3. Is it a generalization to say that Juan Verdades never lies? Why or why not? **Generalize**

4. Reread page 431. Put yourself in the picture when Araceli goes to the kitchen at dawn. What do you see, hear, feel, taste, and smell? **Visualize**

5. **Look Back and Write** Juan Verdades makes an offer that gets him into trouble. Look back at page 434 to find the offer. Write it in his own words, and then write what trouble the offer brings. Provide evidence to support your answer.

   Key Ideas and Details • Text Evidence

Joe Hayes

Because he enjoyed listening to his dad's stories when he was a child in Arizona, Joe Hayes began telling stories to his own two children and then to other children. "I would go anywhere kids were gathered together—the elementary school, the public library, the YMCA, Boy Scouts and Girl Scouts—and offer to tell a story." That's how he got to be a storyteller, particularly of tales of Hispanic culture. Mr. Hayes has advice for young writers. "Always remember that writing is based on speaking. When you write, listen for the sound of the words. When you speak, your language has a rhythm and a flow to it. If you hear a voice in your imagination saying the words as you write, your writing will have that same pleasant cadence." Mr. Hayes lives and tells stories in New Mexico.

Other retold tales: *Watch Out for Clever Women!*
(¡Cuidado con las mujéres astutas!) and *The Crystal Heart*

Use the Reading Log in the *Reader's and Writer's Notebook* to record your independent reading.

Common Core State Standards
Writing 3.b. Use narrative techniques, such as dialogue, pacing, and description, to develop experiences, events, and/or characters. **Also Writing 4., Language 1., 3.**

Narrative

Folk Tale

A **folk tale** is a traditional narrative story that often teaches a moral or a lesson. Folk tales often include mythical or animal characters. The student model on the next page is an example of a folk tale.

Writing Prompt Write a folk tale in which a character learns an important lesson.

Let's Write It!

Key Features of a Folk Tale

- is a traditional narrative story

- may contain a lesson

- may have been passed down for generations, or originate from a particular culture

READING STREET ONLINE
GRAMMAR JAMMER
www.ReadingStreet.com

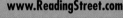

Writer's Checklist

Remember, you should . . .

☑ have a beginning, middle, and end to your story.

☑ write in third-person.

☑ have a character learn an important lesson.

☑ imagine your story being passed on through generations of storytellers.

Long ago, a huge wolf roamed these lands. Every night, he ate a sheep or a cow, but he never ate a pig.

"Why don't the wolves eat pigs?" asked Shaggy Sheep.

"Pigs are smarter than wolves," said Penny Pig.

"That's nonsense!" said Shaggy. "What good is being smart when the wolf is bigger and stronger?"

One day, Penny Pig invited Shaggy Sheep to her house for pizza. When Shaggy knocked, Penny opened the door. To their surprise, the wolf rushed in behind Shaggy.

"Shall I have tender sheep for dinner?" Wolf roared.

"May I offer you pizza instead?" Penny asked. She cut the pizza into four pieces and **set** it in front of the wolf.

"Four pieces is not enough!" Wolf cried. "Give me eight pieces, or I'll eat the sheep instead!"

Penny cut each piece in half. "Here you are," she said.

The wolf gobbled the pizza in one bite. After licking his lips, he declared himself "stuffed full," and **left** in a rush.

"You're right," said Shaggy. "Sometimes it is better to be smart than big and strong."

Writing Trait Voice The story is told with a familiar, informal voice.

Genre A **folk tale** ends with a lesson.

Troublesome verbs are used correctly.

Conventions

Troublesome Verbs

Remember Some pairs of verbs are troublesome because they have similar meanings or look alike. Examples of **troublesome verbs** are *sit/set* and *lie/lay*. When you use one of these verbs, be sure you are using the correct verb for the meaning in the sentence.

443

Common Core State Standards
Literature 2. Determine a theme or central idea of a text and how it is conveyed through particular details; provide a summary of the text distinct from personal opinions or judgments. **Also Literature 10.**

Social Studies in Reading

Genre
Fable

- A fable is a brief story that clearly points to a moral or a lesson.

- Animals are often the main characters in a fable.

- Read "Fox and Little Goat" and see if you can guess the moral or lesson before the story reveals it.

- The moral is usually stated at the end of the story, which underscores its importance.

Fox and Little Goat

retold by Mary Serra

Early one morning, Fox went out for a stroll. But soon it grew hot. It wasn't long before he came to a farm. Fox said, "Oh, look what I see. An old stone well! A perfect place to cool off!"

Leaning over to peer into its depths, Fox said, "If only I could get to that cool water." Alas, poor Fox leaned too far and plummeted in with a SPLASH! Fox struggled, but his paws would not stop slipping on the hard, slick stone walls.

After a while, Little Goat heard Fox splashing about. "Oh, so it's you, Fox," Little Goat called, peering into the well. "Whatever are you doing down there?"

"Cooling off," Fox replied. "Why not jump in and join me?"

So Little Goat did, and he swam around and around in the cool water. Then Fox said, "Well, I'd best be getting home now. Hold still while I stand up on your horns. Then I'll help you up."

Little Goat did his part, but not Fox, who looked down and said, "I'd attempt to help you, but I might fall back in. Good luck, my gullible friend!"

Little Goat splashed around feeling desperate and terrible until the little girl who lived on the farm came to fetch water. She looped a rope over Little Goat's horns, hauled him out, and took him to his mother, who had been wondering where he was.

Little Goat's mother said, "Poor Little Goat! I hope you've learned a lesson: Look before you leap!"

Let's **Think** About...

What features of a fable does this story have? **Fable**

Let's **Think** About...

Reading Across Texts *Juan Verdades* and "Fox and Little Goat" are tales that teach lessons. What lesson does each story teach? Draw pictures and write captions to show the lessons taught.

Writing Across Texts Write a paragraph telling which lesson is more helpful to you and why.

Common Core State Standards
Language 4.a. Use context (e.g., the overall meaning of a sentence or paragraph; a word's position or function in a sentence) as a clue to the meaning of a word or phrase. **Also Literature 10., Speaking/Listening 1.**

Let's Learn It!

READING STREET ONLINE
ONLINE STUDENT EDITION
www.ReadingStreet.com

Vocabulary

Prefixes *re-* and *dis-*

Word Structure When you come to a word you do not know, see if the word begins with a prefix that may help you figure out the meaning of the word. For example, the prefix *re-* adds the meaning "again" to a word, as in *rewrite*, or "back," as in *refund*. The prefix *dis-* adds the meaning "the opposite of," as in *dishonest*, or "remove," as in *dislodge*.

Practice It! Look at the word *repay*. What does the prefix *re-* mean? What does the base word *pay* mean? Explain to a partner why a prefix is important to the meaning of the word.

Fluency

Expression

Remember that when you read aloud, you should change the tone and volume of your voice to express the emotions in the sentences you are reading. Place stress or emphasis on important words and speak characters' words as they might say them.

Practice It! With your partner, practice reading *Juan Verdades: The Man Who Couldn't Tell a Lie*, pages 429–430. Change the tone and volume of your voice to express the emotions in the sentences. Place stress or emphasis on important words.

446

Listening and Speaking

When you tell a story, use appropriate expression and hand gestures to make the story come alive.

Retelling a Story

When you retell a story you know well, your expression and tone should sound as natural as if you were talking to a friend. Retold tales are memorized. They can be family history or traditional literature, but they need a beginning, a middle, a satisfying end—and vivid language to make them come alive.

Practice It! Choose a folk tale or fairy tale you know well. Consider updating it. Outline your tale and then retell it without notes to a partner before you retell it to the class. Ask for and accept suggestions about your retelling.

Tips

Listening . . .

- Listen to identify the speaker's effectiveness as a storyteller.

- Do not interrupt.

- Listen for the structure and the plot of the story.

Speaking . . .

- Use a tone of voice that suits the characters and events in your story.

- Vary the volume of your voice to keep your listeners interested.

- Use appropriate expression and hand gestures.

Teamwork . . .

- Consider your partner's tips.

Common Core State Standards

Language 6. Acquire and use accurately grade-appropriate general academic and domain-specific words and phrases; gather vocabulary knowledge when considering a word or phrase important to comprehension or expression. **Also Speaking/Listening 1.c.**

Let's Talk About

Life Obstacles

- Describe daily obstacles.
- Share ideas about overcoming obstacles.
- Express opinions about what we learn from obstacles.

READING STREET ONLINE
CONCEPT TALK VIDEO
www.ReadingStreet.com

Common Core State Standards
Literature 1. Cite textual evidence to support analysis of what the text says explicitly as well as inferences drawn from the text. **Also Literature 3.**

Skill

Strategy

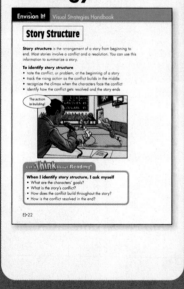

Comprehension Skill

🎯 Draw Conclusions

- When you draw a conclusion, you form a reasonable opinion about something you have read. Drawing conclusions is related to making inferences, or inferring.

- Use what you know about real life to help you draw conclusions.

- When you draw a conclusion, it should make sense. Ask *Is my conclusion based on facts?* or *Does what I have read support my conclusion?*

- As you read the selection, use a graphic organizer like the one below to help you draw a conclusion about why the author titled the selection "Twice Lost; Twice Won."

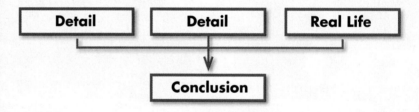

Comprehension Strategy

🎯 Story Structure

A fictional story is often arranged sequentially, or in the order that events happen. Plot is important to a story's structure: the problem, the rising action, the climax, and the outcome or resolution to the problem make up the plot.

TWICE LOST; TWICE WON

My little brother raced into my room, shouting. "I lost another tooth!"

I knew this was big news to him, but it was not the high point of my day. Still, I wanted to show my support. "Great! Don't forget to put it under your pillow tonight." I watched my brother slide the tooth into his shirt pocket and head to the hall. Then I went back to studying for my test.

Skill What can you conclude about where the tooth might be?

Time flew, and I was getting ready to head out for the big basketball game when my brother dashed back into my room. This time, his eyes were red. He sniffled and hung his head. "I lost it," he said.

Strategy What is the problem of the story? How do you think it will be resolved?

"Lost what?" I asked, knowing that I'd have to pack up my uniform and head for the basketball court soon. I hoped this was no big disaster. I couldn't miss the playoff game, and I knew my little brother was looking forward to it too.

Skill Based on this paragraph, what conclusion can you draw about the main character's basketball game? Explain.

"My tooth! I lost my tooth."

I looked at the clock—fifteen minutes until I had to leave. "Okay, where's your shirt, the one you were wearing when you came into my room earlier?"

He led me to a pile of clothes on his closet floor. I rummaged through them but found no tooth. By this time, my brother was sobbing. Then I had an idea. "Where were you when you changed clothes?" I asked.

"In the laundry room," came the muffled reply.

With three minutes to spare, we raced to the laundry room. There, back in a corner, was my brother's tooth. As it turned out, I won twice that day!

Your Turn!

⏸ Need a Review? See the *Envision It! Handbook* for help with drawing conclusions and story structure.

▶ Ready to Try It? Use what you've learned about drawing conclusions as you read *Morning Traffic*.

Common Core State Standards
Language 4.a Use context (e.g., the overall meaning of a sentence or paragraph; a word's position or function in a sentence) as a clue to the meaning of a word or phrase. **Also Language 4.d.**

Envision It! | Words to Know

pawn

remote

rummage

reception

resume

rustling

simultaneous

Vocabulary Strategy for
Antonyms

Context Clues When you find a word you do not know, you can often figure out its meaning by finding a clue in the words around it. The writer may include an antonym, or a word with the opposite meaning, as a clue.

Choose one of the Words to Know and follow these steps.

1. Read the sentence in which the unfamiliar word occurs.

2. Look for a word or phrase that gives a clue to its meaning.

3. Are two things being contrasted? Look for words that point to opposites, such as *unlike, however, but,* or *instead of.*

4. Determine the meaning of the antonym.

5. Give the unfamiliar word the opposite meaning of the antonym. Does this meaning make sense in the sentence?

Read "Lost and Found." Look for antonyms that may give you clues to unfamiliar words' meanings.

Words to Write Reread "Lost and Found." When have you lost something that was important to you? Write a short journal entry to explain. Use words from the Words to Know list in your journal entry.

Lost and Found

It had been an absolutely horrible day. Oscar had lost his prize-winning essay, and he had no idea where it might be. The essay topic was *Literary Elements of The Swiss Family Robinson,* and he was eager to show it to his own family.

Oscar had only discovered the loss when he'd dumped his books out of his backpack at home, rustling through papers as he looked. His sister and her friend had been of little help. They were playing chess, and his sister was very focused on where she'd next move her pawn. His little brother was busy too, playing with his remote-controlled car.

Simultaneously, instead of separately, his sister and her friend waved an absent-minded good-bye as Oscar raced out the door. After tracing his steps to school and back, he found nothing. In a last desperate effort, he rummaged through his backpack again, looking through every folder and book. No luck.

Then, just as he was about to resume his search outdoors, Oscar stopped. He remembered that he'd returned a library book on the way home. He grabbed his phone and called the library. Because of the storm, reception wasn't very good. Still, he frantically explained—and then waited for the librarian to come back to the phone. Hooray! The essay was inside the returned book! Oscar raced out the door again. This time he knew exactly where he was going.

Your Turn!

⏸ **Need a Review?** For help using context clues to determine the meanings of antonyms, see *Words!*

▶ **Ready to Try It?** Read *Morning Traffic* on pp. 454–471.

A **drama** is a story written to be acted for an audience. The story is told by the characters, whose speech is called "dialogue."

Morning Traffic

by Christopher De Paola
illustrated by Frank Morrison

Question of the Week

What obstacles do we face in our daily lives?

455

Characters

David Reyes	An eleven-year-old boy
Karen Reyes	David's mother
Gabe Reyes	David's father
Gil Reyes	David's uncle
Joanna Bates	An eleven-year-old girl
Flower Guy	A young man
Alison Woods	A neighbor
Christine Woods	Alison's eleven-year-old daughter
Arthur Woods	Alison's ten-year-old son

SETTING: A large apartment. A living room with a coffee table and sofa are dominant. A spacious eat-in kitchen can just be seen through a door in the back wall upstage of the living room. A hallway leads to bedrooms and bath. A large casement window is open to the outside.

TIME: Morning.

(DAVID appears in the kitchen wearing a shirt and tie. He is reading a book about chess. He takes a carton of milk out of the refrigerator, places it on the counter and then pours himself a bowl of cereal. He empties the milk and puts the empty carton back in the fridge. Then he wanders into the living room eating his cereal. KAREN enters from the hallway dressed in a business suit and carrying a briefcase.)

KAREN: All right, David, there is tuna in the pantry for lunch.

DAVID: Where's Dad?

KAREN: Getting ready for work. And there are leftovers in the refrigerator for dinner. I hate leaving you alone on teacher workdays.

DAVID: Mom, I'll be fine.

KAREN: Your Uncle Gil is coming over to watch you.

DAVID: Mom, I don't need a babysitter.

KAREN: Well, you're getting one. Your father and I won't be back from the concert until late.

DAVID: I can't believe you got Dad to go watch some guy sing.

KAREN: It's our anniversary. Do you know what I went through to get these tickets? I spent . . .

KAREN *(simultaneously)*:	**DAVID** *(simultaneously)*:
. . . four horrendous hours in line, in the rain . . .	. . . four horrendous hours in line, in the rain . . .

KAREN: . . . to hear Juan Carlos Manuel, the Peruvian tenor.

DAVID: He's just a singer.

KAREN: He's the voice of the century! These tickets sold out in two hours. *(pause)* Why are you all dressed up?

DAVID: No reason.

KAREN *(yelling off)*: Gabriel, I'll see you tonight, honey! At the theater! Seven-thirty!

GABE *(offstage)*: Right! Looking forward to it!

KAREN: Your father's a good liar.

(yelling off) You've got your ticket?

GABE *(off, yelling back)*: Oh, yes!

KAREN: Love you. 'Bye.

(KAREN kisses DAVID. KAREN exits. DAVID takes his cereal bowl into the kitchen. He returns to the living room and sets up a chessboard on the coffee table. After a moment, GABE pokes his head in from the bedroom.)

GABE: Is she gone? Thank goodness.

(GABE runs into the kitchen and begins rustling around, moving papers and opening cabinets.)

GABE: Where is it? I know I left it here on the counter. . . .

DAVID: Shouldn't you be leaving for work, Dad? Because I can't help but notice that you're still here.

GABE: I know, David! But I lost something important. And I have to find it before I can leave for work. *(slight pause)* Why are you all dressed up?

DAVID: No reason. What are you looking for?

GABE: I lost my ticket. The ticket to see this Colombian singer.

DAVID: Peruvian tenor.

GABE: Really?

DAVID: That's what Mom said.

GABE: Do you know what she did for these tickets? She spent . . .

GABE *(simultaneously)* **:**	**DAVID** *(simultaneously)* **:**
. . . four horrendous hours in line in the rain.	. . . four horrendous hours in line in the rain. I know.

GABE: I will have destroyed our anniversary if I don't find this ticket.

DAVID: Maybe you left it at work. You should look there.

GABE: Are you trying to get rid of me? *(slight pause)* Is that my tie?

DAVID: Can't a kid dress up? Can't a kid want to look nice in case he runs into someone he knows?

GABE: You're eleven years old. Who are you running into?

DAVID: I invited a friend over today. But it's not a big deal.

GABE: It's not a big deal?

DAVID: I don't think it's a big deal.

GABE: And yet you're all dressed up.

DAVID: Dad, you're making it sound like a big deal.

(GIL bursts in the front door with a cell phone to his ear. He wanders around the living room, trying to get reception. At one point he leans out the window.)

GIL: No, no. Yes! No, wait, I've got two bars! Can you hear me? No, wait, it's down to one bar. Hello?

GABE: Gil, you're here. Good. You can help me.

DAVID: Uncle Gil, tell Dad he needs to get to work.

GIL: I've got my own problems. My agent is calling me about a job—a new acting job, and you know I haven't had anything since that antacid commercial. Your living room is the only place I can get a connection.

DAVID: I have a guest coming over.

GABE: I can't find my ticket to the concert tonight.

GIL: To see the Chilean?

DAVID *(simultaneously)* :
Peruvian tenor.

GABE *(simultaneously)* :
Peruvian tenor.

GIL: Really?

DAVID: That's what Mom said.

GIL: Do you know that she went through . . .

DAVID *(simultaneously)* :
. . . four horrendous hours in line in the rain. We know.

GABE *(simultaneously)* :
. . . four horrendous hours in line in the rain.

GIL: . . . I was going to say "a lot." She went through a lot to get those tickets. Who's playing chess?

DAVID: I am.

GABE: You don't know how to play chess.

DAVID: I joined the chess club.

GABE: Isn't not knowing how to play going to put you at a disadvantage?

DAVID: That's why I'm reading this book.

GIL: You can't learn the art of chess from a book.

GABE: Your uncle knows how to play.

DAVID: Really? Any advice, Uncle Gil?

GIL: Chess, David, is like an evil queen. With her bishops, her rooks—always needing willing pawns to sacrifice their lives for her.

DAVID: Which one's a rook?

GIL: The one that looks like a little castle. Yes, I played chess. But it was I that was played like a pawn, it was I.

460

GABE: Your uncle was a chess prodigy.

GIL: I was. But the game robbed me of my childhood. . . .

GABE: It wasn't quite that dramatic.

GIL: Mom and Dad let you play baseball! I could've played baseball too, if I hadn't been allergic to grass!

DAVID: It's all right. I'm a quick study. How hard can chess be?

GIL: That's how it all starts. The confidence. Then that first taste of victory. Before you know it, you're sitting alone in the lunchroom, staring into your cottage cheese, wondering where all your so-called friends went. . . .

(GIL's cell phone rings.)

GABE: Would someone please help me locate this ticket?

GIL: Hello. . . ? Can you hear me? I've got half a bar! *(to DAVID)* Get on my shoulders.

DAVID: What?

GIL: Climb on my shoulders. See if there's better reception up high.

(DAVID reluctantly gets on GIL's shoulders. GIL hands DAVID the phone.)

GIL: *(yelling up toward phone)* Can you hear me now!

DAVID: Nothing. No bars.

(The doorbell rings).

GABE: Can someone get that? I'm busy.

GIL: I've got it.

461

(GIL, with DAVID on his shoulders, opens the door. JOANNA stands in the doorway.)

JOANNA: Hey, David.

DAVID: Hi, Joanna.

JOANNA: Are we still playing chess today?

DAVID: Absolutely. Ah, this is my Uncle Gil, and that's my dad. . . .

GIL: Gabe, why don't you ask Joanna if she wants some juice or something?

GABE: Sure. Joanna, come on in. . . .

(JOANNA follows GABE into the kitchen. In the living room GIL lets DAVID off of his shoulders.)

GIL: You didn't tell me your friend was a girl!

DAVID: She's cute, isn't she? I really want to impress her, Uncle Gil. I think I like her.

GIL: I'm going to help you. Listen carefully. A chessboard has eight rows numbered 1 through 8, and eight columns labeled A through H, just like a graph. Make sense?

DAVID: No.

GIL: Do you know which way the pieces move?

DAVID: It's like checkers, right? Don't worry, Uncle Gil. I'll bet you she's not even that good.

(JOANNA returns from the kitchen with a juice.)

JOANNA: I played against my computer last night, and I beat it six times in a row.

DAVID: I'm going to be fine. I'm just going to wing it.

JOANNA: And that was on "expert" difficulty.

(DAVID and JOANNA sit down to play on opposite sides of the coffee table. JOANNA looks at DAVID expectantly.)

DAVID: What?

JOANNA: Choose sides.

(JOANNA holds out both closed hands. DAVID chooses one. It's a black pawn. JOANNA makes the first move. GABE walks in; GIL pulls him aside.)

GIL: We've got to try to stop this disaster.

GABE: I've still got to find this ticket.

GIL: Right! Good call, Gabe. Everyone! If I could have your attention! Gabe here has lost a very important ticket to a concert tonight. We have to find it. Now!

(Everyone scatters. JOANNA looks under the couch.)

JOANNA: I think I see something under the couch. Do you see it?

(Everyone dives to look under the couch and reaches underneath.)

GIL: You're right, I do see something.

DAVID: Yeah, that's got to be it!

GABE: I've almost got it.

JOANNA: Ouch, that's my hand!

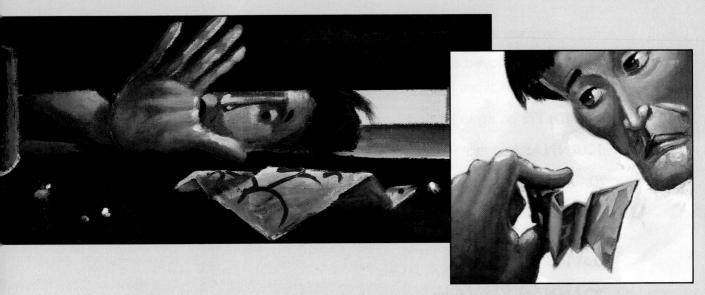

GABE: Sorry. Here it is! Got it! *(Pulls out a small piece of paper.)* Oh, it's only a gum wrapper. I'll check the bedroom again.

(GABE exits. DAVID pulls GIL aside.)

DAVID: Uncle Gil, I appreciate the effort, but. . . .

GIL: Move the pawn—the little one in the front, fifth from the left— move it two squares forward.

(DAVID and JOANNA resume their game. DAVID makes the move. JOANNA makes her second move. It's DAVID's turn again. He puts his hand on a piece. GIL grunts disapprovingly. DAVID switches his hand to another piece. GIL grunts again. The doorbell rings.)

GIL: Saved by the bell! David, why don't you get that?

DAVID: Excuse me a minute, Joanna. Sorry.

(DAVID opens the door. A FLOWER GUY holds a large arrangement of flowers.)

FLOWER GUY: Hi! I've got a delivery for apartment 2-L.

GIL: Right in here. Thanks.

(GABE pokes his head out from the bedroom.)

GABE: Who's that?

GIL: Delivery guy.

FLOWER GUY: I've got a name, you know. Somebody has to sign for these.

GABE: Want to make some extra bucks? Help me find a lost concert ticket?

FLOWER GUY: Sure thing, I got time.

(FLOWER GUY helps rummage through the apartment.)

GIL *(to JOANNA)***:** I believe these are for you. Pretty flowers for a pretty girl, is what David said.

JOANNA: Oh, they're beautiful!

DAVID: Let's keep playing. It's my move.

GIL: I'll put these flowers on the table here.

(GIL purposely puts the flowers on the chessboard. JOANNA and DAVID cannot see each other over the large bouquet. GIL's phone rings and the doorbell rings.)

GIL: Hello? Flower Guy, would you get the door?

FLOWER GUY: I have a name, you know. And someone needs to sign for the flowers.

DAVID: I'll get the door. Sorry, Joanna.

GIL: Can you hear me? I can't. . . .

(DAVID answers the door. ALISON WOODS stands there, with CHRISTINE and ARTHUR WOODS in tow. ARTHUR holds a large model airplane. CHRISTINE holds a remote control.)

ALISON: Hi. You didn't, by any chance, get a delivery of flowers by mistake, did you? I saw the truck out front, but. . . .

CHRISTINE: Hey, David, want to go play at the park?

465

DAVID: Now's not a good time, Christine.

ARTHUR: We just got this new remote-control airplane—check it out!

CHRISTINE: Listen to this . . .

(CHRISTINE pushes a button on the remote. The airplane's motor starts. It makes an extremely loud, whirring sound.)

CHRISTINE: . . . nice, huh?

GIL: Who's that?

ALISON: What did I say about playing with that thing indoors!

ARTHUR: Aw, Mom!

DAVID: *(to JOANNA)* It's Mrs. Woods from across the hall, and Christine and Arthur.

GABE: Alison! Great! Can you help us look for a lost ticket?

GIL: Hello. . . ? How about now . . . can you hear me now?

ALISON: Sure. Are those my flowers?

GIL: I don't think so. Hey, Flower Guy, catch! *(Tosses cell phone to FLOWER GUY.)* Any reception over there?

FLOWER GUY: Hold on! I've got a—no, forget it. *(Tosses cell back to GIL.)* Seriously, will anybody sign for these flowers?

GABE: *(to ARTHUR and CHRISTINE)* Guys, we're looking for a small piece of paper—a concert ticket. . . .

GIL: Alison, how about you? *(Tosses cell to ALISON.)* Anything?

ALISON: Nope. *(Tosses cell back to GIL.)* Are you sure these aren't my flowers?

GIL: Can anybody really be sure of anything?

GABE: Found it! Nope, dry-cleaning receipt.

FLOWER GUY *(exasperated)* **:** You guys have anything to eat here?

(He looks around the kitchen and finds David's box of cereal. FLOWER GUY begins to poke through the refrigerator and cupboards.)

JOANNA: Let's just try to keep playing. It's still your turn. . . .

(DAVID picks up the flowers and looks around for a place to put them. ALISON takes them and reads the tag attached. DAVID and JOANNA try to resume their game. GIL begins to circle the table, still trying for a signal.)

GIL: Wait, I think—yes, yes.

ALISON: Yes, these are mine. They were supposed to come to me in 2-I, see?

(FLOWER GUY pours out a bowl of cereal, rummages in a drawer for a spoon.)

ARTHUR: David, trust me. You're going to want to see this thing fly.

CHRISTINE: It's pretty cool.

(GIL stands on the coffee table, practically on the chessboard.)

GIL: Yes! I can hear you! Finally!

(DAVID stands up, takes GIL's cell phone and tosses it out the window. Everyone stops. Even the model plane sputters to a halt. Silence.)

GIL *(quite calmly)*: Yikes.

DAVID: Can't you all see we're trying to play chess here! This was my one chance to talk to Joanna. She's in the chess club. And even though I don't know how to play chess, looking dumb was worth the chance to say hello. That's all I wanted. And all of you really messed that up for me today.

(Pause. Everyone apologizes to DAVID and JOANNA.)

JOANNA: David, I'm really glad you wanted to say hello.

(KAREN enters).

468

KAREN: Would you believe I forgot—What's going on here?

(FLOWER GUY, holding bowl and spoon, looks in refrigerator for milk.)

GIL: Just a little gathering.

DAVID: Mom, Dad's got something he needs to tell you.

(FLOWER GUY, holding cereal, pulls out the empty milk carton. It has a piece of paper stuck to the bottom.)

FLOWER GUY *(disappointed)***:** Who would put an empty carton of milk back in the refrigerator?

GABE: Honey, I have some bad news. . . .

FLOWER GUY: There's something stuck to the bottom of the carton.

GABE: It's about tonight. . . .

FLOWER GUY *(holding up the missing ticket)***:** Hey, is this the—

GIL: *(Grabs ticket from FLOWER GUY.)* Yes! The Peruvian tenor sings again!

GIL puts the ticket in GABE's hand.

KAREN: You scared me. I thought you were going to say you lost the ticket. You'll never know what I went through to get these tickets.

(DAVID, GIL, and GABE give each other a quick glance.)

(BLACKOUT)

Common Core State Standards

Literature 1. Cite textual evidence to support analysis of what the text says explicitly as well as inferences drawn from the text. **Also Literature 2., Writing 9.**

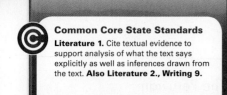

Envision It! | Retell

Think Critically

1. In the play, the mom really wanted to attend the performance of a Peruvian tenor. Name a person or group whose performance you would like to attend, and explain why. **Text to Self**

2. The playwright sometimes has the characters say the same line at the same time. Why do you think he does that? **Think Like an Author**

3. How do you think the ticket ended up on the bottom of the milk carton? **Draw Conclusions**

4. How can you summarize the plot of the play? **Story Structure**

5. **Look Back and Write** What does it usually mean to be stuck in "morning traffic"? Other than on the roads, where was there morning traffic in the play? Before responding, reread pages 456–458 and 464–468. Also note the title and illustration on the opening page. Give specific examples to support your answers.
Key Ideas and Details • Text Evidence

472

Meet the Author

Christopher De Paola

Christopher De Paola grew up in Hollywood, Florida, knowing that he wanted to be in the theater. His father, an accountant, and godfather were actors in community theater, and young Christopher was often backstage, seeing how everything worked. After graduating from Otterbein College, he went to New York City for five years, where he was an actor and a writer. He decided he needed more education, so he earned a master's degree in playwriting from Ohio University. In 2006 he moved to Chicago, where he writes and produces works for the stage and for television. He is also an Emmy Award-nominated actor for a wide variety of roles. Mr. De Paola says, "There are many stories still to be told."

Other books about chess: *Chess for Kids* and *Chess: From First Moves to Checkmate*

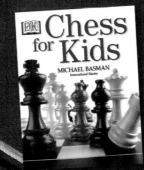

Use the Reading Log in the *Reader's and Writer's Notebook* to record your independent reading.

Common Core State Standards

Writing 3.d. Use precise words and phrases, relevant descriptive details, and sensory language to convey experiences and events. **Also Writing 4., Language 1., 3.**

Let's Write It!

Key Features of a Personal Narrative

- describes an experience or event in the writer's life

- is written in first person

- reveals the writer's thoughts and feelings about the experience

- uses vivid description

READING STREET ONLINE
GRAMMAR JAMMER
www.ReadingStreet.com

Narrative

Personal Narrative

A **personal narrative** tells about a true experience from the writer's life. The student model on the next page is an example of a personal narrative.

Writing Prompt Think about a time when you and friends or family members interacted in a humorous way. Now, write a personal narrative about the experience.

Writer's Checklist

Remember, you should . . .

✓ tell about a real event or experience from your life.

✓ include thoughts and feelings you had as you experienced the event.

✓ write an opening that draws in readers.

✓ use vivid adjectives to help readers picture the scene.

The River Tour

I visited my favorite uncle **in** Chicago last summer, and we took a ride **on** an enormous tour boat. As we walked **up** the steep ramp and hopped **onto** the boat, I felt the rocking motion of the water **below** us. We took a seat **near** the front as sunlight beamed down **through** the clouds.

The tour guide told stories **about** the colorful history **of** Chicago. One I remember **in** particular was about a building **next to** the Sears Tower. Its builders wanted it to stand out, so they put a huge light **on top** of the building. The light was so bright, that birds flying south **for** the winter thought it was the moon! See, birds use the moon to find their way when they fly south, so the light made them get lost. The city made the building dim the light so the birds could find their way. My uncle made a joke afterward about birds and bird-brained builders that had me laughing all day.

After the tour, we ate caramel-and-cheese popcorn **from** a famous Chicago shop. It was one **of** my most memorable, and fun, experiences.

**Writing Trait
Word Choice**
Vivid adjectives are used to give the reader an exact idea of the experience.

Prepositions are used correctly.

Genre
A **personal narrative** tells a true story about an event experienced by the writer.

Conventions

Prepositions

Remember A **preposition** shows a relationship between a noun or pronoun and another word in the sentence, such as a verb, adjective, or other noun. Some examples of prepositions are *in, on, over, under,* and *about.*

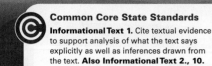
Social Studies in Reading

Genre
Personal Essay

- An essay is a rather brief discussion that uses facts to tell about a specific topic.

- In a personal essay, the writer uses the first-person pronouns *I, my, our,* etc.

- The writer of a personal essay lets the reader feel that he or she is being spoken to directly.

- A personal essay reveals the personal tastes and thoughts of the author.

- Read "Chess—More Than a Game" and see how it qualifies as a personal essay. How does it make you feel about learning how to play chess?

Chess — More Than a Game

By Kaye Segal

Chess, my favorite hobby, is so much more than an ancient game of strategy. Unlike a video game, no two chess games are ever the same. When I am at the board, I am the one in control. Chess teaches a person to slow down and think about the consequences of his or her actions. Studies show that chess can improve concentration, critical thinking, and academic achievement.

So it comes as no surprise that chess is growing in popularity among young players. In New York City, more than twenty thousand students in seventy-six schools learn chess each year. How? Chess-in-the-Schools, a nonprofit group, teaches the game to third and sixth graders across the city. Instructors from the program go to classrooms one day a week for an entire semester. Teachers report that attendance is high on "chess day."

Participating schools have after-school chess clubs that go on year after year. Chess-in-the-Schools also sponsors more than twenty-five tournaments throughout the school year. Hundreds of students, from elementary through high school, get to test their skills at these events.

Every year the U.S. Chess Federation—with programs in major cities, suburbs, and rural areas—holds a national elementary, middle school, and high school tournament. Every four years USCF holds a "supernational" competition for all three grade levels to compete together. Back in 2005, there were more than 5,300 players, all playing in silence. I was one of them.

There is much to be learned about chess, and one way to get better at the game is to read. Books about chess have helped me begin to learn strategies players need to be successful. And chess can engage us in ways that our other classroom subjects don't.

What else does chess do? It has helped me and my fellow players develop confidence and pride in our brainpower. At every move, a person has to think *Why did my opponent do that?* Chess is also a great way to understand that others can have a different point of view.

Chess teaches many skills. Even beginning players learn to use problem-solving strategies and deductive reasoning. Of course, self-discipline is important. There is no talking during a game, and rules of chess make sure that players treat each other with respect. Finally, if a player has the skills, age is not important. As I found out, a more talented sixth grader can crush a high school player!

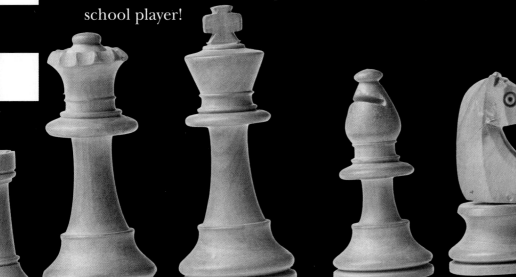

Let's Think About...

What are three examples of ways the author makes this essay personal?
Personal Essay

Let's Think About...

Reading Across Texts What are the differences between how *Morning Traffic* and this essay present chess? Which makes you more interested?

Writing Across Texts Write a comparison of how David in *Morning Traffic* and the author of this essay view chess.

Common Core State Standards
Language 4.a. Use context (e.g., the overall meaning of a sentence or paragraph; a word's position or function in a sentence) as a clue to the meaning of a word or phrase. **Also Literature 10., Speaking/Listening 1.b., Language 4.d.**

READING STREET ONLINE
ONLINE STUDENT EDITION
www.ReadingStreet.com

Vocabulary

Antonyms

Context Clues Antonyms are words that have opposite meanings. Remember that you can use nearby words, such as antonyms, as well as phrases and sentences as you work to determine the meaning of a word. If the first meaning you try in the sentence doesn't make sense, try another.

Practice It! Choose one page of *Morning Traffic* to reread. What context clues did you use to determine the meanings of any words you did not know? Use a dictionary or the glossary if you aren't sure. Then think of an antonym for each new word. Share your results with a partner.

Fluency

Accuracy

Accuracy is being able to read without having to stop often to correct errors or mispronunciations. Two ways to build accuracy are by rereading and also by skimming ahead to look for difficult words.

Practice It! With a partner, practice reading aloud the dialogue between David and Gabe on page 458 of *Morning Traffic*. To speak as the characters might, read over the dialogue before you begin. Be guided by punctuation cues such as ellipses, which signal pauses.

Listening and Speaking

When you take part in a performance, speak loudly enough to be heard.

Readers' Theater

In Readers' Theater, a story is presented in a dramatic form. Actors read from scripts but don't have to memorize their lines.

Practice It! With your group, prepare a Readers' Theater performance about the continuing chess game between Joanna and David. Discuss your ideas, assign roles of characters and a director, and then rehearse. Next present it to the class.

Tips

Listening . . .

- Listen carefully to each speaker.

- Interpret what each speaker says.

Speaking . . .

- When you read your lines, make eye contact with the audience or with the appropriate character.

- Enunciate your words and speak clearly so that the audience can understand you.

Teamwork . . .

- Take turns reading different roles.

Common Core State Standards

Literature 5. Analyze how a particular sentence, chapter, scene, or stanza fits into the overall structure of a text and contributes to the development of the theme, setting, or plot.
Also Literature 4., 10.

Poetry

- A **ballad** is a rhyming narrative poem. It tells a story that can be sung.

- A ballad is dramatic and tells its story without revealing the personal attitudes or feelings of the poet.

- What historic event does the ballad "Concord Hymn" tell about? What does "Abe" tell about?

- Compare the **images** in "Abe" and the poems on pages 482–483 with the images in "Concord Hymn." What differences do you see?

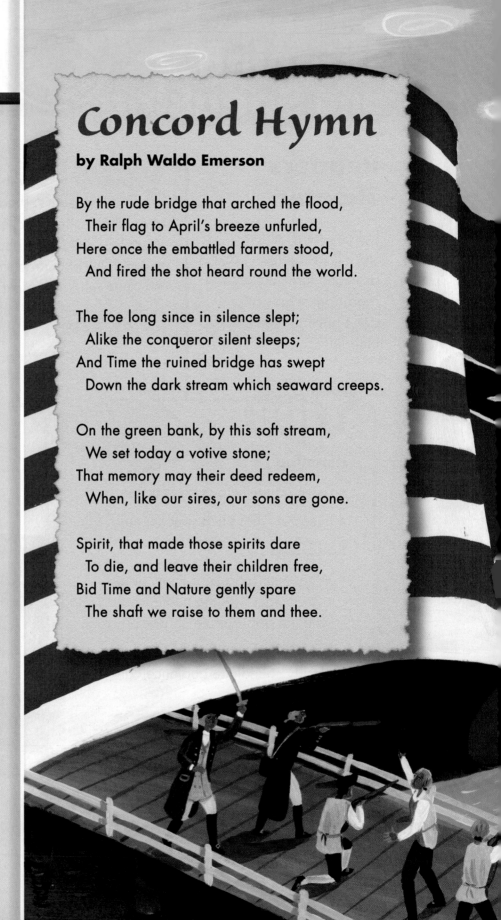

Concord Hymn

by Ralph Waldo Emerson

By the rude bridge that arched the flood,
  Their flag to April's breeze unfurled,
Here once the embattled farmers stood,
  And fired the shot heard round the world.

The foe long since in silence slept;
  Alike the conqueror silent sleeps;
And Time the ruined bridge has swept
  Down the dark stream which seaward creeps.

On the green bank, by this soft stream,
  We set today a votive stone;
That memory may their deed redeem,
  When, like our sires, our sons are gone.

Spirit, that made those spirits dare
  To die, and leave their children free,
Bid Time and Nature gently spare
  The shaft we raise to them and thee.

Abe

by Alice Schertle

And so,
young Abe
      of the too-short pants
      and too-long legs,
young Abe spitting into his palms,
wrapping his bony fingers around
      the handle of an axe,
sinking the bright blade deep
      into heartwood,
young Abe splitting the rails apart

grew into Abe
      of the sad eyes
      of the face carved deep
      by sorrow,
wrapping his strong hands
      around a nation,
trying to hold the bleeding halves
together

until they healed.

Let's **Think** About...

What three elements make "Concord Hymn" a ballad?

Let's **Think** About...

How do "Concord Hymn" and "Abe" both tell about facing life's obstacles? Which do you like better? Why?

481

Martin Luther King, Jr.

by Gwendolyn Brooks

A man went forth with gifts.

He was a prose poem.
He was a tragic grace.
He was a warm music.

He tried to heal the vivid volcanoes.
His ashes are
    reading the world.

His Dream still wishes to anoint
    the barricades of faith and of control.

His word still burns the center of the sun,
    above the thousands and the
    hundred thousands.

The word was Justice. It was spoken.

So it shall be spoken.
So it shall be done.

Another Mountain

by Abiodun Oyewole

Sometimes there's a mountain
that I must climb
even after I've climbed one already
But my legs are tired now
and my arms need a rest
my mind is too weary right now
But I must climb before the storm comes
before the earth rocks
and an avalanche of clouds buries me
and smothers my soul
And so I prepare myself for another climb
Another Mountain
and I tell myself it is nothing
it is just some more dirt and stone
and every now and then I should reach
another plateau and enjoy the view
of the trees and the flowers below
And I am young enough to climb
and strong enough to make it to any top
You see the wind has warned me
about settling too long
about peace without struggle
The wind has warned me
and taught me how to fly
But my wings only work
After I've climbed a mountain

How to Use This Glossary

This glossary can help you understand and pronounce the highlighted words in this book. The entries in this glossary are in alphabetical order. There are guide words at the top of each page to show you the first and last words on the page. A pronunciation key is at the bottom of the following page. Remember, if you can't find the word you are looking for, ask for help or check a dictionary.

The entry word is in dark type. It shows how the word is spelled and how the word is divided into syllables.

The pronunciation is in parentheses. It also shows which syllables are stressed.

Part-of-speech labels show the function or functions of an entry word and any listed form of that word.

con·quer (kong′kər), *V.* to overcome; get the better of: *conquer a bad habit.* ❑ *V.* **con·quered, con·quer·ing, con·querors.**

Sometimes, irregular and other special forms will be shown to help you use the word correctly.

The definition and example sentence show you what the word means and how it is used.

abundant•collapse

Aa

a·bun·dant (ə bun′dənt), *ADJ.* more than enough; very plentiful: *an abundant supply of food.*

al·cove (al′kōv), *N.* **1.** recess or large, hollow space in a wall. **2.** *N.* small room opening out of a larger room: *The piano was in an alcove off the living room.* ❑ *N. PL.* **al·coves.**

ap·par·ent·ly (ə par′ənt lē), *ADV.* seemingly; with the appearance of.

ap·pli·ca·tion (ap′lə kā′shən), *N.* a request for something, such as employment, an award, a loan, etc.: *I filled out an application for a job at the supermarket.*

ap·prox·i·mate (ə prox′sə mit), *ADJ.* nearly correct: *The song ran approximately four minutes.* ❑ *ADV.* **ap·prox·i·mate·ly.**

ar·ti·fact (är′tə fakt), *N.* anything made by human skill or work, especially a tool or weapon. ❑ *N. PL.* **ar·ti·facts.** (*Artifact* comes from two Latin words, *artem* meaning "art" and *factum* meaning "made.")

as·tron·o·mer (ə stron′ə mər), *N.* an expert in astronomy, the science that deals with the sun, moon, planets, stars, etc. ❑ *N. PL.* **as·tron·o·mers.** (*Astronomer* comes from the Greek root *astr* meaning "star.")

Bb

ba·sin (bā′sn), *N.* all the land drained by a river and the streams that flow into it: *The Mississippi basin extends from the Appalachians to the Rockies.*

Cc

char·i·ty (char′ə tē), *N.* **1.** fund or organization for helping the sick, the poor, the helpless, or the environment: *She gives money regularly to the Red Cross and to other charities.* **2.** kindness in judging people's faults: *He showed charity toward the accused thief.* **3.** love of other human beings. ❑ *N. PL.* **char·i·ties.**

col·lapse (kə laps′), *V.* to fold or push together: *The card table would collapse so that it could be stored easily.* ❑ *V.* **col·lapsed, col·laps·ing.**

col·lide (kə līd′), *V.* to hit or strike violently together; crash: *Two ships collided in the harbor and sank.* ❏ *V.* **col·lid·ed, col·lid·ing.**

com·bus·tion (kəm bus′chən), *N.* act or process of burning: *Many houses are heated by the rapid combustion of coal, oil, or gas.*

combustion

com·pact (kom′pakt), *ADJ.* firmly packed together; closely joined: *Cabbage leaves are shaped into a compact head.*

con·fi·dent·ly (kon′fə dənt lē), *ADV.* certainly; surely; with firm belief.

cor·ri·dor (kôr′ə dər), *N.* a long hallway; passage in a large building into which rooms open: *There are many corridors leading from the school's front entrance to the numerous classrooms.* ❏ *N. PL.* **cor·ri·dors.**

cus·tom·ar·y (kus′tə mer′ē), *ADJ.* according to custom; usual: *Ten o'clock is her customary bedtime.*

Dd

dec·ade (dek′ād), *N.* period of ten years: *When you turn 11, you enter your second decade.* ❏ *N. PL.* **dec·ades.** (*Decade* comes from Greek and Latin roots, *deca*, that mean "ten.")

de·cree (di krē′), *N.* something ordered by authority; official decision; law: *The new state holiday was one of three new decrees by the governor.* ❏ *N. PL.* **de·crees.**

des·ti·na·tion (des′tə nā′shən), *N.* place to which someone or something is going or is being sent.

din·gy (din′jē), *ADJ.* lacking brightness or freshness; dirty-looking; dull: *Dingy curtains covered the windows of the dusty room.*

dis·mount (dis mount′), *V.* to get off something, such as a horse or bicycle: *The riders dismounted and led their horses across the stream.* ❏ *V.* **dis·mount·ed, dis·mount·ing.**

dis·tress (dis tres′), *V.* to cause great pain or sorrow; to make unhappy: *Her tears distressed me.* ❏ *V.* **dis·tressed, dis·tress·ing.**

di·vine (də vīn′), *ADJ.* **1.** sacred; holy. **2.** given by or coming from God or a god: *The queen believed that her power to rule was a divine right.* ❏ *ADV.* **di·vine·ly.**

dra·mat·ic (drə mat′ik), *ADJ.* like a drama; of or about plays: *a dramatic actor.*

Ee

em·pha·size (em′fə sīz), *V.* to stress; call attention to: *The number of car accidents emphasized the need for careful driving.* ❏ *V.* **em·pha·sized, em·pha·siz·ing.**

en·rage (en rāj′), *V.* to make very angry; make furious: *The dog was enraged by the teasing.* ❏ *V.* **en·raged, en·rag·ing.**

e·qua·tor (i kwā′tər), *N.* an imaginary circle around the middle of Earth, halfway between the North Pole and the South Pole: *The equator divides the earth into the Northern Hemisphere and the Southern Hemisphere.*

a in *hat*	ėr in *term*	ô in *order*	ch in *child*	ə = a in *about*
ā in *age*	i in *it*	oi in *oil*	ng in *long*	ə = e in *taken*
â in *care*	ī in *ice*	ou in *out*	sh in *she*	ə = i in *pencil*
ä in *far*	o in *hot*	u in *cup*	th in *thin*	ə = o in *lemon*
e in *let*	ō in *open*	u̇ in *put*	ᴛʜ in *then*	ə = u in *circus*
ē in *equal*	ȯ in *all*	ü in *rule*	zh in *measure*	

erosion•immortal

e·ro·sion (i rō′zhən), *N.* the process of gradually eating or wearing away by rain, glaciers, running water, waves, or wind: *Trees help prevent the erosion of soil.*

e·ter·ni·ty (i tėr′nə tē), *N.* the endless time period after death.

e·vap·o·rate (i vap′ə rāt′), *V.* to change from a liquid into a gas: *Boiling water evaporates rapidly.* ❑ *V.* **e·vap·o·rates, e·vap·o·rat·ed, e·vap·o·rat·ing.**

ex·ca·va·tion (ek′skə vā′shən), *N.* the act of or process of uncovering by digging: *The excavation revealed an ancient, buried city.*

ex·port (ek spôrt′ *or* ek′spôrt), *V.* to send goods out of one country for sale and use in another: *The United States has exported corn for many years.* ❑ *V.* **ex·port·ed, ex·port·ing.**

ex·tract (ek strakt′), *V.* to pull out or draw out, usually with some effort: *extract iron from the earth.* ❑ *V.* **ex·tract·ed, ex·tract·ing.**

Ff

fixed (fikst), *ADJ.* steady; not moving:*a fixed gaze.* ❑ *ADV.* **fix·ed·ly.**

fix·ture (fiks′chər), *N.* thing put in place to stay: *a bathroom fixture, light fixtures.* ❑ *N. PL.* **fix·tures.**

flim·sy (flim′zē), *ADJ.* easily torn or broken; not strongly made: *I accidentally tore the flimsy paper.* ❑ *ADV.* **flim·si·ly.**

flour·ish (flėr′ish), *V.* to grow or develop well; thrive: *His radishes flourished with the right conditions.* ❑ *V.* **flour·ished, flour·ish·ing.**

for·mal (fôr′məl), *ADJ.* **1.** according to set customs or rules: *The ambassador paid a formal call on the prime minister.* **2.** done with or having authority; official: *A written contract is a formal agreement to do something.* *ADV.* ❑ **for·mal·ly.**

fran·tic (fran′tik), *ADJ.* very much excited; wild with rage, fear, pain, or grief: *The trapped animal made frantic efforts to escape.* *ADV.* ❑ **fran·ti·cal·ly.**

ful·fill (fůl fil′), *V.* to perform or do a duty, command, etc.: *She felt she was able to fulfill all the teacher's requests.* ❑ *V.* **ful·filled, ful·fill·ing.**

furious (fyür′ē əs), *ADJ.* **1.** very angry; full of wild, fierce anger. **2.** of unrestrained energy, speed, etc.: *furious noises, a furious storm.* ❑ *ADV.* **fur·i·ous·ly.**

Gg

gal·ax·y (gal′ək sē), *N.* **1.** group of billions of stars forming one system: *Earth and the sun are in the Milky Way galaxy. Many galaxies outside our own can be seen with a telescope.* **2.** the Milky Way. (*Galaxy* comes from the Greek word *galaktos* meaning "milk.")

galaxy

grope (grōp), *V.* to feel about with the hands: *He was groping in the dark for a flashlight after the lights went out.* ❑ *V.* **groped, grop·ing.**

Hh

hatch·et (hach′it), *N.* a small axe with a short handle, for use with one hand: *He used the hatchet to chop wood.*

Ii

ig·nite (ig nīt′), *V.* to set on fire: *A spark from a campfire can ignite dry grass.* ❑ *V.* **ig·nit·ed, ig·nit·ing.**

im·mor·tal (i môr′tl), *ADJ.* living forever; never dying; everlasting: *Most religions teach that the soul is immortal.* (*Immortal* comes from the Latin word *mort* meaning "death.") ❑ *ADV.* **im·mor·tal·ly.**

in·ci·dent (in′sə dənt), *N.* something that happens; event: *an exciting incident.* (*Incident* comes from the Latin word *incidentem* meaning "happening, befalling.")

in·dus·tri·al (in dus′trē əl), *ADJ.* engaged in or connected with business, trade, or manufacturing: *industrial worker, industrial development.* ❏ *ADV.* **in·dus·tri·al·ly.**

Ll

lunge (lunj), *V.* to move suddenly forward; thrust: *The dog is always lunging at strangers.* ❏ *V.* **lunged, lung·ing.**

Mm

me·chan·i·cal (mə kan′ə kel), *ADJ.* **1.** of or involving a machine or machinery: *The flight was delayed because of mechanical problems with the plane.* **2.** like a machine; automatic; without expression: *His acting was very mechanical.* ❏ *ADV.* **me·chan·i·cal·ly.**

men·ac·ing (men′is ing), *ADJ.* threatening: *The dog had a menacing growl.* ❏ *ADV.* **men·ac·ing·ly.**

mo·men·tous (mō men′təs), *ADJ.* very important: *Choosing between peace and war is a momentous decision.* ❏ *ADV.* **mo·men·tous·ly.**

mon·grel (mong′grəl), *N.* animal or plant of mixed breed, especially a dog.

morsel (môr′səl), *N.* a small portion of food: *The turtle ate every morsel of the lettuce.*

Nn

ne·go·ti·ate (ni gō′shē āt), *V.* to talk over and arrange terms; confer; consult: *The two countries came together to negotiate for peace.* ❏ *V.* **ne·go·ti·at·ed, ne·go·ti·at·ing.**

nub (nub), *N.* lump or small piece; knob: *He worked so hard he felt worn down to a nub.*

nudge (nuj), **1.** *V.* to push slightly to attract attention: *She nudged me when it was my turn.* **2.** *N.* slight push: *The director gave him a nudge.* ❏ *V.* **nudged, nudg·ing.**

Oo

obsidian (ob sid′ē ən), *N.* a hard, dark, glassy rock that is formed when lava cools.

obsidian

op·er·a (op′ər ə), *N.* a play in which music is an essential and prominent part, featuring arias, choruses, etc., with orchestral accompaniment: *Her favorite opera is* Porgy and Bess.

Pp

pains·tak·ing (pānz′tā′king), *ADJ.* very careful; particular; diligent: *a painstaking painter.* ❏ *ADV.* **pains·tak·ing·ly.**

par·ti·cle (pär′tə kəl), *N.* a very little bit: *I got a particle of dust in my eye.* ❏ *N. PL.* **par·ti·cles.** (*Particle* comes from the Latin word *partem* meaning "part.")

pawn (pȯn), *N.* **1.** (in chess) one of the 16 pieces of lowest value. **2.** an unimportant person or thing used by someone to gain advantage: *The dictator used the peasants as his pawns.* ❏ *N. PL.* **pawns.**

per·mis·sion (pər mish′ən), *N.* consent; leave: *My sister gave me permission to use her camera.*

per·sist (pər sist′), *V.* to keep on; refuse to stop or be changed: *Though we'd asked her not to, she persisted in reading at the table.* ❏ *V.* **per·sist·ed, per·sist·ing.**

plea (plē), *N.* request or appeal; an asking: *The firefighters heard many pleas for help.* ❏ *N. PL.* **pleas.**

pot·ter·y (pot′ər ē), *N.* pots, dishes, vases, etc., made from clay and hardened by heat. *N. PL.* **pot·ter·y.**

pre·his·to·ric (prē′hi stôr′ic), *ADJ.* of or belonging to times before histories were written: *Prehistoric peoples used stone tools.* ❏ *ADV.* **pre·his·to·ri·cal·ly.**

prejudice•simultaneous

prej·u·dice (prej′ə dis), *N.* **1.** unreasonable dislike of an idea, group of people, etc.: *It can be difficult to set aside prejudice.* 2. an unfair, usually bad opinion. ❑ *N. PL.* **prej·u·dice.**

priv·i·leged (priv′ə lijd), *ADJ.* having some special rights, advantage, or favor: *The nobility of Europe was a privileged class.*

pueb·lo (pweb′lō), *N.* **1.** a Native American village built of homes of adobe and stone. **2. Pueblo,** member of any Native American group living in such villages, including the Hopi and Zuni of the southwestern United States and northern Mexico. ❑ *N. PL.* **pueb·los; Pueb·lo** or **Pueb·los.**

Qq

qui·et·ly (kwī′ət lē), *ADV.* making no sound: *He waited quietly.*

quill (kwil), *N.* a stiff, sharp hair or spine like the pointed end of a feather: *A porcupine releases quills on its back when it feels threatened. N. PL.* **quills.**

quills

Rr

re·cede (ri sēd′), *V.* to go backward; move backward; withdraw: *When the tide receded, we dug for clams.* ❑ *V.* **re·ced·ed, re·ced·ing.**

re·cep·tion (ri sep′shən), *N.* quality of the sound and picture reproduced in a television receiver or cellular phone: *Reception was poor inside the store.*

re·cit·al (ri sī′ tl), *N.* a musical entertainment, given usually by a single performer. ❑ *N. PL.* **re·cit·als.**

re·cy·cle (rē sī′kəl), *V.* to collect, process, or treat something so that it can be used again: *The town recyles paper, aluminum, and glass.* ❑ *V.* **re·cy·cles, re·cy·cled, re·cy·cling.**

reg·is·ter (rej′ə stər), *V.* to have some effect, to make an impression: *The President's intelligence registered on the students.* ❑ *V.* **reg·is·tered, reg·is·ter·ing.**

reign (rān), *V.* to rule: *The king and queen reigned over the kingdom.* ❑ *V.* **reigned, reign·ing.**

re·mote (ri mōt′), **remote control,** *N.* device used to control a TV set, garage door opener, toy, etc., from a distance.

re·pay (ri pā′), *V.* to do something in return for something received: *No thanks can repay such kindness.* ❑ *V.* **re·paid, re·pay·ing.**

re·store (ri stôr′), *V.* to bring back to a former condition: *The ancient figures are being restored by archaeologists.* ❑ *V.* **re·stored, re·stor·ing.**

re·sume (ri züm′), *V.* to begin again; go on: *Resume reading where we left off.* ❑ *V.* **re·sumed, re·sum·ing.**

romp (romp), *V.* to play in a rough, boisterous way; rush and tumble. ❑ *V.* **romped, romp·ing.**

row·dy (rou′dē), *ADJ.* rough; disorderly; sometimes quarrelsome: *The gym was full of rowdy kids.* ❑ *ADV.* **row·di·ly.**

ruff (ruf), *N.* a collarlike growth of long or specially marked feathers or hairs on the neck of a bird or other animals: *The little girl held on to the dog's ruff until she could attach his leash.*

rum·mage (rum′ig), *V.* **1.** to search thoroughly by moving things about: *I rummaged through three drawers before I found my gloves.* **2.** to search in a disorderly way. ❑ *V.* **rum·maged, rum·mag·ing.**

rus·tle (rus′əl), *V.* to make or cause a light, soft sound of things gently rubbing together: *The leaves rustled in the breeze. The wind rustled my papers.* ❑ *V.* **rus·tled, rus·tling.**

Ss

si·mul·ta·ne·ous (sī′məl tā′nē əs), *ADJ.* done, existing, or happening at the same time: *The two simultaneous explosions of the dynamite sounded like one.* ❑ *ADV.* **si·mul·ta·ne·ous·ly.**

slung (slung), *V.* past tense and past participle of **sling** (sling), *V.* to hang so as to swing loosely, to hang in a sling: *They slung their packs over their shoulders. The man had slung his jacket across a chair.*

smol·der (smōl′dər), *V.* to burn and smoke without flame: *The campfire smoldered for hours after the blaze died down.* ❑ *V.* **smol·dered, smol·der·ing.**

speck·led (spek′əld), *ADJ.* marked with many small spots: *A speckled bird flew out of the bush.*

stif·fen (stif′ən), *V.* to make or become rigid, fixed: *Her muscles stiffened in the cold wind.* ❑ *V.* **stif·fened, stif·fen·ing.**

stoop (stüp), **1.** *V.* to bend forward: *She stooped to pick up the kitten.* **2.** *ADJ.* **stooped** (stüpt), bent over, as from age: *The old man was stooped from years of gardening.*

stun (stun), *V.* to daze; bewilder; shock; overwhelm: *She was stunned by the news of her friend's injury.* ❑ *V.* **stunned, stun·ning.**

sub·scribe (səb skrīb′), *V.* to give your consent or approval; agree: *She does not subscribe to my opinion.* ❑ *V.* **sub·scribed, sub·scrib·ing.** (*Subscribe* comes from two Latin words, *sub* meaning "under" and *scribe* meaning "to write.")

su·per·sti·tious (sü′pər stish′əs), *ADJ.* having belief or practice based on ignorant fear or mistaken reverence. ❑ *ADV.* **su·per·sti·tious·ly.**

sur·vive (sər vīv′), *V.* to continue to exist; remain; to continue to live after: *No one thought the old, bent tree would survive being hit by lightning.* ❑ *V.* **sur·vived, sur·viv·ing.**

Tt

terra cotta (tər′ə kot′ə), **1.** *N.* kind of hard, often unglazed, brownish-red earthenware, used for flowerpots, vases, statuettes, building decorations, etc. **2.** *ADJ.* a dull, brownish red.

trav·erse (trav′ərs), *V.* to pass across, over, or through: *Explorers traversed the desert by truck.* ❑ *V.* **tra·versed, tra·vers·ing.**

tread (tred), **1.** *V.* to set a foot down; walk; step: *Don't tread on the flower beds.* ❑ *V.* **trod, trod·den. 2.** *V.* tread water; to keep the body straight in the water with the head above the surface by moving the arms and legs. ❑ *V.* **tread·ed, tread·ing.**

trop·ics (trop′iks), *N. PL.* the regions between the equator and imaginary circles 23.45 degrees north and south of the equator, where the sun can shine directly overhead: *The hottest part of the Earth is in the tropics.*

tropics

trow·el (trou′el), *N.* tool with a flat, usually wide blade used for spreading or smoothing plaster or mortar: *They used trowels to lift out the artifacts.* ❑ *N. PL.* **trow·els.**

Vv

vig·il (vij′el), *N.* act of staying awake for some purpose; act of watching.

vig·or·ous (vig′ər əs), *ADJ.* full of vigor; strong; active; energetic; forceful: *At 72, he still is a vigorous jogger.* ❑ *ADV.* **vig·or·ous·ly.**

Ww

waft (wäft), **1.** *V.* to carry over water or through air: *A breeze wafted the aroma of fresh bread to me.* ❑ *V.* **waft·ed, waft·ing. 2.** *N.* a breath or puff of air, wind, scent, etc.: *Wafts of fresh air came through the window.* ❑ *N. PL.* **wafts.**

wane (wān), *V.* **1.** to go through the moon's regular reduction in the amount of its visible portion. The moon wanes when the side facing the Earth moves gradually out of the sun's light. **2.** to lose strength or intensity; to draw to a close: *Daylight wanes after the sun sets.* ❑ *V.* **wanes, waned, wan·ing.**

watch·ful (wäch′fəl), *ADJ.* watching carefully; on the lookout; wide-awake ❑ *ADV.* **watch·ful·ly.**

work·shop (wėrk′shop′), *N.* shop or building where work is done.

489

Unit 1
Old Yeller

English	Spanish
lunge	embestir
nub	nudillo
romping	retozando
rowdy	alborotado
slung	colgué
speckled	moteada

Mother Fletcher's Gift

English	Spanish
apparently	aparentemente*
fixtures	accesorios
flimsy	frágil
incident	incidente*
subscribe	suscribir*
survive	perdurar

Viva New Jersey

English	Spanish
corridors	pasillos
destination	destino*
groping	agarrando a tientas
menacing	amenazador
mongrel	perro callejero
persisted	persistió*
pleas	súplicas

Saving the Rain Forests

English	Spanish
basin	cuenca
charities	organizaciones benéficas
equator	ecuador*
erosion	erosión*
evaporates	evapora*
exported	exportados*
industrial	industrial*
recycled	reciclada*
tropics	trópico*

* English/Spanish cognate: A **cognate** is a word that is similar in two languages and has the same meaning in both languages.

Hachiko: The True Story of a Loyal Dog

English	Spanish
fixed	fijados
furious	furioso*
morsel	bocado
nudge	un codazo ligero
quietly	silenciosamente
ruff	collar
stooped	encorvado
vigil	vigilia*

Unit 2
The Universe

English	Spanish
astronomers	astrónomos*
collapse	colapsa*
collide	chocan
compact	compacto*
galaxy	galaxia*
particles	partículas*

The Emperor's Silent Army

English	Spanish
approximately	aproximadamente*
divine	divino*
excavated	excavados*
mechanical	mecánico*
pottery	cerámicas
restore	restaurar*
superstitious	supersticiosos*
terra cotta	terracota*
watchfully	vigilantemente

Stones, Bones, and Petroglyphs

English	Spanish
alcoves	huecos
decades	décadas*
obsidian	obsidiana*
prehistoric	de la prehistoria*
Pueblo	Pueblo*
trowels	paletas

Good-bye to the Moon

English	Spanish
combustion	combustión*
dingy	deslucidos
negotiate	negociar*
traversed	atravesaba
waft	aroma
waning	menguando

Egypt

English	Spanish
abundant	abundantes*
artifacts	artefactos*
decrees	decretos*
eternity	eternidad*
immortal	inmortales*
receded	retrocedían
reigned	reinaron*

Unit 3
Hatchet

English	Spanish
hatchet	hacha*
ignite	encender
painstaking	esmerado
quill	púa
registered	se registraron*
smoldered	humearon
stiffened	se paralizó

When Marian Sang

English	Spanish
application	solicitud
dramatic	dramático*
enraged	enfurecidos
formal	formal*
momentous	de suma importancia
opera	ópera*
prejudice	prejuicios*
privileged	privilegiado*
recital	recital*

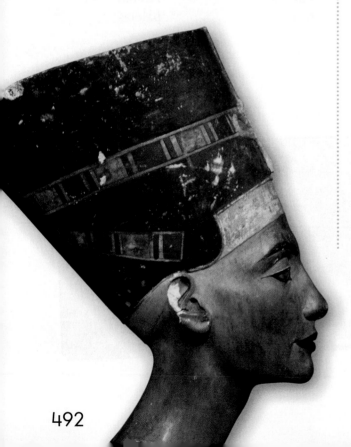

Learning to Swim

English	Spanish
customary	habitual
emphasized	enfatizaba
frantic	frenéticos
stunned	estupefactos
treaded	se mantenían a flote

Juan Verdades: The Man Who Couldn't Tell a Lie

English	Spanish
confidently	con seguridad
dismounted	desmontó*
distressed	angustiado
flourish	florear
fulfill	satisfacer
permission	permiso*
repay	reembolsar
vigorously	vigorosamente

Morning Traffic

English	Spanish
pawn	peón
reception	recepción*
remote	remoto*
resume	reanudar
rummage	revolviendo todo
rustling	crujido
simultaneous	simultáneo*

Acknowledgments

Acknowledgments

Photographs

Every effort has been made to secure permission and provide appropriate credit for photographic material. The publisher deeply regrets any omission and pledges to correct errors called to its attention in subsequent editions.

Unless otherwise acknowledged, all photographs are the property of Pearson Education, Inc.

Photo locators denoted as follows: Top (T), Center (C), Bottom (B), Left (L), Right (R), Background (Bkgd)

CVR Shutterstock; **4, 18** Vince Maggiora/San Francisco Chronicle/Corbis; **8, 174** Shutterstock; **12, 328 328** djgis/Shutterstock; **18** (Bkgd) TongRo Image Stock/Fotosearch.Com; **20** (B) altrendo images/Getty Images; **20–21** Suzanne Long/Alamy; **21** (TR) Mitch Diamond/Alamy; **23** (BR) W. Perry Conway /Corbis; **24** (BL) Jupiter Images; **24** (TL) Brian Tan/Shutterstock; **24** (CL) Laurence Mouton/Photo Alto/Jupiter Images; **25** (TR) Getty Images/Blend Images; **41** Thomas D. Mcavoy/Time Life Pictures/Getty Images; **44** (B) Getty Images; **45** (BR) Corbis; **45** (TR) Pat Doyle/Corbis; **46** (TL) George D. Lepp/Corbis; **46** (BL) (BR) Getty Images; **47** (CR) Tom Nebbia/Corbis; **47** (B) Ariel Skelley/Corbis; **50** (B), **51** (B) Jim West/Alamy; **50–51** kali9/iStockphoto/Getty Images; **54** (BL) Gianni Muratore/Alamy; **54** (CL) Lisa F. Young/Alamy; **54** (TL) Peter Anderson/DK images; **55** Lee Snider/Corbis; **73** Charles Sykes/AP Images; **76** (BR) Corbis; **77** (TR) Henri Cartier-Bresson; **77** (B) Bettmann/Corbis; **80** (B) david hancock/Alamy; **80–81** Charles Register/Alamy; **81** (B) Jupiter Images; **84** (TL) Jupiter Images; **84** (CL) Stockbyte/Getty Images; **84** (BL) Ralph A. Clevenger/Corbis; **85** (CR) Sam Diephuis/Getty Images; **104** Getty Images; **108–109** Paul Harris/Photolibrary; **109** (C) Michael Willis/Alamy; **109** (B) Peter Pinnock/Getty Images; **111** (T) Natalie Fobes/Corbis; **111** (Bkgd) Ludovic Maisant/Getty Images; **112** (TL) Chris Howes/Wild Places Photography/Alamy; **112** (BL) (CL) Jupiter Images; **113** (BR) santiphoto/Fotolia; **113** (CR) Brand X Pictures/Thinkstock; **114–115** Gerard Lacz/AGE Fotostock/Superstock; **116** John Wang/Corbis; **117** (CL) Thinkstock; **117** (TL) Michael & Patricia Fogden/Corbis; **117** (R), **118** (R), **125** (TR), **129** (TR) Chase Swift/Corbis; **118** (TL) Jack Jeffrey/Alamy; **118** (B) Gustavo Gilabert/Corbis; **120** Charles O'Rear/Corbis; **121** (BR), **137** (BR) Kevin Schafer/Corbis; **121** (TR) Corbis; **121** (CL) Getty Images; **122** (CR), **130** (BL) Jolly Photo/Shutterstock; **122** (BR) Wayne Lawler/Corbis; **124, 128** (CL) Wayne Lawler/Corbis; **125** (TL) David Reed/Panos Pictures; **125** (B) Jeremy Horner/Panos Pictures; **126** (BL), **490** (BR) Paul Harris/Alamy; **126** (TL), (CL) Getty Images; **127** (TR), **136** (CR) Kevin Schafer/Corbis; **127** (B), **128** (BL) Fred Hoogervorst; **138–139** Ryan McVay/Getty Images; **139** (T) Frank Gaglione/Getty Images; **139** (B) John Giustina/Getty Images; **141** (TL) Marc Henrie/DK Images; **141** (BR) Getty Images; **142** (TL) Tetra Images/Getty Images; **142** (CL) Arco Images GmbH/Alamy; **142** (BL) Wilmar Photography/Alamy; **143** Hunt/Fotolia; **164** (B) DLILLC/Corbis; **165** (T) Eric and David Hosking/Corbis; **165** (L) Royal Geographical/Getty Images; **165** (C) Getty Images; **166** (TR) David Fleetham/Alamy; **166** (B) Ched Bradley/The Elephant Sanctuary in Tennessee; **167** Juniors Bildarchiv/Glow Images; **174** Shutterstock; **176–177** NASA; **176** (C) Jupiter Images; **177** (B) Andersen Ross/Jupiter Images; **179** (BR) Comstock/Thinkstock; **179** (TL) David Parker/Photo Researchers; **180** (CL) Eric Van Den Brulle/Getty Images; **180** (BL) Tony Gentile/Reuters/Corbis; **180** (BL), **486** Jupiter Images; **181** (T) ESA/NASA/P. Anders/Corbis; **181** (B) Galaxy Picture Library/Alamy; **182–183** Corbis; **184** (T) (B) Mark McCaughrean (Keele University/C. Robert O'Dell (Vanderbuilt University)/NASA/Space Telescope Science Institute; **185, 194** (TL), **196** (BL) Royal Observatory. Edinburgh/AAO/SPL/Photo Researchers; **186, 201** (R) Jess Hester and Paul Scowen (ASU)/NASA/AURA/Space Telescope Science Institute; **188–189** C. Robert O'Dell (Vanderbilt University)/Kerry P. Handron (Rice University) and NASA/Space Telescope Science Institute; **188** (TR), **194** (CL) David A. Hardy/SPL/Photo Researchers; **190** Image courtesy of NRAO/AUI/NSF/National Radio Astronomy Observatory; **193, 194** (BL) Dana Berry/Space Telescope Science Institute; **195** David A. Hardy/SPL/Photo Researchers; **198–199** JPL/NASA; **199** (T) Ames Research Center/NASA; **202—203** Casey Christie/ZUMAPRESS/Newscom; **203** (B) Jason Edwards/Getty Images; **203** (C) Best View Stock/Alamy; **205** (T) DK Images; **205** (Bkgd) demarco/Fotolia; **205** (BR) DBA Images/Alamy; **206** (CL) Phil Schermeister/Corbis; **206** (BL) Shutterstock; **206** (TL) Ira Block/National Geographic Image Collection/Alamy; **207** Tomb of Qin shi Huang Di, Xianyang, China/Bridgeman Art Library; **208–209** iemily/Fotolia; **210** (TC) Zhuge Ming/Imagine china; **210** (B), **215** (B), **218, 220** (TR) (BR), **221**(CR), **222** (L), **224** (BL), **226** (BL), **231** (BR), **491** (BL) O. Louis Mazzatenta/National Geographic Stock; **211, 212–213, 219** (T) Zhou Kang/Imaginechina;

WORDS!

Vocabulary Handbook

Antonyms

Synonyms

Base Words

Prefixes

Suffixes

Context Clues

Related Words

Word Origins: Roots

Multiple-Meaning Words

Dictionary

Thesaurus

Antonyms

An antonym is a word that has the opposite meaning of another word. *Day* is an antonym for *night*.

whisper

blare

Antonym = Opposite

Strategy for Antonyms

1. Identify the word for which you want to find an antonym.
2. Think of other words or phrases that have the opposite meaning.
3. Use a thesaurus to help you find antonyms.
4. Use a dictionary to check antonyms' meanings so that you use the word that best communicates your ideas.

Synonyms

Synonyms are two or more words that have the same meaning or nearly the same meaning.

display

Synonym = Same

show

Strategy for Synonyms

1. Identify the word for which you want to find a synonym.
2. Think of other words or phrases that have the same, or almost the same, meaning.
3. Use a thesaurus to help you find more synonyms, and make a list.
4. Use a dictionary to find the word that best communicates your ideas.

Base Words

A base word is a word that can't be broken into smaller words.

lock

unlock

Lock is the base word.

Strategy for Base Words

1. Look for a base word in the unknown word.
2. Determine the meaning of the base word.
3. Guess the meaning of the unknown word. Does it make sense in the sentence?
4. Check your guess in a dictionary.

Prefixes

A prefix is a word part added onto the front of a base word to form a new word.

cap

uncap

Strategy for Prefixes

1. Look at the unknown word and identify the prefix.
2. What does the base word mean? If you're not sure, check a dictionary.
3. Use what you know about the base word and the prefix to figure out the meaning of the unknown word.
4. Use a dictionary to check your guess.

Common Prefixes and Their Meanings

un-	not
re-	again, back
in-	not
dis-	not, opposite of
pre-	before

Suffixes

A suffix is a word part added to the end of a base word to form a new word.

coatless

coat

Common Suffixes and Their Meanings

-ly	characteristic of
-ation	act, process
-able	can be done
-ment	action or process
-less	without

Strategy for Suffixes

1. Look at the unknown word and identify the suffix.
2. What does the base word mean? If you're not sure, check a dictionary.
3. Use what you know about the base word and the suffix to figure out the meaning of the unknown word.
4. Use a dictionary to check your guess.

W•6

Context Clues

Context clues are the words and sentences found around an unknown word that may help you figure out a word's meaning.

My mother and I bought some delicious fruit today. We bought bananas, grapes, apples, and my favorite—kiwis!

SALE

Strategy for Context Clues

1. Look for clues in the words and phrases around the unknown word.
2. Take a guess at the word's meaning. Does it make sense in the sentence?
3. Use a dictionary to check your guess.

Related Words

Related words are words that all have the same base word.

invent

invention

inventor

Strategy for Related Words

1. Find the base word in your unfamiliar word.
2. Identify the meaning of the base word.
3. Guess the meaning of the unfamiliar word. Does it make sense in the sentence?
4. Use a dictionary to check your guess.

Word Origins: Roots

Many English words contain
Greek and Latin roots.

microscope

dentist

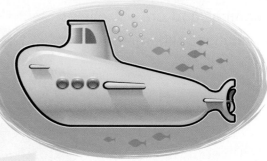

submarine

Latin Roots

dent	tooth
dict	to say; to speak
scrib	to write
sub	under; below
tract	to pull
vis	to see

Greek Roots

auto	self
bio	life
micro	very small
ology	the study of
phon	sound; voice
scope	see
tele	far

Strategy for Roots

1. Using what you know about roots, guess the meaning of the unknown word.
2. Does your guess make sense in the sentence?
3. Use a dictionary to check your guess.

Multiple-Meaning Words

Multiple-meaning words are words that have different meanings depending on how they are used. Homographs, homonyms, and homophones are all multiple-meaning words.

Homographs

Homographs are words that are spelled the same but have different meanings and are sometimes pronounced differently.

bow

bow

Some Common
Homographs

bass
close
contract
lead
live
present

Strategy for Homographs

1. Read the words and phrases near the homograph.
2. Think about the homograph's different meanings and decide which one makes the most sense in the sentence.
3. Reread the sentence with your guess to see if it makes sense.
4. Check your guess in a dictionary.

Homonyms

Homonyms are words that are pronounced the same and have the same spelling, but their meanings are different.

row

row

Strategy for Homonyms

1. Read the words and phrases near the homonym.
2. Think about the homonym's different meanings and decide which one makes the most sense.
3. Reread the sentence with your guess to see if it makes sense.
4. Use a dictionary to check your guess.

Some Common Homonyms

pen
duck
mail
ear
bank
bark

Homophones

Homophones are words that are pronounced the same way but have different spellings and meanings.

flour

flower

Some Common Homophones

ate	eight
bored	board
brake	break
knight	night
weight	wait

Strategy for Homophones

1. Think about the different spellings and meanings of the homophone.
2. Check a dictionary for the definitions of the words.
3. Use the word that best fits your purpose.

This chart can help you remember the differences between homographs, homonyms, and homophones.

Understanding Homographs, Homonyms, and Homophones

	Pronunciation	Spelling	Meaning
Homographs	may be the same or different	same	different
Homonyms	same	same	different
Homophones	same	different	different

Homograph

dove

dove

Homonym

mail

mail

Homophone

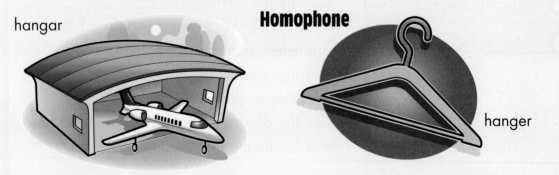

hangar

hanger

Dictionary

A dictionary is a reference book that lists words alphabetically. It can be used to look up pronunciation, parts of speech, definitions, and spelling of words.

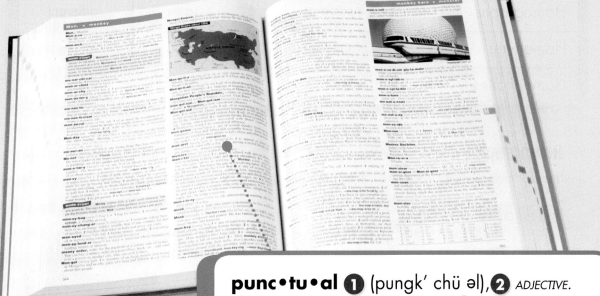

punc•tu•al ❶ (pungk′ chü əl), ❷ *ADJECTIVE.*
❸ prompt; exactly on time: ❹ *He is always punctual.*
❺ ✳ *ADVERB* **punc′tu•al•ly.**

❶ Pronunciation

❷ Part of speech

❸ Definitions

❹ Example sentence

❺ Other form of the word and its part of speech

Strategy for Dictionary

1. Identify the unknown word.
2. Look up the word in a dictionary. Entries are listed alphabetically.
3. Find the part of the entry that has the information you are looking for.
4. Use the diagram above as a guide to help you locate the information you want.

Thesaurus

A thesaurus is a book of synonyms. A thesaurus may also list antonyms for many words.

cute
adjective
attractive, appealing, amusing, charming, adorable, enchanting.
ANTONYMS: plain, ugly

Strategy for Thesaurus

1. Look up the word in a thesaurus. Entries are listed alphabetically.
2. Locate the synonyms and any antonyms for your word.
3. Use a dictionary to help you choose the word with the exact meaning you want.